In recent years, there has been a renewed interest in the military history of the English Civil War and its associated conflicts in Ireland and Scotland. Historians are increasingly paying attention to the 'actualities of war' (to use Sir Basil Liddell Hart's phrase) during these conflicts, and this has given rise to an accompanying recognition that the better-studied political, social and religious developments of the mid-seventeenth century cannot be divorced from military events. Thus, this volume this is a timely evaluation of a selection of distinct, yet interrelated, military aspects of the Civil War. It commences with two studies that re-evaluate our understanding of two key battles. Peter Gaunt sheds new light on the little-studied (but vitally important) battle of Middlewich on 13 March 1643, which kick-started the Civil War (political, as well as military) career of Sir William Brereton and played a key role in establishing parliamentary dominance in the strategically significant county of Cheshire. Malcolm Wanklyn reappraises the bridge-building exercise over the rivers Teme and Severn at Powick that made Cromwell's tactical plan for fighting the Scots at Worcester on 3 September 1651 possible. The volume then moves on to consider ideology in practice. Many who formed the nucleus of royalist and parliamentarian armies had fought in the English regiments in the service of the Dutch Republic prior to the Civil War. Ismini Pells investigates how these men looked back to their shared experiences on the Continent to establish networks and working relationships both with those in their own armies and the armies of their adversaries. Tim Jenkins provides a reminder that military outcomes were often dependent on civilian actions. Focusing on one of Shrewsbury's leading inhabitants, William Rowley, Jenkins explores the role of religious ideology in the corporate politics and Civil War allegiances of a town that remained under royalist occupation from September 1642 to February 1645. By comparing the instructions in seventeenth century military manuals with the evidence from conflict archaeology, Warwick Louth demonstrates how his groundbreaking methodology can improve our investigation and interpretation of the events that took place on the Civil War battlefields of Britain. Finally, this volume considers the care and welfare provided for the Civil War's participants: nowhere are the actualities of war more apparent than in a conflict's casualties. Stephen Rutherford assesses the battlefield surgery of both sides during the war. He considers the types of wounds that were inflicted and highlights the biomedical significance of the treatments available, many of which have remained unchanged until the twentieth century and even to the present day. Eric Gruber von Arni examines royalist hospital provision during the Civil War, evaluating the attitudes and achievements that accompanied it and contrasting these with the attitudes and achievements of parliamentary medical care. Christopher Scott concludes with a short but lively chapter offering a new explanation for Sir William Waller's defeat at Roundway Down on 13 July 1643, which rests on the destitute condition of the horses in Waller's cavalry.

Ismini Pells obtained her PhD from the University of Cambridge in 2014. Her doctoral thesis examined the religious and political thought and military career of Philip Skippon - commander of the infantry in the New Model Army. She is currently working on turning her thesis into a monograph, which will be the first dedicated biography of Skippon. She has already published a study of Skippon s annotations in his personal Bible, as 'Scriptural Truths? Calvinist Internationalism and Military Professionalism in the Bible of Philip Skippon' in *Writing the lives of people and things, AD 500-1700* by (ed.) R.F.W. Smith and G. Watson (Ashgate, Farnham: 2016). Ismini is currently an Associate Research Fellow in the Centre for Medical History at the University of Exeter, where she is working on the project The Medical World of Early Modern England, Ireland and Wales, c. 1500-1715, which has been funded by the Wellcome Trust. She is particularly interested in the medical developments that resulted from the military events of the 17th century and the political roles and networks of medical practitioners during and after the civil war. Ismini is also an academic advisor at the Wolfson Centre for Care, Welfare and Medicine at the National Civil War Centre in Newark.

NEW APPROACHES TO THE MILITARY HISTORY OF THE ENGLISH CIVIL WAR

NEW APPROACHES TO THE MILITARY HISTORY OF ENGLISH CIVIL WAR

*Proceedings of the First Helion & Company
'Century of the Soldier' Conference*

Wolverhampton Military Studies No.25

Edited by Ismini Pells

Helion & Company Limited

Helion & Company Limited
26 Willow Road
Solihull
West Midlands
B91 1UE
England
Tel. 0121 705 3393
Fax 0121 711 4075
Email: info@helion.co.uk
Website: www.helion.co.uk
Twitter: @helionbooks
Visit our blog at http://blog.helion.co.uk/

Published by Helion & Company 2016
Designed and typeset by Mach 3 Solutions Ltd (www.mach3solutions.co.uk)
Cover designed by Paul Hewitt, Battlefield Design (www.battlefield-design.co.uk)
Printed by Lightning Source Ltd, Milton Keynes, Buckinghamshire

ISBN 978-1-911096-44-3

British Library Cataloguing-in-Publication Data.
A catalogue record for this book is available from the British Library.

For details of other military history titles published by Helion & Company Limited, contact
the above address, or visit our website: http://www.helion.co.uk

We always welcome receiving book proposals from prospective authors.

Contents

List of Figures

List of Tables

List of Contributors

Prof. Peter Gaunt

Peter Gaunt is professor of early modern history at the University of Chester. He has published widely not only on military and other aspects of the Civil War in England and Wales, and in Britain as a whole, but also on Oliver Cromwell and aspects of the Cromwellian regime of the 1650s. His most recent book, *The English Civil War, A Military History*, was published in 2014. Prof. Gaunt is a past chairman and current president of The Cromwell Association.

Prof. Malcolm Wanklyn

Malcolm Wanklyn's research interests are in the military history of Britain 1639-52 and in the history of the river Severn and its environs from *circa* 1550. He has published books and articles in academic journals on strategy and tactics in the English Civil War and on many aspects of social, economic and religious development in the counties of Shropshire, Worcestershire, Cheshire, and Warwickshire from *circa* 1550. He managed the ESRC- and Leverhulme Trust-funded Gloucester Port Book Programme between 1984 and 1996, and he lectures and publishes extensively on the history of the river ports of the Severn and aspects of the economic, political and religious history of the counties listed above. Currently, Prof. Wanklyn is working on further articles on armies, generals and politicians in the British wars of 1639-52 and the definitive officer lists of the New Model Army.

Dr Ismini Pells

Ismini Pells is Associate Research Fellow on the Wellcome Trust-funded project 'The Medical World of Early Modern England, Ireland and Wales, c. 1500-1715' at the University of Exeter. She was awarded her PhD by the University of Cambridge in 2014 for her thesis 'The military career, religious and political thought of Philip Skippon, c. 1598-1660'. She has recently published 'Scriptural Truths? Calvinist Internationalism and Military Professionalism in the Bible of Philip Skippon' in *Writing the Lives of People and Things, AD 500-1700*, ed. R.F.W. Smith and G.L. Watson (Ashgate, 2016) and is currently working on turning her research on Skippon into a monograph. Her current research interests lie in the impact of warfare on the development of medicine and surgery in the early modern period and in examining cases of potential psychological trauma from the English Civil War and its associated conflicts. Dr Pells is a trustee of the Society for Army Historical Research and The Cromwell Association, as well as an academic advisor at the Wolfson Foundation Research Centre for Care, Welfare and Medicine at the National Civil War Centre in Newark.

Prof. Tim Jenkins
Tim Jenkins is a self-confessed 'prac-ademic' combining academic research with professional heritage management skills to explore new historical perspectives within the context of the built environment. Following the completion of a PhD at the University of Birmingham, he has worked extensively in the fields of history and heritage incorporating broad research interests that include British military history and the origins of conflict. Prof. Jenkins is currently Associate Professor in Design, Heritage and Built Environment at University Centre Shrewsbury and a Visiting Professor in History and Archaeology at the University of Chester.

Warwick Louth
Growing up amongst the ruins and stories of the English Civil War in Hampshire, it is no surprise that Warwick Louth became fascinated with the period. He gained a degree in Archaeological Practice from the University of Wales Trinity Saint David, Lampeter, followed by a masters degree in Conflict Archaeology at the Centre for Battlefield Archaeology at the University of Glasgow. He is a founder member, archaeological advisor and trustee for Glasgow and South-West Scotland with the Scottish Battlefields Trust. Warwick now writes, researches and talks on a freelance basis – both for enthusiasts and in academic circles – on conflict archaeology, military history and The Wars of the Three Kingdoms. When not engaged in this, he takes part in military modelling, wargaming and is also a member of a range of re-enactment societies. He also works as a Battlefield Coordinator at the Battle of Bannockburn Visitor Centre for the National Trust for Scotland. He lives in Glasgow, on the fringes of the Kilsyth battlefield.

Dr Stephen M. Rutherford
Stephen Rutherford is a Senior Lecturer and Deputy Director of Undergraduate Education at the School of Biosciences, Cardiff University. Stephen undertook his first degree and PhD at the University of York. After a brief period working in the Registrar's Department at the Royal Armouries Museum, Leeds, Stephen undertook post-doctoral research fellowships at University of Nevada, Reno (USA) and the University of Oxford. Stephen has been a member of the faculty at Cardiff University since 2005. Stephen's research background is in genetics and cell biology and he is closely involved in the teaching of cell biology and associated subjects to bioscience, medicine and dentistry undergraduate students. In particular, Stephen has an interest in the development of military surgery and wound care through the ages, and lectures to medical students on the history of military surgery.

Dr Eric Gruber von Arni

Eric Gruber von Arni served for 31 years as a nursing officer in the medical services of the British army and reached the rank of Colonel, before retiring from the service in 1996. His career included service in Germany, Hong Kong, the Sultanate of Oman and the Kingdom of Saudi Arabia, as well as within the United Kingdom and Northern Ireland. In 1982 he was decorated with the Royal Red Cross (2nd Class) for his work in the reception of evacuated casualties in the UK during the Falklands War. In 1991, he was decorated with the Royal Red Cross (1st Class) for his work during the 1990-1 Gulf War as the army's senior nurse in the Middle East. His final military appointment was as the army's Director of Nursing Studies at the Royal Army Medical College in London. Dr Gruber von Arni was awarded a doctorate in military medical history at the University of Portsmouth in 1999. His book *Justice to the Maimed Soldier* was published in 2001 followed by a sequel, *Hospital Care and the British Standing Army, 1660-1714*, in January 2006. He has also contributed chapters to J. Henderson, P. Horden and A. Pastore, eds *The Impact of Hospitals, 300–2000* (2007); G. L. Hudson, ed., *British Military and Naval Medicine, 1600-1930* (2007). Most recently, he has written on the treatment of injuries and disease during the reign of Henry VIII in *Henry VIII, Arms and Man* (the Royal Armouries' celebratory publication commemorating the five hundredth anniversary of the coronation of Henry VIII). He is currently researching for a second sequel to *Justice to the Maimed Soldier* covering the period 1714 to 1780. Dr Gruber von Arni is a Fellow of the Royal Historical Society and has assisted in supervising two doctoral candidates.

Dr Christopher L. Scott

Christopher Scott was Head of Education for the Royal Armouries at Her Majesty's Tower of London and is a member of the Battlefielda Trust, the Royal Historical Society, the Guild of Battlefield Guides and the British Commission for Military History. He has represented Britain at the International Historical Sciences Congress and is a published writer and authority on many aspects of the social and military history of the English Civil Wars, the Monmouth Rebellion and the War of the Spanish Succession. He has an extensive list of book and television credits and has guided bodies of international historians, senior officers and battlefield experts over sites of Cromwell's, Marlborough's, and Wellington's victories. Dr Scott has been walking battlefields for over forty years, analysing ground and tactics and has developed an established academic critique for battlefield study. He gained his doctorate under Professor Richard Holmes at Cranfield University with a ground-breaking investigation into the Restoration Militia. Currently, Dr Scott is working as a freelance lecturer, battlefield guide, author, and museology consultant. He is also a wargamer, retired Lord General of the Roundhead Association and a good storyteller – he won the Cameron Mackintosh Contemporary Playwright Award and has had his plays performed in London and at the Edinburgh Fringe.

The Wolverhampton Military Studies Series
Series Editor's Preface

As series editor, it is my great pleasure to introduce the *Wolverhampton Military Studies Series* to you. Our intention is that in this series of books you will find military history that is new and innovative, and academically rigorous with a strong basis in fact and in analytical research, but also is the kind of military history that is for all readers, whatever their particular interests, or their level of interest in the subject. To paraphrase an old aphorism: a military history book is not less important just because it is popular, and it is not more scholarly just because it is dull. With every one of our publications we want to bring you the kind of military history that you will want to read simply because it is a good and well-written book, as well as bringing new light, new perspectives, and new factual evidence to its subject.

In devising the *Wolverhampton Military Studies Series*, we gave much thought to the series title: this is a *military* series. We take the view that history is everything except the things that have not happened yet, and even then a good book about the military aspects of the future would find its way into this series. We are not bound to any particular time period or cut-off date. Writing military history often divides quite sharply into eras, from the modern through the early modern to the mediaeval and ancient; and into regions or continents, with a division between western military history and the military history of other countries and cultures being particularly marked. Inevitably, we have had to start somewhere, and the first books of the series deal with British military topics and events of the twentieth century and later nineteenth century. But this series is open to any book that challenges received and accepted ideas about any aspect of military history, and does so in a way that encourages its readers to enjoy the discovery.

In the same way, this series is not limited to being about wars, or about grand strategy, or wider defence matters, or the sociology of armed forces as institutions, or civilian society and culture at war. None of these are specifically excluded, and in some cases they play an important part in the books that comprise our series. But there are already many books in existence, some of them of the highest scholarly standards, which cater to these particular approaches. The main theme of the *Wolverhampton Military Studies Series* is the military aspects of wars, the preparation for wars or their prevention, and their aftermath. This includes some books whose main theme is the technical details of how armed forces have worked, some books on wars and battles, and some books that re-examine the evidence about the existing stories, to show in a different light what everyone thought they already knew and understood.

As series editor, together with my fellow editorial board members, and our publisher Duncan Rogers of Helion, I have found that we have known immediately and almost by instinct the kind of books that fit within this series. They are very much the kind of well-written and challenging books that my students at the University of Wolverhampton would want to read. They are books which enhance knowledge, and offer new perspectives. Also, they are books for anyone with an interest in military history and events, from expert scholars to occasional readers. One of the great benefits of the study of military history is that it includes a large and often committed section of the wider population, who want to read the best military history that they can find; our aim for this series is to provide it.

Stephen Badsey
University of Wolverhampton

Introduction

Dr Ismini Pells

Charles Carlton once admitted, in a review in the *Journal of the Society for Army Historical Research*, that whilst reading a recent publication on the English Civil War, he 'often wanted to ask the authors that old Second World War catch phrase, 'Don't you know there's a war on?''. He expressed some exasperation that the discussion of the politics surrounding the war could 'take place as if the background was a college library, rather than a brutal, bloody civil war'.[1] It was Carlton himself who, back in 1992, observed that 'there can be no doubt' that 'the debate over the causes and nature of the crisis that engulfed the British Isles during the middle of the seventeenth century will continue' but in essence, 'they were a complex series of wars, in which men and women killed and were killed, had their bodies maimed, and had to endure some of the most traumatic experiences any human being can face'.[2] Indeed, there is a strong argument for the case that for all the impassioned debate in Westminster and beyond, the outpourings from the political and popular press, and the religious and literary creativity that blossomed as a result of the mid-seventeenth century crisis, the decisions that really counted, those upon which all other matters depended, were made on the battlefield.

Of course, it would be wrong to view military matters in isolation from the political, social or religious events of the period. Military history in general has undergone something of a renaissance over the past 25 years or so and much of this can be attributable to the refashioning of the subject itself to incorporate broader political and cultural themes. Traditionally, military history was a subject with which few serious scholars concerned themselves; the preserve of journalists and retired soldiers and tainted as 'an ideal source of pleasure for the layman with a genuine interest in the 'passionate dramas' of the past'.[3] It was, in John Child's words 'looked down upon by

---

1   C. Carlton, 'Review: The English Civil War, Conflicts and Contexts, 1640-49', *Journal of the Society for Army Historical Research*, 89:358 (2011), p. 185.

2   C. Carlton, *Going to the Wars: The Experience of the English Civil Wars, 1638-1652* (London, Routledge: 1992), p. 2.

3   M. Howard et al., *What is Military History?*, History Today, 34:12 (1984), pp. 9-13, at pp. 6 and 8.

the historical profession and regarded as not quite respectable… something for old soldiers to compile during their retirement'.[4] Traditional military history was equated with military antiquarianism.[5] It was a subject largely concerning itself with such matters as tactics, strategy, uniforms and maps with arrows. Moreover, as John Keegan noted, traditional military history was seldom able to explain what it was actually like to be in the middle of these episodes of extreme violence.[6] However, 'When academics invaded military studies' as Childs put it, 'they immediately connected them with other branches of history. Suddenly, social, political, and economic historians realised that their subjects possessed military dimensions and so military history lost some of its isolation and became linked to its own parent discipline'.[7] Most military historians are now concerned to place operations and the specifically professional sides of fighting a war within their historical context of political aims, the economic and social structure of the conflicting states and the interaction between war and civil society.[8] Armed forces and the conduct of war do and must remain at the heart of military history (which can continue to 'produce a faintly unpleasant odour in the senior common room') but there is now a prevailing awareness that wars are fought by large numbers of men and women 'whose needs and concerns can place unprecedented demands on the structures of society and the state'.[9] It is within this context that this volume is placed.

The majority of the chapters contributed to this volume are extended versions of papers delivered to the Helion and Company English Civil War Conference, held at Rowley's House in Shrewsbury on 19 September 2015. The conference was inspired by Helion's 'Century of the Soldier' series, which was launched to re-examine military history during the period c. 1618–1721. Dubbed the 'golden era' of pike and shot warfare, this period witnessed the development of standing armies, the emergent dominance of gunpowder weapons and the growth of professionalism and a distinctive culture amongst military personnel. Yet, the developments resulting from this period of 'military revolution' were not merely confined to military matters. This was an era of great social, political and religious upheaval, the causes and consequences of which were inextricably linked to military issues.[10] The 'military revolution' had a profound impact on the English Civil War and the associated conflicts in Scotland and Ireland, whilst our understanding of the ramifications of these conflicts is crucial to our interpretation of the nature and characteristics of this phenomenon. The chapters in this volume address several of the themes integral to the 'military revolution'

---

4   Ibid., p. 9.
5   Ibid., p. 7.
6   Ibid., p. 9.
7   Ibid., p. 10.
8   Ibid., p. 7.
9   Ibid., pp. 9-10.
10   G. Parker, 'The "Military Revolution", 1560-1660 – a myth?', in P. E. J. Hammer, ed., *Warfare in Early Modern Europe 1450-1660* (Aldershot, Ashgate: 2007), pp. 1-20.

and in keeping with our understanding of this notion, their focus is not confined to what may be viewed as purely military matters, with political, social and religious considerations explored too.

This volume opens with a section devoted to what might be considered more traditional military history: the reassessment of two key military encounters in the Civil War. Peter Gaunt re-examines the events of the battle of Middlewich, fought on 13 March 1643. In order to shed new light on the day's proceedings, Professor Gaunt utilises the evidence provided by a hitherto neglected but invaluable contemporary plan of the battle, which was most likely prepared by or for Sir Thomas Aston, commander of the royalist forces at Middlewich, to accompany his written account of the engagement. However, Professor Gaunt also explains how the consequences of this rather obscure and disjointed encounter extended far beyond purely military affairs. Victory established the not only parliamentary control of Cheshire but also forced an end to the political neutralism that has prevailed throughout the North West in winter 1642-3. It helped establish the reputation of Sir William Brereton and confirmed his place as leading political as well as military figure in the parliamentarian cause. Moreover, as one of the earliest clear parliamentarian successes of the Civil War, Middlewich provided the London newsbooks with the perfect demonstration of the divine approval of the parliamentarian cause, a conviction made no less significant by Aston's support for the king's religious policies.

Malcolm Wanklyn's chapter, reminding us of the British dimension to the Civil Wars, reflects upon the battle of Worcester (3 September 1651) and its place as the culmination of Cromwell's last military campaign. This chapter forms an addendum to Professor Wanklyn's paper delivered to the conference, which detailed the significance of Cromwell's amphibious assault on the coast of Fife in July 1651 during his campaigning in Scotland. At Worcester, Cromwell faced similar challenges to those posed by the crossing of the Firth of Forth the previous summer, in that he was forced to overcome the problems presented by water hazards in the landscape over which his campaign was to be fought. Professor Wanklyn uses the events at Worcester to make the case for Cromwell's place in the pantheon of military greats, on the basis of his ability to overcome the tactical problems of the landscape, his observance of a flexible strategy and his refusal to rely on his cavalry, the wing of his army with which he was most familiar. However, as Carlton pointed out, 'for most soldiers generals remain remote, even unimportant figures'.[11] Indeed Peter Newman argued that no assessment of a general can be made without acknowledging the role of the men who actually fought the war and 'upon whose efforts and achievements great reputations were founded'.[12] Thus, Professor Wanklyn also takes the time to examine the role of the Cheshire militia in Cromwell's 'crowning mercy', highlighting the experience and

11   Carlton, *Going to the Wars*, p. 180.
12   P. R. Newman, *The Old Service: Royalist Regimental Colonels and the Civil War, 1642-46* (Manchester, Manchester University Press: 1993), p. 1.

bravery of many of the soldiers as well as officers who comprised the regiments of this force.

The second section of this volume considers some of the social and cultural ideals that inspired men to fight in the Civil War and influenced and constrained their actions once the fighting begun. My own chapter investigates the influence of the experiences of fighting in the English regiments under the command of first Sir Francis Vere and later his brother Sir Horace Vere, largely in the Netherlands, on many of the men who formed the officer corps of both sides during the Civil War. At the start of the war, the military experience of these men was much sought after and their personal relationships with other veterans exploited in the recruitment processes. Yet, equally importantly, much of the ideology that governed the relationships within and between Civil War armies, as well as those relationships between these armies and civilian societies, was based upon these men's previous service under the Veres. Naturally, theory did not always translate into practice and many Vereronian veterans struggled at times to implement the codes they had learnt in the Netherlands in the context of the English environment. Nevertheless, a study of this kind can serve as a useful reminder that by placing military conflicts within their social and cultural contexts, we can better understand not just why men fought but the manner in which they fought.

As Christopher Hill once warned, we must be guard against the danger 'of forgetting those who fought well because they thought they were fighting God's battles'.[13] It is almost impossible to contemplate the actions of Civil War armies without also considering the religious ideals that inspired the soldiers who fought in them. Richard Baxter was undoubtedly one of the leading theological lights during the Civil War years, who also had strong links to the parliamentary army. He preached weekly sermons to the parliamentarian garrison at Coventry, helped to establish another parliamentarian garrison at Wem and visited the New Model Army's quarters in Leicester after the battle of Naseby, before accepting the appointment of chaplain to Edward Whalley's Regiment.[14] Baxter was born in the county of Shropshire and it was whilst visiting members of the godly community in Shrewsbury, men such as William Rowley in whose house the conference was held, that Baxter began to develop his religious convictions. Tim Jenkins explores the role of the godly community within Shrewsbury to shed light on their influence in this town in terms of societal and religious innovation, as well as the tensions these men and women caused during the royalist occupation of Shrewsbury during the Civil War.

---

13   T. Liu, *Discord in Zion: The Puritan Divines and the Puritan Revolution 1640-1660* (The Hague: 1973), p. xii.
14   N. H. Keeble, 'Baxter, Richard (1615–1691)', *Oxford Dictionary of National Biography* (Oxford, Oxford University Press: 2009), online edn, http://www.oxforddnb.com/view/article/1734, accessed 21 July 2016.

Religious ideals aside, drillbooks and manuals might be considered the bibles of the military revolution. The proliferation of printed drillbooks, with detailed, step-by-step illustrations, enabled the dissemination of the tactics and strategy of leading Continental armies, such as the Dutch army of William of Nassau, which had the effect of institutionalising and unifying military action. However, as Warwick Louth argues in his complex and challenging chapter, the ability to be able to complete the movements outlined in military manuals whilst under enemy fire may be another matter entirely. Thus the instructions in such books may represent the ideal, rather than the reality, and their enactment on the battlefield may have been truncated and simplified according to the situation and time constraint. Nevertheless, Mr Louth demonstrates the archaeological usefulness of military manuals in their ability to dictate artefact recovery on Civil War battlefields. He uses the evidence provided by drillbooks to illustrate when and how an individual performing drill movements might deposit artefacts, as well as examining the spatial distribution of these artefacts to find common arrangements that mirror the tactical formations used by the army in which that individual fought. The outcome is the development of a series of rules and guidelines, based on the nature and use of manual trends on Civil War battlefields, which can be used to identify sites relevant to conflict, thus enabling heritage boundaries to be tightened and further archaeological exploration undertaken.

Nowhere are 'the actualities of war'[15] more apparent than in a conflict's casualties. The final section of this volume, 'Medicine and Welfare', investigates the care available to those who made up the Civil War armies. In his chapter, Stephen Rutherford, argues against the unfavourable reputation of early modern military surgeons as men who were being poorly trained, overly reliant on traditional theories and bizarre practices, and lacking in skill. He maintains that far from the unflattering popular image of leeches, amputations and unsanitary conditions, military surgeons in the Civil War were potentially highly-skilled and well-trained individuals. In particular, Dr Rutherford is able to show that the key methodologies of Civil War practitioners were based on scientific principles and evidence-based methodology. He uses the writings of Civil War surgeons to demonstrate the extent to which surgery adapted to changes in the requirements of medical practice prompted by the development of the increasingly sophisticated weaponry of the military revolution and the monumental impact this had of the population of the British Isles. Astonishingly, Dr Rutherford reveals that few breakthroughs in surgery or medical practice were made after the early modern period until the discovery of bacteria and the development of anaesthetics in the mid-nineteenth century and much of the practice of Civil War surgeons is still in evidence today with only modest refinements.

Despite the evident skill of parliamentarian and royalist surgeons alike that Stephen Rutherford demonstrates, Eric Gruber von Arni paints a rather bleak picture of the attention and financial resources that were devoted to medical administration on the

15 Carlton, *Going to the Wars*, p. 3.

royalist side in Civil War. In comparison to the detailed and numerous records that provide a comprehensive record of medical administration on the parliamentarian side, few such documents survive for their opponents. Nevertheless, piecing together the few remaining references to medical and nursing care in the royalist camp, Dr Gruber von Arni examines the philosophy and measures adopted by the king and his council of war to provide hospitals and care for their army's sick and wounded in the royalist capital of Oxford. He argues that flaws in the royalist command structure, namely the council of war exercising centralised control under the king's autocratic personal direction, created severe difficulties for administrating a coordinated casualty care policy.

Finally, as Gavin Robinson has recently reminded historians, it was not just humans but also horses who played a vital role in the military outcomes of the Civil War.[16] Thus, the care and welfare of these animals must have been of comparable importance to that provided for people. This volume concludes with Chris Scott's short but lively reassessment of Sir William Waller's defeat at the battle of Roundway Down on 13 July 1643. In this chapter, Dr Scott acknowledges the significance of the traditional explanations given for Waller's defeat: the experience and expertise of the royalist horsemen, their impetus in the battle and the cowardice of their parliamentarian counterparts However, he argues that the key factors in determining the result of the battle are to be found firstly in the parliamentarians' deployment of the inferior Dutch firepower system against the royalists' use of Swedish cavalry tactics but also, most crucially, the dilapidated physical condition of the parliamentarian horses as a result of sustained summer campaigning.

Taken as a whole, these chapters aim to stimulate interest, open discussion and provoke debate. As the first conference volume in this series, it is hoped that other scholars will pick up and engage with the themes raised here and that together we might, in some small way, pay tribute to those brave men and women for whom the Civil War was not a subject for academic discussion but a bloody reality.

---

16   G. Robinson, *Horses, People and Parliament in the English Civil War: Extracting Resources and Constructing Allegiance* (Farnham, Ashgate: 2012).

Part I

New Perspectives

————————————————————————————————————

1

'Wedged up in the church like billetts in a woodpile': New light on the battle of Middlewich, 13 March 1643

Prof. Peter Gaunt

Just as he was putting to bed his edition of *Certaine Informations from Severall Parts of the Kingdome* for the week 13-20 March 1643, the editor of this London-based and pro-parliamentarian newspaper picked up the first reports reaching the capital of a victory for parliament's forces in far off Cheshire. The editor, William Ingler, tacked onto the final page of the newspaper the brief report that:

> Out of *Cheshire* they write, that the Commissioners of Array sent out of *Chester* 7 or 800 horse, and 3 peeces of Ordnance to *Middlewich* to guard and fortifie that Town, which Sir *William Brereton* having notice of, made out of *Namptwich* with his forces, met with them, fought with them, took 80 of them prisoners, with all their Ordnance and powder, slew some of them, and put the residue to shamefull flight.[1]

Similarly, but from a very different viewpoint, Peter Heylyn, the editor of the Oxford-based and pro-royalist weekly newspaper *Mercurius Aulicus*, squeezed a brief but troubling report of the engagement onto the penultimate page of the edition which went to press on 18 March:

> This day we had an uncertaine rumour, of a disaster that had befallen His Majesties forces in *Cheshire*, under the conduct of Sir Thomas Aston: the true circumstances of which, if upon further information, it shall prove considerable, shall be told hereafter.[2]

---

1   *Certaine Informations from Severall Parts of the Kingdome*, 9 (13-20 March 1643), p. 72.
2   *Mercurius Aulicus*, 11 (11-18 March 1643), p. 137.

Both reports, of a parliamentarian victory and royalist defeat at Middlewich, proved to be true, but while the parliamentarian presses were kept busy providing their readers with further details of the battle and its outcome, nothing more was said in *Mercurius Aulicus* and the Oxford editors quickly moved on to other, happier news. In contrast, parliamentarian newspapers waxed lyrical about the victory. Several stressed the number and value of the prisoners: 'about five hundred, whereof many were commanders and Gentlemen' reported one, going on to predict that this royalist defeat 'will much asswage the malice and cruelty of the enemy in those parts'.[3] The editor of another London-based newspaper thought that since the start of 'this unnaturall war God hath not given many more complete victories',[4] while a further account printed as a pamphlet in London a few days after the event reckoned, perhaps somewhat imaginatively, that:

> The same morning we set upon them, *Sir Tho: Aston*, and the rest drank to *Billie Brereton*, as they called him, and said they would give him a Breakfast anon, but such was the good hand of God upon us, that we fared better then they would have had us: Their Word [the single word or short phrase adopted by each side before an engagement so that in the heat of battle friend could be distinguished from foe] was Prince *Rupert*; Ours, *The Lord of Hosts*: And so you see that *The Lord of Hoasts* overcame Prince *Rupert*.[5]

This was a nice piece of wishful thinking, of course, as Prince Rupert himself, clearly already parliament's *bête noire*, played no part at Middlewich.

The engagement fought at Middlewich in mid-March 1643 to which these reports relate was not part of the major, national campaign of that year; that did not really begin until well into April, when the king's main Oxford-based army and the main parliamentarian army under Lord General Essex clashed around Reading. Instead, it formed one facet of a number of regional struggles which began in several English

---

3   *A Perfect Diurnall of the Passages in Parliament*, 40 (20-27 March 1643), unpaginated.
4   *A Perfect Diurnall of the Passages in Parliament*, 42 (20-27 March 1643), unpaginated (despite sharing the same title and dates, this newspaper is different from that cited in the previous note). Brief reports of the battle appeared in several other parliamentarian newspapers, including *The Kingdomes Weekly Intelligencer*, 12 (14-21 March 1643), p. 95, *A Continuation of Certaine Speciall and Remarkable Passages from Both Houses of Parliament*, 3 (16-23 March 1643), p. 5 and *The Kingdomes Weekly Intelligencer*, 13 (21-28 March 1643), p. 99.
5   Anon., *Cheshires Successe Since their Pious and truly Valiant Collonell Sir William Brereton Barronet, came to their Rescue* (London: 1643), the first part of the pamphlet is very irregularly paginated and it is unpaginated at this point. Parts or all of the text of this pamphlet were subsequently reproduced and included in slightly later military accounts, notably in John Vicars's account of the battle of Middlewich in his broader history of the early stages of the civil war: J. Vicars, *God on the Mount, or a Continuation of Englands Parliamentary Chronicle* (London: 1643), pp. 289-92.

regions, especially Yorkshire, the far South-West and Gloucestershire and its environs, in the opening weeks of 1643. The North West as a whole, including Shropshire, Staffordshire and Lancashire too, appeared divided and disputed during winter 1642-43, with plenty of uncertainty and an unwillingness firmly to commit to either side.[6] In Cheshire, pockets of active royalism and parliamentarianism certainly existed by this stage but they were overshadowed by a good deal of apathy, non-engagement and neutralism. Indeed, Cheshire is one of those counties in which, during winter 1642-43, a more formal and organised attempt was made to demilitarise and to keep the county out of the unfolding war via a neutrality treaty, concluded at Bunbury just before Christmas. That attempted neutrality was ended and Cheshire was dragged more firmly into the civil war by the return to the county in late January 1643 of Sir William Brereton of Handforth, a middling Cheshire landowner and one of the county's MPs. He returned to Cheshire from London, bringing with him a small body of a few hundred mounted troops – some raised in the London area, others picked up *en route* in Shropshire and Staffordshire – together with supplies of arms and ammunition for the further troops, especially infantry, which he hoped to raise in his native county. He and his men entered Cheshire from the east, via Congleton, where he was likely to encounter little initial resistance and some support, as it fell to some extent under the sway of the Manchester, Salford and Stockport area, which had already shown strong pro-parliamentarian sympathies, and was also furthest from Chester and the county's western border with North Wales, where royalism and royalists were much stronger. Brereton's chief opponent as he moved from east to west across the county was another Cheshire landowner, Sir Thomas Aston of Aston Hall, a former MP and sheriff, who had already shown himself to be a firm and active supporter of the king and his policies, especially his religious policy, within Cheshire during the year or so before the outbreak of war.[7] While Brereton's attempts to recruit for parliament in and around Chester in early August 1642 had fallen very flat,[8] from summer

---

6   See P. Gaunt, *The English Civil War. A Military History* (London, I B Tauris: 2014), chapter 4, especially pp. 126-41 for the various regional campaigns of winter and early spring 1643.

7   For Brereton, see J. Morrill, 'Sir William Brereton and England's wars of religion', *Journal of British Studies*, 24 (1985), pp. 311-32; J. Morrill, 'Brereton, Sir William, first baronet (1604-1661)', *Oxford Dictionary of National Biography* (60 vols, Oxford, Oxford University Press: 2004) [hereafter *ODNB*]; R. N. Dore, ed., *The letter books of Sir William Brereton* (2 vols, Record Society of Lancashire and Cheshire: 1984 and 1990), especially the introductions to both volumes. For Aston, see E. C. Vernon, 'Aston, Sir Thomas, first baronet (1600-1646), *ODNB*. Both men are assessed in J. Morrill, *Cheshire, 1630-1660: County Government and Society during the English Revolution* (Oxford, Oxford University Press: 1974) and in R. N. Dore, '1642: the coming of the civil war to Cheshire: conflicting actions and impressions', *Transactions of the Antiquarian Society of Lancashire and Cheshire*, 87 (1991), pp. 39-63.

8   British Library [hereafter BL], Harleian MS 2155, fol. 108 (Account of the Civil War in Chester in August 1642).

1642 onwards Aston had supported the king militarily and had in turn been supported and empowered by the king to serve as a prominent military officer within Cheshire.[9] In January 1643 he received further direction and authorisation in his military capacity, both from the king himself and from Prince Rupert.[10]

There followed between late January and mid-March 1643 a series of engagements and stand-offs within Cheshire in which Brereton generally outmanoeuvred and repulsed Aston and quite quickly secured eastern and central Cheshire. The series began with an evening street fight in Nantwich which, confused and rather amateurish though it seems to have been in the darkness of a winter's evening, nonetheless set the tone for the short campaign, as it ended in the complete

Figure 1.1 Sir William Brereton, the parliamentarian commander-in-chief in Cheshire, as depicted in an illustrated volume describing the achievements of parliament's leading generals compiled and published by Josiah Ricraft in 1647. (J. Ricraft, *A Survey of Englands Champions*, London: 1647)

defeat of the royalists. The king's men reportedly panicked and fled when Brereton fired his small field guns in their general direction, 'which wrought more terror than execution', and when some loose parliamentarian horses galloped towards them. The parliamentarian account of the action claimed that one royalist officer 'crawled away on all foure[s], lest he should be discern'd, & then ran on foot bare headed' for six miles and that Aston himself ran three miles on foot before finding a horse and riding away into Shropshire.[11] Even if we discount some of this as parliamentarian propaganda, it was not an auspicious beginning for Aston and his men. The battle of Middlewich of mid-March, which ended with another street fight, is best seen as the culmination of this series of engagements; the final, biggest and most decisive battle of this six-week campaign, which saw Brereton's parliamentarians secure most of the county, including establishing garrisons in the newly-fortified towns of Nantwich and

---

9   BL, Additional MS 36913, fols. 90-6 and 101-3 (Letters and warrants relating to Sir Thomas Aston's command in Cheshire, 1642).

10   BL, Additional MS, fol. 105 (Rupert's orders to Aston of 17 January, addressed to him as colonel of a regiment of cuirassiers), fol. 107 (Rupert's further orders to Aston also dated 17 January, addressed to him as colonel of a regiment of horse) and fol. 110 (the king's orders to Aston of 19 January, addressed to him as colonel both of a regiment of horse and of a regiment of dragoons).

11   *Cheshires Successe*, pp. 2-3.

Northwich and a forward base at Beeston Castle, overlooking Chester, west Cheshire and the Dee valley, which remained in royalist hands.

The surviving written sources for the battle of Middlewich are heavily skewed towards the parliamentarians. From Nantwich on 15 March, Brereton wrote to his fellow north-western MP, William Ashhurst, giving an account of the battle. What may be the original letter survives[12] but in any case, the text (with only very minor variations from the manuscript version) was quickly published, both as a separate pamphlet[13] and within a wider compilation of material describing Brereton's successful Cheshire campaign.[14] Brereton was based at Northwich immediately before the attack on Middlewich and led the initial assaults on the western side of the town. His letter to Ashhurst focuses on this element of the engagement. The pamphlet, which prints a range of sources covering Brereton's wider county campaign of early 1643, includes a second, different and in some ways more detailed account of the battle. This is apparently written by a parliamentarian based at Nantwich – his identity is never revealed in the pamphlet and no extant manuscript version has been found – and who participated with fellow-Nantwich troops in the second wave of the parliamentarian attack, on the southern side of the town. As one would expect, this account focuses on that element of the parliamentarian operation.[15] These two principal parliamentarian accounts can be supplemented by other, briefer descriptions. These include a short letter 'from a man of note', again found within the pamphlet giving a broader account of Brereton's Cheshire campaign;[16] a handful of short reports in London-based, pro-parliamentarian newspapers, most of which have already been quoted or noted; and two short accounts of the battle found within wider chronicles of the civil war in and around Cheshire, namely Edward Burghall's 'Providence improved; being remarks taken from his diary' and Thomas Malbon's 'Memorials of the civil war in Cheshire and the adjacent counties'.[17]

On the other hand, we have only one surviving royalist written account of any detail. It was put together just a few days after the battle – one version claims it was written at Pulford on 17 March – by Sir Thomas Aston himself. Two apparently contemporary manuscript versions survive, with generally only very minor textual

12   BL, Additional MS 34253, fol. 23 (Letter from Sir William Brereton to William Ashhurst, MP for Newton-in- Makerfield, giving an account of his victory over the royalist Forces at Middlewich, 15 March 1643).

13   A. Goodwin, *Two Letters of Great Consequence to the House of Commons* (London: 1643), pp. 3-5; the other letter transcribed in this pamphlet concerns developments in Buckinghamshire.

14   *Cheshires Successe*, unpaginated at this point.

15   Ibid., pp. 2-13 [sic] – irregular pagination at this point.

16   Ibid., unpaginated at this point.

17   Both are printed in J. Hall, ed., *Memorials of the Civil War in Cheshire, and the adjacent counties, by T. Malbon, and, Providence Improved, by E. Burghall* (Record Society of Lancashire and Cheshire: 1889), the two accounts of events at Middlewich, which are very similar in content, length and detail, are interspersed by Hall on pp. 39-42.

variations between them.[18] This account does not appear to have been printed at the time and not until well into the nineteenth century was the text transcribed and published.[19] Another extant, if brief, royalist account, apparently written by a group of commissioners of array and pro-royalist Cheshire gentlemen somewhat later in 1643 and providing a critique of the whole royalist campaign in Cheshire down to that point, includes an interpretation and explanation of the royalist defeat at Middlewich. However, this does not itself supply or add significant details of the battle or of the events which unfolded in and around the town on 13 March.[20]

The various written sources, especially the three main accounts – Aston's, Brereton's and the anonymous Nantwich parliamentarian's – display differences in tone and style. Most obviously, the two principal parliamentarian accounts have a triumphant air about them, entirely and understandably absent from Aston's version of events. The parliamentarian authors were keen to stress that the victory achieved at Middlewich had been more divine than mortal and, while in places the courage of their own troops and the shortcomings of their royalist opponents were duly acknowledged and the former praised, the emphasis was on the way in which the Lord had shaped events and had bestowed victory on His favoured troops, those fighting for a godly cause. Thus, in his letter, Brereton was clear that victory was a gift from the Lord and stressed that 'I desire the whole praise and glory may be attributed to almighty God, who infused courage into them that stood for his cause, and strucke the enemie with terror and amazement'. The anonymous Nantwich account likewise noted that although the royalists' initial positions had seemed very strong and almost impregnable, 'God lead on our men with incredible courage' and that when they were short of gunpowder 'God supplied us more then treble out of our Enemies store', whilst it further reported that, with victory secured, 'we turned our prayers into prayses, sent for the *Belman* to warne the Towne to the Church, to returne God thanks for such an unparalel'd mercy, which they did with great alacritie, and joyfull acclamations in a full *Congregation*'.[21]

Divine will played no part in Aston's account, which has an altogether different tone and thrust. Aston's purpose was to excuse himself and to stress that the blame for the royalist defeat at Middlewich could not be laid at his door. The tone was set in the opening paragraph, in which Aston appealed that he should not be condemned

18   BL, Additional MS 36913, fols 120-1v (Sir Thomas Aston's account of the battle of Middlewich, 1643); Harleian MS 2135, fols 102-3v (Letter from Sir Thomas Aston defending his conduct at the battle of Middlewich, 17 March 1643).

19   G. Ormerod and T. Helsby, *The History of the County Palatine and City of Chester* (3 vols, London, G. Routledge: 1882), III, pp. 178-80; J. R. Phillips, *Memoirs of the Civil Wars in Wales and the Marches, 1642-1649* (2 vols, London, Longmans Green & Co: 1874), II, pp. 56-61.

20   BL, Additional MS 36913, fol. 122 ('A representation of the state of the kings affaires in the County Palatine of Chester, and parts adjacent, tendred by divers of the Commissioners of Array and Gentry of that County', 1643).

21   *Cheshires Successe*, p. 13 [sic] and unpaginated at this point.

for his failure in battle until 'truth may bee knowne, and let that [ac]quit or condemne mee'. For Aston, the truth was that his mid-Cheshire foray had been much slower than intended through no fault of his own, that his departure from Middlewich had been similarly delayed because of the action or inaction of others and that the decision to remain in the town, to make a stand there and to fight to hold it had been taken with the 'joynt consent' of Aston and the other senior officers and royalist officials who were with him. In the ensuing engagement he had been let down by the failure of royalist troops from Whitchurch to march on Nantwich and thus distract the parliamentarian forces based there, by the inexperience and mistakes of his infantry officers and by the woeful performance of his infantry, both his Welsh foot and members of the Cheshire trained bands or militia, who had moved forward and taken up position unwillingly and had then proved hopeless in battle. Aston alleged that they shot in the air or randomly, went to ground and took cover unnecessarily, and generally proved cowardly and prone to run. As a consequence, Aston claimed that his cavalry, repeatedly praised in this account and to whom no blame should be attached, he felt, were let down and left in the lurch. Equally, several of his artillery pieces were left unmanned or almost unguarded. Conversely, Aston portrayed himself as a vigorous and diligent commander, moving around the field and moving men to shore up his defences, attempting to rally his crumbling forces, at one point riding amongst his cowering foot with drawn sword in an effort to get them to stand and fight. Even once the town's defences had failed and the enemy were breaking through, he bravely stayed and organised a last stand around the church, he claimed, so that he 'was the last [royalist] horseman in the towne' that day. Having reluctantly quit the town, Aston suggested that he hoped to rally his remaining horse outside Middlewich but, failing to locate them, only then did he ride off to Whitchurch, in order to find or to raise men there. Aston closed his account of events with a series of self-justificatory assertions.

> Where the occasion of this disaster can fix on mee, I shall gladly bee informed. The designe was sure approved, desired by all. The stay att Middlewich, which was not occasioned by mee, was necessary, was assented to by all... The intelligence failed not, but was seasonable, thoughe raw men with unreadie officers were long in answering the alarme, and drew out without either powder or shot. The horse could doe noe more, unlesse there had beene place for it, nor could any horse suffer with more unmoved courage, till they were clearly deserted by the foot. And I thinke noe man there will denie, but I was to my best asisting every part of the action...

To corroborate his account, Aston included at several points in the margin the names of a handful of his men, most or all of them his junior officers, who could or would support his version of events, some of whom added their signatures at the foot of the last sheet to confirm that 'The particulars here recited are justified by us whose names are subscribed according to our severall knowledge attested in the Margin'. The names appearing in the surviving versions of Aston's account vary slightly, but they include Francis Aston, Robert Chetwood, Thomas Holme or Holmes, Nathaniel, Thomas and William Naper or Napier, Thomas Prestwich, William Ratcliffe, Thomas Roston and Richard and John Wiltshire.[22] Aston ended by pointing out that 'If the event must condemn the man, the service of this Countrey will be but an uncomfortable undertaking' and by reiterating that any failure was 'not brought by the good will or default of' himself. The whole document might succinctly but accurately be summarised as 'it was not my fault'.[23]

As well as differences in perspective and purpose, the main surviving written accounts of the battle also differ in terms of the clarity of the narrative. The two principal parliamentarian accounts provide a fairly clear story of the battle as it unfolded between early morning and early afternoon on 13 March, albeit one containing a few gaps. They appear to supply a crisp narrative of the successive phases of the engagement and there is a clear chronological thread and sequence which can be followed. Aston's account is not only longer, mentioning developments omitted from the two parliamentarian narratives, but also in places a little harder to follow. Just as Aston took an interest in different parts of the battlefield during the day, so his narrative seems a little jumbled at times, or at least it tells the story of one phase before jumping or returning to a somewhat earlier phase underway elsewhere. This is especially true in his account of the closing phases of the engagement, once his outer defences had been overwhelmed and broken. Nonetheless, keeping in mind the differences and issues already noted, it is possible to run together all the main extant texts to produce a reasonably consistent and plausible version of the events which unfolded 13 March. However, in the case of this battle, we possess another vital and precious source which can greatly expand our knowledge and strengthen our grasp of events.

Surviving contemporary plans of civil war battles are as rare as hen's teeth. We possess the stylised Sir Bernard de Gomme watercolours of the royalist army or of both armies arrayed before a handful of major battles including Edgehill and Naseby, the detailed but in some ways distorted and misleading Streeter bird's-eye view of both armies deployed at Naseby and the composite engraving showing several stages of the battle of Dunbar.[24] But it is very rare to have an extant contemporary battle

---

22   See the lists of Aston's forces at BL, Additional MS. 36913, fols 145-59; I am most grateful to Professor Malcolm Wanklyn for discussion of this point.

23   BL, Additional MS 36913, fols 120-1v (Sir Thomas Aston's account of the battle of Middlewich, 1643); BL, Harleian MS 2135, fols 102-3v (Letter from Sir Thomas Aston defending his conduct at the battle of Middlewich, 17 March 1643).

24   All have been reproduced in several modern works, perhaps most accessibly in, for the de Gomme plans, P. Young, *Edgehill 1642, the Campaign and the Battle* (Kineton, The Roundwood Press: 1967), plate 9; G. Foard, *Naseby, the Decisive Campaign* (Whitstable, Prior Publications: 1995), figures 54 and 55; for versions of the Streeter image, C. Carlton, *Going to the Wars, the Experience of the British Civil Wars, 1638-1651* (London, Routledge: 1992), plates 4 and 5; and for Dunbar, Ibid., plate 14.

plan from the civil war and that makes the plan of Middlewich all the more valuable. Hitherto rarely noted and little used by historians,[25] it survives amongst one of the volumes of Aston papers now held by the British Library, whose catalogue correctly identifies it as a plan of the battle of Middlewich.[26] It carries no date, title, scale, orientation or the name or initials of the cartographer but given its provenance, it was presumably prepared by or for Aston in order to illustrate and to accompany his written account of the engagement. It is in ink on paper and now measures around sixteen inches by twelve inches – in modern terms, around A3 size – though it is just a little frayed and rough around the edges and corners, so it is possible that the original would have been a little bigger and that there has been some minor loss of paper and of illustration and annotation. However, in the main it is sound, in good condition and provides a clear image. Although the location portrayed is not identified on the plan and the word 'Middlewich' never appears, sufficient topographical clues are given firmly to locate and to orientate the plan. Thus, close to one edge it has an image of a twin-gabled timber-framed house labelled 'Kinderton House' and, a little to the left of it, a bridge over a waterway is labelled 'Byley Bridge', while a road running away to the right of and passing Kinderton House is identified as 'The way to Brereton'. If that edge becomes the top of the plan, a road heading off the right hand edge is labelled 'Holmes Chappel Lane' and a second road running off the bottom right corner is called 'Nantwich way'.

Kinderton Hall is the best starting point for locating the plan. Rebuilt in the early eighteenth century as a grand brick farmhouse – the gardens, earthworks and remains of a possible medieval moat surviving immediately west of the Georgian house may indicate the site of its predecessor shown on the Aston plan, which was demolished around 1700 – it still stands just outside Middlewich and so confirms that Middlewich is the town shown in the centre of the plan. This also gives some indication of orientation and scale. Taking the parish church of St Michael and All Angels as the centre of Stuart Middlewich, Kinderton Hall stands around half a mile north-east of that point. The modern road system running into and out of Middlewich and around the area has been subject to significant changes and accordingly, it is dangerous and misleading to attempt to equate the named roadways shown on the Aston plan with modern A- and B- or more minor roads, but Holmes Chapel lies to the east and Nantwich to the south of Middlewich. So all those features would be more or less correctly placed and labelled if north is roughly top left of the plan and south ('Nantwich way') is bottom right. However, the other two named features do not fit so well. On the basis of this orientation, Byley bridge is shown a little way north-north-west of Kinderton Hall and that is incorrect. Byley bridge (see Figure 1.3) still carries a roadway over the river Dane, but it is situated around half a mile north-east of Kinderton Hall and thus

25   The plan was reproduced and briefly discussed by me in an article entitled 'Four churches and a river: aspects of the civil war in Cheshire', *Cromwelliana*, series 2, vol. 5 (2008), p. 17.
26   BL, Additional Ms. 36913, fols 129v-30 (Plan of the battle of Middlewich, 1643).

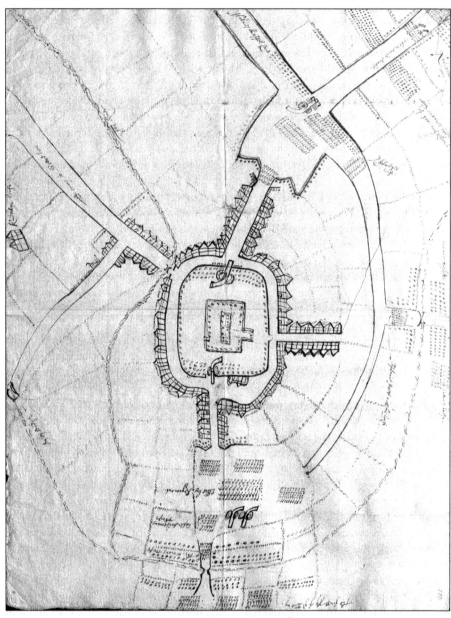

Figure 1.2 The contemporary sketch plan of the battle of Middlewich, drawn from a royalist perspective and almost certainly by or for Sir Thomas Aston, which survives amongst his papers at the British Library. (© The British Library Board: British Library, Additional MS 36913, fols 129v–130)

around a mile north-east of the centre of Middlewich. Is it possible that Aston or his cartographer confused Byley with the next crossing point of the Dane downstream and that the bridge labelled 'Byley' here is in fact Ravenscroft bridge (see Figure 1.4), which does cross the Dane a little under half a mile west-north-west of Kinderton Hall and a little over half a mile north of the town centre? That would fit quite neatly with the proposed orientation and scale of the plan. Equally, the roadway marked 'The way to Brereton' is problematic, unless a rather circuitous route was intended, for although the village of Brereton and nearby Brereton Hall do lie roughly east of Middlewich, they are a little beyond and south of Holmes Chapel, whereas the Aston plan seems to suggest that the Brereton route lies parallel to but clearly north of the road to Holmes Chapel.

Middlewich and its hinterland were extensively redeveloped post-civil war, from the eighteenth century onwards. The huge expansion of salt-working and the arrival of other large chemical works, the cutting of the Trent and Mersey Canal and the Middlewich branch of the Shropshire Union Canal, together with the redirection of various natural waterways and the creation of new watercourses and reservoirs, the arrival of the railway, and the substantial demographic and physical expansion of the town have between them hugely altered the layout and topography of the whole area. Just as we cannot securely identify the various roads shown on the Aston plan either with modern roads and with those shown on the earliest detailed maps of Middlewich, dating from the nineteenth century, so the fields and field boundaries shown on the Aston plan cannot help us much, as they had largely been overrun or greatly changed by urban expansion and other developments by the time of the Victorian ordnance survey and tithe maps.

Similarly, we cannot always neatly and with confidence identify the waterways shown on the Aston plan with modern or known rivers. One, labelled simply 'The River', enters at the top right hand corner of the plan, clips the corner of the town where a crude and small bridge is drawn, presumably intending to show the road being carried over the river, and then flows on around one side of the town to join another river further on. This may be intended as the then route of the river Croco, a small river which rises in mid Cheshire, east of Middlewich, runs around the north-east side of the town and flows into the river Dane to the north-north-west of the town centre, though its current course has clearly been altered and artificially rechannelled in places as its flows through the outskirts of the modern town (see Figures 1.5 and 1.6). The river into which it flows and which is shown entering on the top edge of the plan where it is crossed by 'Byley' – perhaps in reality Ravenscroft – bridge must be the Dane. A little further west and slightly under one mile north-west of the town centre, the Dane (having already absorbed the Croco) merges with and receives the waters of the river Wheelock. This river flows from south to north through southern Cheshire and runs around the western side of Middlewich, at its closest point a little over half a mile from the town centre, before flowing into the Dane a little under a mile north-west of Middlewich (see Figure 1.7). This must be the other unnamed river shown on the Aston plan looping around the bottom and left hand side of the

Figures 1.3 and 1.4 The rebuilt or heavily restored Byley bridge (Figure 1.3) still carries a road over the river Dane north-east of Middlewich. However, given its position, the bridge labelled 'Byley' on the plan of the battle is more likely to be Ravenscroft bridge (Figure 1.4), also rebuilt or at least heavily restored since the time of the civil war, which spans the Dane much closer to and north of the town. (Author's photograph)

Figure 1.5 Part of the now rather sad and much depleted river Croco, rerouted past various industrial estates on the north-eastern outskirts of Middlewich. (Author's photograph)

Figure 1.6 The river Dane flowing from east to west across the northern outskirts of the town, around the point where in the seventeenth century – though no longer – it would have received the waters of the Croco. (Author's photograph)

Figure 1.7 A stretch of the river Wheelock, flowing from south to north past the western outskirts of the town, shown here a little south of to its junction with the Dane. Although the creation of the Trent and Mersey Canal and its offshoots and of various reservoirs around the town means that probably less water is now carried by the Wheelock and the Dane around Middlewich than would have been the case at the time of the Civil War, this photograph still gives a sense of how the river and its modest but significant valley would have been defensible by Aston and presented an obstacle to Brereton's attacking force. (Author's photograph)

plan and thus roughly around the western side of the town. Once again, and allowing for some give and take on what was clearly intended as a sketch plan, the orientation and scale already established in our discussion of the relationship of Kinderton Hall to the town centre seem to work.

The Aston plan also depicts the town itself, showing houses lining both sides of four roads running into the centre and around the outer edge only of a continuous roadway which encircles and encloses the church and churchyard. Despite redevelopment of the road system, including the brutish A54 which now roars past just north of the church, something of this arrangement survives today. St Michael's church is very clearly portrayed on the Aston plan and is apparently shown quite accurately, complete with the large projecting porch close to the west end of the south wall, which is still there. Like most churches, St Michael's is aligned almost exactly east-west. Thus the Aston plan seems to be an amalgam of different scales and orientations. The urban centre – the church, the churchyard, the encircling road and probably the four streets

Figure 1.8 The south side of St Michael's Church, with its projecting porch and quite lofty, battlemented tower (left) and its series of large, late medieval, Perpendicular-style windows. (Author's photograph)

running into it – are portrayed at a much larger scale than the area around but outside the town. The church and perhaps the centre are also depicted on a more traditional orientation, with the top of the plan being north, the bottom south and so on, while the northing for the outer area turns approximately 45 degrees anti-clockwise, so that the top left is north, the bottom right south and so on.

The military details and annotations on the plan make clear that it was drawn up from a royalist perspective. Several bodies of royalist soldiers are identified through their commanding officer – 'The Maiors Troope', 'Capt. Bridgmans Troope', 'Ellis his Regiment', 'Captaine Prestwich his horse' and 'Ld Cholmleyes horse'. Conversely, the parliamentarians are always simply the enemy – 'The first pty of the Enemy', 'Enemies horse', 'Enemies musketrs', 'The enemyes body of 300 musketeers' and 'The enemies Drakes'. The plan also uses symbols to show where different types and blocks of soldiers were deployed, employing identical symbols for both royalists and parliamentarians – a lower case 'h' for horse, 'p' for pikemen and 'o' or a small circle for musketeers. While these annotations seem to provide a reliable indication of the different types of royalist and parliamentarian soldiers deployed around Middlewich and of where they were deployed at various times during the operation – as we shall see, they often correspond to and are thus confirmed and corroborated by details of deployment given in the written accounts – and they also seem to give a rough indication of the size and density of the deployments, they almost certainly do not provide an accurate indication of numbers. In other words, although (employing a magnifying glass) it is possible carefully to count the number of lower case letters or small circles shown on the plan, for each individual block of soldiers and in total, the figures reached in this way almost certainly do not equate to the actual numbers of troop deployed on the ground, even on the royalist side. In any case, Aston or his cartographer would presumably have had only a hazy grasp of the numbers of parliamentarians who opposed and engaged them in the course of 13 March.

Even without any accounts of the battle to flesh things out, the plan reveals that the engagement was fought in distinct areas and even gives a rough indication of chronology. To the north-west of the town, the armies are shown confronting each other either side of and across a key bridge, which is depicted carrying the roadway over the Wheelock. The plan suggests that Aston stationed two troops of horse to hold the bridge and the townward side, with musketeers lining the hedges or ditches on either side of the bridge along the eastern bank of the river. Three further bodies of horse, a stand of pikemen and two pieces of artillery are shown drawn up in a larger enclosed area behind the bridge, while more royalist musketeers appear lining the townward side of that area, where it narrowed into one of the house-lined streets running into Middlewich. Against them, the parliamentarians are depicted with musketeers lining hedges or ditches either side of the bridge on their western bank and with three bodies of horse in support. The plan suggests that the battle began here, for the parliamentarians are referred to as the first party of enemy troops to attack Aston's positions. To the south-west of the town, the armies are also shown confronting each other either side of another bridge over the Wheelock. Again, the plan depicts Aston seeking to hold his side of the bridge with a body of horse, flanked by musketeers lining hedges or ditches. On their side of the bridge, the parliamentarians are shown having two bodies of musketeers and, on their northern flank, a body of horse. The plan gives the impression that fewer men were deployed (on both sides) here compared with the north-western and southern engagements. To the south, along 'Nantwich way' – also known as Booth or Booth's Lane – there is shown and there was no waterway and bridge which Aston could easily defend and instead the plan indicates that he sought to hold the top of that road, at its junction with Holmes Chapel Lane, where it opened out to form a large enclosed area, before narrowing on the townward side to form another house-lined street running into the centre. The plan indicates that the royalists placed an artillery piece pointing down the road, flanked by bodies of musketeers and, behind them, two bodies of horse, with a further body of Lord Cholmondeley's horse on the western flank. Ahead of this main body of royalist troops, smaller numbers of royalist musketeers are depicted in a more advanced position lining the hedges or ditches on either side of the road, while further musketeers are shown lining the enclosed area where most of Aston's forces had drawn up; according to the plan, further royalist musketeers and a body of pikemen were positioned to protect the point at which this area narrowed to form the street running into Middlewich. The opposing parliamentarian force is shown to comprise two smaller guns (drakes) and musketeers with horse behind them in the road and on both sides of the road substantial bodies of musketeers. The plan also shows that Aston made provision to hold the town centre. Royalist musketeers are depicted lining the churchyard wall and two guns are shown pointing down the north-western and southern approach roads. Further musketeers are shown inside the church. Conversely, apart from a small number of presumably royalist musketeers depicted stationed behind hedges or ditches on either side of the road running eastwards out of the town, supposedly towards Brereton, just beyond the final houses, no troops, either royalist or parliamentarian, appear on the northern and eastern sides of the town.

The plan almost certainly provides a composite image of the day's key actions and flash-points, showing troops drawn up and ready to fight at different stages of the battle. As we will see, the parliamentarian attackers and royalist defenders were in position to the north-west of the town by early morning and fighting began there. Conversely, while Aston, anticipating an assault from the south may well have drawn up troops on that side of the town early in the day, we know that the parliamentarian force did not arrive, marching along 'Nantwich way' and deploying in and on either side of that road, until much later in the morning. Although from the outset Aston may well have had an eye on making a stand closer to the town centre, should his outer defences fail in one or more areas, it is likely that the arrangement shown on the plan, with significant numbers of musketeers lining the churchyard wall and within the church, represents not Aston's initial deployment at the beginning of the day, but the position which developed in late morning, as many of Aston's musketeers fell back into the centre. Equally, the two royalist artillery pieces shown mounted in or adjoining the churchyard wall, and pointing down two of the main streets leading into the town centre, are probably two of the three pieces of ordnance which had begun the battle positioned further out, shown here defending the north-western and southern approaches to Middlewich. In other words, the plan is almost certainly depicting the same artillery pieces but is showing them in the two different spots where Aston positioned them during the course of the battle, rather than indicating that Aston had a total of five pieces of ordnance.

Overall, therefore, and despite some uncertainties and limitations, the Aston plan provides a wealth of information about the battle, which can be employed to support the more traditional printed and archival sources available to us. Running those sources together, what do we know and what can we reconstruct about the short campaign and decisive battle which took place in and around Middlewich in March 1643?

The parliamentarians explained their attack on royalist-held Middlewich in both general and more specific terms. Broadly, they condemned the royalists for the raiding, the plundering and the heavy taxes that they were allegedly inflicting on the people of mid-Cheshire and thus in turn, they portrayed themselves as spurred into action in order gallantly to save civilians from the suffering, depredations and 'wicked out-rages' being endured at the hands of Aston's royalists. More specifically, the parliamentarians moved to counter a royalist thrust into central Cheshire. Aston's

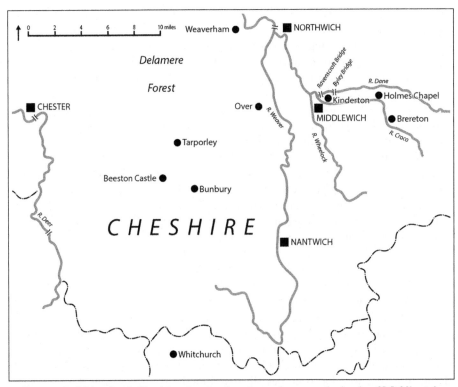

Figure 1.9 Map of mid-Cheshire, showing locations relevant to the battle of Middlewich, 13 March 1643.

royalists were pushing eastwards into the heart of the county, up to and over the line of the river Weaver. In the process, parliamentarian sources alleged, they plundered Weaverham and took prisoner some elderly male townsmen, who had reportedly been tightly bound, tied to a cart, driven 'through mire and water, above the knees' and carried off to an unidentified dungeon, 'where they lie without fire or light, and now through extremities are so diseased that they are readie to yield up the Ghost'; they occupied Over, where they not only plundered mercilessly but also supposedly 'left Ratbane in the house[s] wrapt in papers for the Children' so that they would eat the poison in mistake for sweets, though even the parliamentarian source admitted that the parents returned home in time to save their children from that fate; and they raided and occupied Middlewich itself, which the royalists allegedly plundered very thoroughly, loading their ill-gotten goods onto carts and dispatching the plunder to Tarporley, where they held an impromptu fair to sell it.[27] But above all, as Brereton

27 *Cheshires Successe*, pp. 2-13 [sic].

relayed in his letter to Ashhurst, he felt that the royalists' occupation of Middlewich and any attempt by them to hold and to fortify the town were 'of most dangerous consequence',[28] not only representing a very unwelcome royalist intervention in newly-secured parliamentarian territory but also driving a wedge between the parliamentarian bases and freshly-established garrisons of Nantwich and Northwich.

Not surprisingly, Aston explained the background to the battle very differently. In his account, his move into mid-Cheshire was designed as a brief raid, a very temporary and short-lived thrust eastwards, which turned into something bigger and longer through no fault of his own. The expedition was held up when some of his soldiers mutinied on Friday 11 March because of lack of pay and although the mutiny quickly subsided on promise of speedy payment, so that Aston and most of his men moved on and quickly occupied Middlewich unopposed and without a fight, Aston claimed that he was forced to divide his troops and to leave a body of cavalry at Over to guard the pay waggons. More usefully, although Aston did not say this, a body of troops stationed in and around Over would help to guard Aston's rear and his natural line of retreat back westwards, over the Weaver and into and through Delamere Forest, returning to his base in the still secure royalist territory of western Cheshire and Chester. In his account, Aston stressed that he intended his occupation of Middlewich to be very brief because he was aware how vulnerable he and his men were sitting in an 'open' – that is, undefended – town, sandwiched between parliamentarian troops and garrisons at Northwich and Nantwich. But, he claimed, he was compelled to hang on in Middlewich much longer than anticipated because of two developments. Firstly, Sir William Brereton's distant kinsman, William second Baron Brereton, who has been described as 'quietly royalist' during the civil war,[29] had just contacted the Chester royalists offering to supply troops and equipment to support the royalist war effort on condition that Aston would provide a convoy so that his wife and children and his precious possessions could be safely transported from Brereton Hall, which then as now stands a few miles east of Middlewich in what had become parliamentarian territory, to the relative safety of royalist-held Chester. The offer was accepted and so, having consulted other officers and the sheriff of Chester, who was with him at Middlewich, Aston decided to stay in the town through the rest of Saturday 11 March and overnight, expecting Lord Brereton and his entourage to come into Middlewich on Sunday morning, whereupon they would all withdraw and pull back westwards. Aston also claimed that, in order to make this lengthier stay in Middlewich less perilous, he requested that royalist troops stationed in Whitchurch, just over the border in north Shropshire, should move north-eastwards as if to

28   Ibid., unpaginated at this point.
29   By Anita McConnell, referring to the family as a whole, in her biography of this Lord Brereton's son and successor, 'Brereton, William, third Baron Brereton of Leighlin (*bap.* 1631, *d.* 1680)', *ODNB*; William, second Baron Brereton does not have an *ODNB* biography of his own.

threaten parliamentarian Nantwich, thus deterring any attack upon Middlewich from the Nantwich garrison. However, Aston's plans fell apart when Lord Brereton came into Middlewich on Sunday 12 March, as requested, but alone and not with his family and possessions, apparently just to confer and to discuss his family's safe conveyance in the near future rather than being ready to move at once, and when such royalist forces as remained at Whitchurch – in fact, the royalists were running down their military presence there – failed to move towards Nantwich. Secondly, at this point the pro-royalist sheriff made clear that he too wanted more time in the area, as he was planning to summon the civilians in and around Middlewich to provide support, financial and human, to the royalist cause and war effort. Accordingly, Aston and his rather mixed force – he had with him his own horse, some Welsh infantry and units of the Cheshire trained bands, in total perhaps a little over 1,500 men – stayed in Middlewich throughout Sunday 12 March and overnight and they were still there as Monday 13 March dawned.[30]

Meanwhile, the Cheshire parliamentarians, well aware of Aston's presence, responded to it, initially not with a full attack – Brereton admitted to being wary of attacking a well-prepared body of troops, particularly strong in foot, he thought – but with giving alarms, harrying and raiding the royalists' outer defences, particularly the western defences. This was undertaken by parliamentarian units of cavalry and dragoons which Brereton led or sent out from Northwich, where he was then based, during Saturday night and Sunday afternoon. Yet, with the royalists still sitting tight in Middlewich, Brereton laid plans for a bigger and more concerted attack, to be launched early on Monday. He hoped to mount a coordinated assault upon the outer defences of Middlewich around dawn on Monday morning. He would lead the Northwich parliamentarians in attacking the western approaches to the town, while at the same time a larger parliamentarian force, having marched up from Nantwich, would attack from the south. That at least twin-pronged attack seems to have been the intention from the outset – or at least, that is the impression conveyed by the parliamentarian sources – rather than a revised plan adopted on the hoof in the course of Monday morning when the two bodies of parliamentarians failed to coordinate their arrival. For whatever reason, and it is never fully explained in the surviving accounts, when Brereton and his Northwich troops – perhaps not much more than 300 men – arrived outside the town early on Monday morning, they found that they were alone, with no sign of their Nantwich colleagues. The Nantwich parliamentarian's account perhaps comes closest to clarifying this misunderstanding in noting that 'wee could not easily communicate our purposes one to another'. Nonetheless, Brereton decided to attack without delay with his modest Northwich force, assaulting the western side

---

30   BL, Additional MS 36913, fols 120-1v (Sir Thomas Aston's account of the battle of Middlewich, 1643); BL, Harleian MS 2135, fols 102-3v (Letter from Sir Thomas Aston defending his conduct at the battle of Middlewich, 17 March 1643).

of the town, beginning sometime between 6 am and 8 am and fighting alone for between three and four hours.[31]

Why did Brereton choose to attack the western approaches to Middlewich? He did, after all, control Northwich and its bridge over the Dane there, so he had the option of keeping to the east of the Dane and thus approaching Middlewich from the north or, indeed, then sweeping round to attack from the east. However, the ground between Northwich and Middlewich on the eastern side of the Dane is flat and low-lying, crossed by several brooks and today peppered with ponds and meres. It was likely to have been slow going for both horse and foot in late winter 1643. Moreover, approaching from that direction Brereton's men would have to cross and doubtless fight their way over not only the Dane – which having run more or less north-south from Northwich to a position just north-west of Middlewich, at that point effectively turns a right angle to run more or less west-east across the north side of Middlewich and beyond – but also, across most of that front, the river Croco as well. Both in his sparring during the weekend and in his concerted attack on Monday morning, Brereton preferred to approach keeping to the west of the Dane, where there is a distinct ridge above the river and a line of higher ground. This probably offered much better ground for the march and certainly meant that Brereton would be approaching Middlewich along the ridge overlooking the western side of the town, affording good views over the royalist positions and defences below. Turning to attack downhill south of the point at which the Wheelock flowed into the Dane, Brereton's forces would only have to fight their way across that single river.

Although the parliamentarian sources do not mention it, Aston claimed that he had not been idle and that he had sent out bodies of troops both to harass the parliamentarians and to serve as advance outposts. One mounted force, under Captain Spotswood, had been dispatched to give Brereton's men 'an alarme att Northwich', where their advance was rather bolder than he had intended, Aston claims, while another body of horse, under Captain Prestwich, was sent to defend one of the approaches to the town. These men were caught by surprise by the advancing parliamentarians and were attacked 'ere they could cleare theire scattered quarters', Aston relates, and although they were able to drive off the parliamentarians and to rescue some royalist prisoners, Prestwich and his men were forced to fall back to the main royalist defensive line protecting the bridge over the Wheelock.[32]

The first and main parliamentarian attack, by Brereton and the bulk of the force he had brought from Northwich, took place at this bridge, where the road from Northwich descended the hillside through Stanthorne parish to cross the Wheelock at a point around two-thirds of a mile west-north-west of the centre of the town

---

31   *Cheshires Successe*, p. 12 [sic] and unpaginated.
32   BL, Additional MS 36913, fols 120-1v (Sir Thomas Aston's account of the battle of Middlewich, 1643); BL, Harleian MS 2135, fols 102-3v (Letter from Sir Thomas Aston defending his conduct at the battle of Middlewich, 17 March 1643).

Figures 1.10 and 1.11 Dropping down from the hillside north-west of Middlewich, the main road now crosses the Wheelock via a modern bridge to enter the outskirts of the town. Brereton's initial attack early on the morning of 13 March probably occurred around or close to this spot, so his musketeers, with horse in the rear, probably drew up in the sloping fields on the western (far) side of the river, while Aston's troops occupied the near bank and sought to hold the adjoining crossing-point. (Author's photographs)

(continuing to take the church as the centre point). Aston does not give very much detail about the early phases of this engagement but he notes that, having fallen back to this position, Prestwich's horse did good work in keeping the parliamentarians 'att a stande'. However, his Welsh foot took up their positions there 'soe unwillingly (though it were but to line hedges)', Aston notes, 'that 2 troopes of horse, the Maiors and Capt Bridgmans, were sent downe to face the enemy in a narrow passage within halfe musquet shot, wherein severall of them were shot, otherwise the foot would not have advanced or stayed by it'.[33] Brereton's letter to Ashhurst also gives only limited information about this assault. Deploying a force of parliamentarian musketeers there, they 'behaved themselves very gallantly', he noted, and resolutely stood their ground in the face of royalist artillery, which Brereton claimed inflicted very few casualties, 'there being only one or two men hurt, but not mortally'.[34] This is all consistent with the plan of the battle, which depicts this first parliamentarian assault led by musketeers lining hedges or ditches west of the river on either side of the bridge, with parliamentarian horse behind them. Lining the hedges or ditches on either side of the bridge on the other bank of the river are royalist musketeers – presumably including the reluctant Welsh foot – with the Major's and Bridgman's troops of horse in the roadway next to and immediately behind the foot, while two artillery pieces are depicted just south of Bridgman's horse. Other unnamed royalist horse and Ellis's pikeman hold positions further back, almost as a reserve.

At some point during the morning, starting later than and secondary to Brereton's main assault at this bridge, Brereton dispatched a smaller mixed force of Northwich musketeers and horse to threaten a second crossing of the Wheelock. This must be the bridge a little over half a mile upstream along the Wheelock and about three quarters of a mile south-west of the town centre. The main parliamentarian accounts make little reference to this attack on a second bridge but Aston is much fuller. He records how 'An other part of the enimy approaching another passage called Waring bridge, Capt Prestwich his troope was commanded thither to stay by the foote, which were of Capt Massies companie, which hee did'.[35] Again, all this is consistent with the plan, which shows unidentified royalist musketeers – they must be Massey's men – defending the hedges or ditches on either side of the bridge, while Prestwich's horse hold the bridge itself. Against them are ranged two bodies of parliamentarian musketeers, stationed in fields on either side of the roadway leading to the bridge, with a body of parliamentarian horse on their northern flank.

33 BL, Additional MS 36913, fols 120-1v (Sir Thomas Aston's account of the battle of Middlewich, 1643); BL, Harleian MS 2135, fols 102-3v (Letter from Sir Thomas Aston defending his conduct at the battle of Middlewich, 17 March 1643).
34 *Cheshires Successe*, unpaginated at this point.
35 BL, Additional MS 36913, fols 120-1v (Sir Thomas Aston's account of the battle of Middlewich, 1643); BL, Harleian MS 2135, fols 102-3v (Letter from Sir Thomas Aston defending his conduct at the battle of Middlewich, 17 March 1643).

The general impression at this stage as conveyed by the written accounts is of something approaching stalemate on the ground – Malbon wrote of this first phase of the battle, 'the fighte contynuynge longe betwixt theim equall'[36] – but one favouring the royalists, for as the morning wore on Brereton's supplies of gunpowder became depleted, partly simply through use but partly because of an accidental spillage – the Nantwich parliamentarian's account records how 'this accident fell out, that his powder was all spilt excepting about 7 pound'. Accordingly, some of Brereton's officers began advising that the attack should be ended and they should retreat 'but Sir *William* was resolute not to retreit, but to send to Northwich for more powder, and to keep them in play as well as they could till the Powder came, which accordingly they did'.[37] There is a hint, therefore, that the Northwich parliamentarians were playing for time, eking out their remaining gunpowder and hoping that their Nantwich colleagues would tardily arrive.

Sometime in late morning, between 11 am and 12 noon, the Nantwich force, numbering at least 800 men, perhaps rather more than that, did arrive and began attacking the southern approaches of the town, where despite – or more probably because – there was no defendable bridge, Aston had stationed a very strong defensive force. The single roadway was protected by ditches and banks on both sides but had been further strengthened by 'the addition of some small trenches', he wrote. Aston says he deployed two trained bands companies there, numbering 200 men, a forward unit of 60 horse, with further horse behind them in reserve, and 120 musketeers to line the hedges flanking the road.[38] He also had an artillery piece here, described by Malbon as 'a good Brasse peece of ordnance'.[39] The parliamentarians admitted that 'The Enemy had chief advantages [there], their Ordinance planted; we had none, they layd about 150 Musquetiers in an hole convenient for them, they layd their Ambuskadoes in the hedges… and had every way so strengthened themselves, that they seemed impregnable'. But a parliamentarian troop of horse stood firm in the face of royalist artillery, emboldened by the failure of Aston's gun to do much damage – 'which once grazed before them, and then mounted cleare over them, in another that it dasht the water and mire in his [Captain George Booth's] and two other Captaines faces, but there it dies: this was no discouragement to our men'.[40] Once more, the depiction of the rival forces on the Aston plan is broadly consistent with this, although it gives a clearer sense of the composition and arrangement of the troops, provides a number for the main body of parliamentarian musketeers – 300 of them – and also suggests that, contrary to the Nantwich parliamentarian's account, they did possess

36   Hall, *Memorials of the Civil War in Cheshire*, p. 40.
37   *Cheshires Successe*, p. 12 [sic].
38   BL, Additional MS 36913, fols 120-1v (Sir Thomas Aston's account of the battle of Middlewich, 1643); BL, Harleian MS 2135, fols 102-3v (Letter from Sir Thomas Aston defending his conduct at the battle of Middlewich, 17 March 1643).
39   Hall, *Memorials of the Civil War in Cheshire*, p. 40.
40   *Cheshires Successe*, pp. 12-13 [sic].

and deployed two small field pieces, namely drakes, to counter the royalists' single but clearly much bigger artillery piece on this side of the town.

At and from that point, with Brereton's Northwich forces maintaining their attack on two points of Aston's western defences and with the Nantwich parliamentarians now attacking from the south, the tide of battle turned decisively and apparently quite quickly in parliament's favour on all fronts. The parliamentarian accounts attribute this to God's support and to the courage of their soldiers, such that Aston's defences crumbled and both the Nantwich and the Northwich parliamentarians moved forward and entered the town more or less simultaneously, meeting little further resistance until they approached the town centre and the area around the church. It is Aston's account which gives fuller details of the royalist collapse, even though at this stage the text becomes a little harder to follow in places and to arrange in strict chronological order – probably a fair reflection of how disorder descended on the royalist side from this point onwards and of how, writing a few days later, Aston struggled clearly to reconstruct this phase of the battle or was troubled by his memories of it. Aston claimed that on the north-western side of the town, where his Welsh foot had already performed poorly and from which Prestwich's troop of horse had already been withdrawn in order to defend the second bridge, Bridgman's horse too now had to be removed and redeployed to prop up the royalist position on the southern side of the town. Thus further depleted, Aston describes how his north-western defences buckled and broke. Major Gilmore ordered the Welsh foot to fall back, which allowed the parliamentarian musketeers to move forward through the hedged fields either side of the roadway, threatening to outflank the remaining royalist horse, who were unable to counter-charge because of the enclosed nature of the ground occupied by the parliamentarians. Accordingly, the remaining royalist horse (and presumably also the block of pikemen shown on the plan) fell back towards and into the town. A body of royalist musketeers were left protecting 'a breast worke', presumably an earthwork thrown up where the large area in which Aston had initially drawn up most of his force narrowed to form one of the house-lined streets into Middlewich. Although the Aston plan does not clearly depict this or any other battlefield earthworks, it does show a body of musketeers stationed at this point. However, those royalist musketeers, 'after once discharging att randome, they quit the worke and ranne away', alleged Aston.

Aston goes on to describe how his south-western and southern defences crumpled at around the same time. On the south-western side, where Prestwich's horse had been supporting Massey's foot in trying to hold the bridge, the pressure of the parliamentarian attack again forced them to retreat, though Aston gives few details. He is far fuller on how and why, for all his efforts to provide a strong defence in the area, his southern flank broke. Despite stationing or moving additional musketeers there, supported by further horse, when the parliamentarians began moving forward 'with a great body of musqueters on either side [of] the lane' while the parliamentarian horse waited well to their rear, the royalist position collapsed. As soon as the parliamentarians opened fire, the royalist musketeers and their commanding officer 'fell downe, and crept away leaving their armes'. As on the north-western side, the advance of the parliamentarian foot through the fields on both sides of the road threatened to outflank the royalist horse, who in turn could not counter-charge because the parliamentarians had advantage of enclosed ground. Without infantry support and protection, the royalist horse fell back and they also wheeled away in the hope that the single royalist artillery piece stationed in this area could be employed by Captain Ellis in an effort to halt, or at least to disrupt and slow, the parliamentarian advance.[41] From a parliamentarian perspective, Malbon reported that, faced with such an initially strong royalist position, the Nantwich troops decided not to mount a frontal attack up the road but instead 'with theire horse & foote leape into the fields on both sides of the Lane'. Malbon also suggests that the key turning-point here was the parliamentarian capture of the royalist ordnance, for eventually, after a fierce exchange, they got so close to the royalist artillery piece that 'they did dryve the mr Gunner from yt; And seazed the same, & havinge gotten ytt, the adversaryes all fledd'.[42]

With the royalist outer defences now collapsing or collapsed and with the parliamentarians entering Middlewich and converging on the town centre along three streets, the royalist hold on Middlewich was fragile. Royalist officers and troops fell back towards the town centre. Aston tries to make this sound like a wise and initially quite orderly phase of the royalist operation, portraying himself as organising the defence of the churchyard by a body of royalist dragoons, ordering artillery pieces to be drawn up in the churchyard and ordering a mixed body of musketeers and other trained bandsmen to defend both the approaches to the church and the ordnance. However, the reality was probably much more disorganised and *ad hoc*, as chaos increasingly overtook the royalist forces, and this is perhaps unconsciously revealed by the structure of Aston's account at this point. This is the densest part of his narrative, although the overall impression he was seeking to convey is clear: as a diligent commander several times he tried to get his remaining foot, both musketeers and pikemen, to make a stand with cavalry in support but the royalist foot repeatedly broke and ran, leaving the brave royalist horse exposed and with little choice but to fall back. Nevertheless, exactly where and when these failed stands occurred and the precise narrative sequence of this phase are difficult to reconstruct. Aston claims that most of his remaining musketeers were useless and had no will to fight on – at first they threw themselves to the ground, laying themselves down 'in a valley' and even when Aston had forced them to get up and join other royalist musketeers lining a hedge, they did not dare 'put up theire heads, but shot their peeces up into the ayre, noe one foot officer being by them, to ranke or order them'. In contrast, much of the royalist horse, drawn up in the streets, stood their ground bravely, Aston claimed. However, the wayward firing of the remaining royalist artillery and the

41   BL, Additional MS 36913, fols 120-1v (Sir Thomas Aston's account of the battle of Middlewich, 1643); BL, Harleian MS 2135, fols 102-3v (Letter from Sir Thomas Aston defending his conduct at the battle of Middlewich, 17 March 1643).
42   Hall, *Memorials of the Civil War in Cheshire*, p. 40.

speedy advance of the victorious parliamentarians, shouting as they did so, caused most of the remaining royalist foot to turn and flee. 'Our foot... all instantly forsooke theire stand and ran away', including the Welsh and the Cheshire trained bandsmen from Broxton hundred, 'all the whole stand of pikes in the reare of the horse clearly ran away' and 'all the musqueteers placed for the defence of the street ende quit theire trenches, haveing never discharged a shot, or never seene the enimy or cause of feare, but their fellowes flying'.

Aston's increasingly disjointed account then describes how, having overseen the rescue of one of the royalist artillery pieces and the orderly retreat of his horse into the High Street, he went to the churchyard, expecting to find it well defended. Instead, he found 'all the foot wedged up in the church like billetts in a woodpile, noe one man att his armes'. With the parliamentarians quickly advancing along three streets and with a risk that his horse would find themselves 'as sheep in a pen exposed to slaughter', Aston ordered them to withdraw to a field 'att the end of the towne', though in fact they became separated and disordered as they did so. Finding the artillery which he had drawn up around the churchyard unmanned and deserted and himself alone, isolated and now directly exposed to enemy fire, Aston claimed that he had little choice but to withdraw from the town, riding off in the hope of finding his surviving horse.[43] In contrast, the Nantwich parliamentarian's account focuses on the energy and bravery of the Nantwich foot at this stage of the battle, and especially 'our *Major* (a right *Scottish* blade)', in forcing their way into and through the streets 'upon the mouth of the Canon, and storme of the muskets'. This account also puts a different slant on Aston's final moments in Middlewich, claiming that the royalist commander sought refuge with some of his foot inside St Michael's church, 'but they durst not let him in, lest we should enter with him', so that 'he mounted his Horse, and fled with all speed by *Kinderton*'.[44]

The royalist foot, including many officers, who had occupied and sought refuge in the church, held out there for up to an hour. Brereton reported that royalist musketeers, firing out from the body of the church and from the 'steeple', 'did much annoy us for some short time'. But the parliamentarians picked off some of the royalists, 'fired the *Church-doore*, and thrust at them with swords as they lookt out of the Windowes', so that the defenders quickly lost heart and 'they cride for quarter, which was granted them'.[45] At that point, sometime in the early afternoon, the fighting ended and parliament, having secured a complete and decisive victory, gained full control of Middlewich. Fatalities were surprisingly light, with the parliamentarians suggesting that they had lost just six men themselves, though equally claiming only around thirty royalist dead. But while Aston and much of his horse got away, the battle produced a rich haul of prisoners, including Colonel Ellis, Sergeant-Major Gilmore, eleven

---

43   Ibid.
44   *Cheshires Successe*, p. 13 [sic].
45   Ibid., p. 13 [sic] and unpaginated.

captains and six lieutenants, together with abundant cash, arms and powder. A parliamentarian account also claims that many of the surviving royalist foot captured in the church felt let down by Aston, upset that he had run away without informing them of his flight, 'that they might have shifted for themselves, as well as he'. They allegedly proclaimed that 'they would never [again] fight for Sir *Tho: Aston* without a promise under his hand that he would not run away'.[46]

Middlewich was not a major battle in Civil War terms. The two sides had in total somewhere around, and probably no more than, 1,500 men apiece. It was also a fairly static and disjointed battle, with much of the action occurring at three separate stand-offs on the outskirts of, or approaches to, the town, followed by a much swifter and one-sided street fight. Nonetheless, the battle had a clear and decisive outcome. It confirmed and cemented not only the parliamentarians' dominance of central as well as eastern Cheshire but also Brereton's dominance of the parliamentarian war effort within the county. It was not the first clear parliamentarian success during the Civil War – Brereton had gained a victory at Nantwich several weeks before, whilst also during January 1643 Sir Thomas Fairfax had humiliated royalist forces at Leeds and by the time of the battle of Middlewich parliament had recently captured Lichfield. Yet it was a significant fillip for the parliamentarian cause both locally and nationally. The buoyant mood is reflected in the way that Brereton closed his letter to Ashhurst, in which he had conveyed news of the victory – 'We heare nothing from London how things goe there, but our confidence is in the Lord of heaven, to the protection of whose Providence I desire to commend you, and so conclude, and Rest...'.[47]

Conversely, Middlewich left the royalist cause in much of Cheshire in disarray, broken and bereft, and it underlined the fact that the king's men were now penned up in the western part of the county. It was a personal disaster for Aston, whose military career continued until the closing stages of the war but who never again was given an independent command of the sort he had held in 1642-3 and who never again played a significant role in the war in his native county. Despite his long and complex self-justificatory account, some mud may have stuck. Near the end of that account, Aston claimed that

> It is the plaine truth, the enimy haveing noe diversion, butt att liberty with theire full power to fall on us from all parts, were much too hard for us in a place not defensible. And without some more experienced foot officers, I must freely say, noe number will bee found sufficient to withstand readie men.

Other contemporary accounts partly support Aston's assessment, notably the paper drawn up by, or in the name of, some of the royalist commissioners of array and gentlemen of Cheshire. The authors point to the malign influence of Orlando

46   Ibid.
47   Ibid.

Bridgeman – the son of the bishop of Chester but an outsider, from a Devon family, who was at that stage in effect (co-)governor of Chester – and his clique, many of whom were also non-Cheshire men, who had allegedly fallen out with local royalist figures such as Aston. As a consequence of this factional division and of Bridgeman's focus upon defending Chester and prioritising resources on strengthening the city, Aston was allegedly left out in the cold, unsupported, unaided and starved of men and resources. Thus Aston and his men 'were ordered to march out, neither money nor provision ready...', they were 'delayed at Middlewich', far from being sent to their aid by distracting the Nantwich garrison the royalist force at Whitchurch was in the process of being disbanded and 'soe the Rebels [were] left loose to assaile our men in an unfenc'd towne on 3 sides... soe that few of those that suffered there considered themselves any other then betrayed by this action, the reasons whereof they think very enquirable'.[48] For some, Middlewich had confirmed 'our confidence... in the Lord of heaven'; for others, it left a very bitter taste, with feelings of being 'betrayed'. For historians, it has produced a rich crop of source material, not least the rare, valuable and informative contemporary battle plan, which allows us to reconstruct in such detail the decisive engagement which unfolded in and around this modest market town on a late winter's Monday morning over 370 years ago.

48   BL, Additional MS 36913, fols 120-1v (Sir Thomas Aston's account of the battle of Middlewich, 1643); BL, Harleian MS 2135, fols 102-3v (Letter from Sir Thomas Aston defending his conduct at the battle of Middlewich, 17 March 1643).

2

Some Further Thoughts on Oliver Cromwell's Last Campaign

Prof. Malcolm Wanklyn

Introduction

The paper that I delivered to the conference at Rowley House in September 2015 cannot be transformed into a chapter in a book of the conference. It would be in breach of copyright, as the most substantial part of the paper, an account of how the deadlock in Cromwell's campaign in Scotland was broken by an amphibious assault on the coast of Fife in July 1651, had been published earlier in the year in series III volume 4 of *Cromwelliana*, the journal of the Cromwell Association. However, the editor's kind offer for me to contribute a chapter to the book of the conference does give me the opportunity to reflect on the battle of Worcester, the culmination of the 1651 campaign, which I had intended to do at the conference had time been available. The reason why it was to have formed the final section of my paper is that it was complementary to the stratagem for crossing the Firth of Forth, in that Cromwell's engineers modified the landscape over which the battle of Worcester was to be fought so as solve the tactical problems caused by a water hazard. Writing about Worcester also gives me the opportunity to bring into the public domain a 'spin-off' from some research on the Cheshire militia which I undertook during my doctorate studies many years ago, when post-graduate regulations gave students the chance to range widely around their chosen topic instead of being forced by the four-year deadline to focus exclusively on their research question.

I

War between the English republic and Scotland became inevitable once the Scottish government allowed Charles, Prince of Wales to leave France in the summer of 1650 to be crowned king at Scone in succession to his executed father. Charles was sure to want to extend his rule over England and Ireland in due course. Moreover, the leaders of Church and State in Scotland had for years held the view that Scotland's liberties would not be secure until Presbyterianism had become the state religion throughout the British Isles. To achieve this, it would first be necessary to destroy the New Model Army and the English Republic committed as they both were to a wide measure of toleration for more radical forms of Protestantism. Sir Thomas Fairfax, the commander of the New Model Army since 1645, took charge of the preparations for war but, although happy to defend England against a Scottish invasion, he refused to lead a pre-emptive strike against fellow-Protestants and former allies. He was therefore allowed to resign on the grounds of ill-health and Oliver Cromwell, his second-in-command, succeeded him as lord general less than a month before the New Model Army crossed the border.[1]

Cromwell's Scottish campaign began well with an unexpected victory at Dunbar on 3 September 1650, when his army was trapped between the mountains and the sea and outnumbered by a factor of three to two. However, the follow-up was less successful.[2] He should have headed straight for Stirling, where a formidable castle guarded the only bridge over of the river Forth that gave overland access to the lowlands of northeast Scotland (to which the survivors of Dunbar had retreated) and that was capable of carrying the weight of an artillery train. Instead, he was bedazzled by the prospect of occupying Edinburgh. The Scottish capital surrendered without a fight, though its castle was to remain in enemy hands for a further three months.

When Cromwell marched against Stirling a fortnight later, the Scots had recovered their nerve and he drew back. A siege was impossible as he could not surround the castle without first capturing the bridge, which was on the north side of the town, and a storm, though considered, was rejected probably on account of the losses likely to be incurred. Only six months earlier his failed assault on Clonmel in Ireland had resulted in the deaths of between 500 and 2000 of his soldiers.

There followed ten months of stalemate. The Scottish army had regrouped behind the lines of Stirling and by the summer of 1651 it was not much inferior in size to the forces commanded by Cromwell. However, its commanders refused to be tempted into fighting another battle. Meanwhile, English attempts to seize a port in Fife, which would have enabled the New Model Army to bypass the bottleneck, failed in the execution. The end came with the arrival from England of purpose-built flat-bottomed boats, which enabled troops to be landed on the open beach at North Queensferry on the far side of the Firth of Forth. Some of these had been constructed from scratch at Newcastle. The rest came from boatyards along the Thames estuary.

1   M. Wanklyn, *The Warrior Generals: Winning the British Civil Wars* (New Haven, Yale University Press: 2010), pp. 216-17. For the growth of anxiety about the intention of the Scottish government from March 1650 onwards, see B. Whitelock, *Memorials of the English Affairs* (London: 1732), pp. 446-58.

2   The narrative of the campaign in Scotland and the convergence of the armies on Worcester that follows are based largely on Wanklyn, *Warrior Generals*, pp. 219-24 updated in places by M. Wanklyn, 'Cromwell's Generalship and the Conquest of Scotland 1650 – 1651', *Cromwelliana*, ser. 3, vol. 4. (2015), pp. 36-50.

Oddly, the latter were less expensive and the contract for them was with a number of boat-builders, rather than one. Possibly they were barges that normally traded in the Thames estuary along the coasts of Kent and Essex, which were then modified for the carrying of troops and horses.[3]

There followed the battle of Inverkeithing, fought on 20 July, at which Lieutenant General Lambert managed to defeat the small Scottish force sent to contain the bridge-head. He then quickly forced the surrender of the deep-water port of Burntisland close by. Cromwell immediately abandoned the stand-off at Stirling, shipped most his army across the Firth of Forth and headed north for the city of Perth and the crossing of the river Tay. The Scottish commanders were thus offered the chance to fight him in a conventional battle somewhere in Fife. Yet, the 'bread basket of Scotland' was mainly open country where Cromwell would be able to make effective use of his cavalry, superior to the Scots' in both quality and quantity. Alternatively, King Charles's generals could have wrong-footed him by leading their army south towards England. This might have resulted in a royalist uprising against the New Model Army but to the duke of Hamilton, it was an act of despair, everything else having failed.[4]

Elsewhere, I have suggested that it was probably not Cromwell's intention to leave the door to England wide open (as it were) to tempt the Scottish army into an action that would lead to its utter destruction but if it was, he never expected they would march as far south as Worcester before he could bring them to battle. There were sufficient cavalry regiments in southern Scotland and northern England commanded by generals Harrison and Lambert to delay their advance until he caught them up with the rest of the army. Yet, in the event, the English cavalry were positioned to defend the east-coast route via Berwick and Newcastle and the ports along the south coast of the Firth of Forth, which the forces in Fife would use to shorten their march. When the Scots chose the west-coast route via Carlisle and Preston as the Engagers' army had done in 1648, Cromwell's subordinates were unable to assemble sufficient infantry support to prevent the Scots crossing the Mersey at Warrington bridge.

Harrison and Lambert were wise not to have tried to use dismounted cavalry for that purpose. Such troops were occasionally employed in close combat situations where the fighting would be virtually hand-to-hand, such as the storming of a breach in a town's defences. However, what had happened on the battlefield at Newbury in 1643 had shown the heavy casualties that horse soldiers were likely to incur if they were used instead of infantry in an attacking role, whereas if cavalry were ordered to play a defensive role against infantry attack, whether mounted or dismounted, they would quickly find that pistols and swords were no substitute for muskets and

---

3   I am grateful to Dr. Chris Scott for this suggestion made during the discussion at the conference.
4   National Archives Scotland, GD 406/1/ 5956.

pikes.[5] It therefore seems likely that Cromwell had instructed Harrison and Lambert to hold back if they could not collect together sufficient infantry to face the Scottish onslaught, as heavy losses in the mounted arm was the last thing he wanted when he eventually faced the Scots in battle.[6]

The Scottish army duly made its way south as far as Lichfield, which it reached on 19 August 1651. It was theoretically possible that it could have reached the London area before the New Model Army caught up with it but Cromwell was marching fast down the Great North Road and it was therefore more likely that a battle would take place in the open field country of the South Midlands, where the Scottish lack of cavalry would put their army at a distinct disadvantage. The king and his advisers therefore decided to change the direction of their army's march from southeast to southwest and to make for the enclosed countryside of north and west Worcestershire. It duly marched via Wolverhampton, Kidderminster and Ombersley to Worcester, where it arrived on 22 August.

The king and his military advisers probably hoped that a defensive position centred on the city, with its strong fortifications defending the only bridge over the river Severn between Bewdley and Upton, would give their army time to recuperate. During the long march south, the royal army had only had a single day's rest. Moreover, the Severn in Worcestershire marked the edge of a large area of country to the west of the river Severn in Herefordshire, Monmouthshire and the counties of southeast Wales which had been solidly royalist in sympathy in 1642 and under royalist control for almost the whole of the First Civil War. If the Scottish army could maintain its position, it might be possible within four to six weeks to raise an army large enough to take on Cromwell's forces in battle. However, the king and his advisers failed to take into account the experience of the *pays* to the west of Severn during the latter stages of the first war. Plundering by the king's forces there in the winter of 1644-5 had led to the rise of neutralist sentiment. Resentment at this treatment by the soldiery burst forth in the form of armed assemblies of clubmen, which had been put down by force by Princes Rupert and Maurice in the spring. There followed in the late summer the abortive siege of Hereford conducted by a Scottish army, which was unpaid and therefore lived off the countryside. Although the Scots seem to have shown little or no violence towards the civilian population, their systematic seizure of horses and

5   M. Wanklyn, *Decisive Battles of the English Civil Wars* (Barnsley, Pen & Sword: 2006), p. 79.
6   The fact that cavalry were scarcely mentioned in accounts of the battle at Worcester on 3 September was not because Lambert and Harrison were in disgrace but because in the event, it turned out to be an infantry engagement in which cavalry played very little part. Lambert was wounded in the fighting on the west bank of the Severn, whilst Harrison was charged with pursuing the Scots as they retreated, the most likely option in the opinion of the Council of State in London and probably Cromwell also.

foodstuffs and their plundering of church plate and vestments was still remembered hundreds of years later.[7]

A second attraction of Worcester as an army base was the topography of the middle Severn valley. By 1651, after almost ten years of fighting, the senior officers who accompanied King Charles would have had a very sound knowledge of the landscape of the English/Welsh borderland. They are likely to have considered that Worcester would have been a good place from which to conduct a defensive campaign, not only because of the many possibilities of impeding an enemy advance in the enclosed country that lay to the west of the Severn but also because of the river itself. Rivers do not usually serve as effective constraints on military operations if they are as narrow as the Severn is in its lower reaches but there were few fords and south of the Shropshire county line, the only bridges were at Bewdley, Worcester, Upton and Gloucester.

As soon as the Scottish army arrived in Worcester, bodies of their men were sent to break down the bridge at Upton and also, it seems, the one at Bewdley. Nothing, however, could be done about the bridge at Gloucester, as the city was garrisoned by a battalion of New Model Army foot commanded by Sir William Constable.[8] Finally, as the river was navigable, it could be used for transporting infantry and military hardware up or downriver as required. The royalists had moved troops from Shrewsbury to Bridgnorth in 1642 and from Bewdley to Worcester in 1644, whilst artillery pieces and cannonballs cast in the blast furnaces of south Shropshire had gone by river to Worcester on the first stage of their journey to the king's headquarters at Oxford during 1643 and 1644.

As the Scots army headed towards Worcester, Cromwell's army continued on its way south through Ripon, Macclesfield and Leicester, rendezvousing with Harrison and Lambert's cavalry at Warwick on 25 August. It then moved forward to Evesham in the Avon valley, a position that would force the Scots to fight should they decide to resume their march towards London, as it lay astride the road from Worcester to the capital. There, the New Model Army paused for a week, which is hardly surprising as it had marched over 300 miles in nineteen days. The rest also allowed time for reinforcements in the shape of militia regiments to arrive from Cheshire, Essex and a number of other counties, whilst the Worcestershire militia withdrew behind the walls of Gloucester, which was thought to be the Scots' next target.[9]

7   R. Hutton, *The Royalist War Effort 1642-6* (London, Longman: 1982), pp. 169-172; J. Webb and T. Webb, *Memorials of the Civil War between King Charles I. and the Parliament of England as it affected Herefordshire and Adjacent Counties* (2 vols, London, Longman: 1879), II, pp. 221-3 and 391-8.

8   C. Firth and G. Davies, *The Regimental History of Cromwell's Army* (2 vols, Oxford, Clarendon Press: 1940) II, pp. 399-401.

9   M. Atkin, *Worcestershire under Arms* (Barnsley, Pen & Sword: 2004), p. 139; *Calendar of State Papers Domestic* [hereafter *CSPD*], 1651, pp. 340-415 contains numerous orders and correspondence concerning the militia regiments.

Soon after arriving at Evesham, Cromwell and his senior officers agreed on a plan of attack. A direct advance on Worcester was not the best way of achieving closure, as the Scots could withdraw with some confidence into the countryside to the west of the city, where the enclosed landscape favoured defence. The most important priority was therefore to move substantial numbers of troops onto the far bank of the river, so as to cut off this possible line of retreat but the nearest bridge, that at Upton, had been broken down and marching via Gloucester could be foolhardy. Getting to the far side of Worcester by that route would take several days, during which the Scottish king's army might carry out a successful attack on the forces left at Evesham and then march towards London, confident that it had stolen a march on a much depleted New Model Army.

However, on 29 August General Lambert managed to establish a toehold on the west bank of the river Severn at Upton. A file of dragoons used a plank placed across the hole made in the roadway of the bridge and took up position in Upton Church, which they defended against Scottish counterattack until 150 more of their comrades arrived, having crossed the Severn with considerable difficulty on horseback via a ford that was little used because it could not be crossed on foot.[10] The bridge was then repaired such that troops and their heavy equipment could be moved to the west bank of the Severn in force. This effectively put an end to any idea of the Scottish army falling back from Worcester into Herefordshire, which its commanders recognised by breaking down the bridges at Powick and Bransford over the river Teme, which joined the Severn from the west two miles south of the city. However, they still retained the option of retreating along the north bank of the Teme towards the uplands of mid-Wales.

II

The battle that followed on 3 September is unusual in a number of important respects. Firstly, it was fought on two fronts: one in the Teme valley to the south west of the city and the other in the open ground to the south east of the city, separated from one another by the river Severn. This complicated matters for the commanders-in-chief, Cromwell and King Charles, who had to devise ways of transferring units from one front to the other as and when necessary once the battle started. This was comparatively easy for Charles, who controlled the bridge at Worcester – all he had to worry about was congestion in the city's narrow streets – but not for Cromwell, as there were no fords across the Severn usable by an army for miles to the south of Worcester.

Secondly, cavalry played very little part in the fighting on either front once fighting commenced. Stray comments that horse were of significance in the New Model Army,

10   Whitelock, *Memorials*, p. 505. Some of the soldiers are said to have swum across.

beating off enemy attacks, do not count for much.[11] In fact, the outcome of most battles was decided either by infantry alone (as at Dunbar, Preston, the first battle of Newbury and Edgehill) or by infantry and cavalry working together (as at Marston Moor and Naseby). However, despite Worcester being largely an infantry battle, there were few casualties amongst the officers on the Cromwellian side. Was Cromwell being economical with the truth? He had underplayed the casualties sustained in the Second Civil War at Preston and in South Wales in 1648, as well as at Drogheda in Ireland the following year, whilst we have no record of his report on the casualties sustained in the failed storming of Clonmel in May 1650. However, my recent work reconstructing the officer corps of the New Model Army suggests that he gave the correct impression. I have only discovered a single company commander in the New Model Army regiments present at Worcester who was killed in the battle.[12] On reflection, this may not be all that surprising, as at no time did Cromwell's regiments have to assault a prepared position guarded by troops who were ready to repel an attack. Worcester was a series of encounter engagements in which there was no time for the Scots to get into proper defensive mode. However, this may not be the whole story. My research did not extend to the officers of the militia regiments which fought at Worcester. It was they who led the only textbook infantry assaults that took place during the course of the battle – those on Fort Royal and Sudbury Gate – though they too may have been defended primarily by scratch forces driven back by the failed assault on Cromwell's army drawn up on the high ground to the east of the city.

One final point needs to be made before turning to the battle itself. As day dawned on 3 September, it is by no means certain that Cromwell saw the campaign against the Scots as ending that day in a decisive battle. The forces on the east bank were to remain in position. Those on the west bank were to advance on Worcester from the south, crossing the river Teme as they progressed and then, if the Scots failed to make a stand, to take up positions blocking the roads leading towards Worcester bridge. In the event of a siege, they could cut the city off from supplies of foodstuffs and fodder coming from the west but if the Scots decided to retreat, they would lose their last remaining escape route towards Wales along the north bank of the Teme towards Ludlow. To me, it all looks like the first stage in an operation to starve the Scots into surrender without fighting a battle, and this hypothesis is not contradicted by the

11   H. Cary, *Memorials of the Great Civil War in England from 1646 to 1652* (2 vols, London, Colburn: 1842) p. 358; M. Atkin, *Cromwell's Crowning Mercy: the Battle of Worcester 1651* (Thrupp, Sutton: 1998), p. 98.

12   This was Captain Jones of Ralph Cobbett's regiment: *Mercurius Politicus*, no. 66 (4 to 11 September 1651), p. 1054. John Moseley, a staff officer, who was also killed at Worcester, may have commanded a company in the first regiment of foot: Firth and Davies, *Regimental History of Cromwell's Army*, I, p. 331.

exercise in military engineering that immediately preceded the battle which is to be discussed below.[13]

III

The first stage in confronting the Scottish army took place over much of the same ground as the first major engagement in the First Civil War almost exactly nine years earlier and for the same reason. In September 1642, the earl of Essex, parliament's first lord general, was approaching the city from the east. His objective was to surround and destroy a small enemy force, which had taken refuge in the city on its way from Oxford to join the royal army at Shrewsbury To do so, he needed to secure the west bank of the Severn to prevent it escaping. Cromwell had the same objective but with a much bigger prey, so it is not surprising that fighting on 3 September 1651 began at the crossing of the river Teme as it had done on 23 September 1642.

Cromwell also used the bridge at Upton, eight miles to the south of Worcester, to move forces to the west bank whilst the rest occupied the high ground just to the east of the city but whereas Essex's force was small and made up entirely of cavalry and dragoons, Cromwell's comprised well over 5,000 men, most of which were infantry. However, splitting his forces in this way was potentially dangerous, as the Scots could use interior lines to throw their strength against one part of the army or the other. His regiments on the east bank, for example, were potentially open to attack from almost the whole of the royalist army as the king's commanders could rely on holding the line of the Teme for some time, and after that the west end of Worcester bridge almost indefinitely, with nothing stronger than an infantry brigade. However, although the militia regiments made up much of the first line of battle on the east bank, the second line was stuffed with New Model foot, whilst regiments of New Model cavalry were in close support.[14] Moreover, the Cromwellian forces deployed on the high ground to the east of Worcester probably outnumbered the Scottish army and its English supporters. They also had an advantage in the lie of the land, as the latter would have to advance uphill against a position that the Commonwealth forces had had several days to put into a state of defence.

Cromwell's forces on the west bank faced more of a threat of coming under attack from almost the entire enemy army, though the enclosed landscape along both banks of the Teme almost as far as its junction with the Severn would make it easier to mount an effective defence. However, this cut both ways. The river was also a major obstacle in the way of the advance towards the western end of Worcester bridge, as Essex had

---

13   In a letter written to Admiral Blake just prior to the battle, the Council of State in London foresaw three possibilities – a battle, a siege, or the flight of the Scottish army northwards – and they presumably based their reasoning on intelligence from Cromwell's headquarters: *CSPD*, 1651, p. 407.

14   Atkin, *Cromwell's Crowning Mercy*, pp. 92 and 175.

found in 1642, and the Scots had already made it more difficult by destroying the bridges at Powick and Bransford. The classic response if the enemy was threatening to overwhelm his troops on the west bank of the Severn would be for Cromwell to distract them by threatening to storm the city from the east but that was no guarantee of success, as no attempt had been made to create a breach with artillery fire and to do so would almost certainly take several days. Even then, if his forces did manage to enter the city, it would be comparatively easy for the Scots to withdraw across the bridge, breaking it down behind them. Instead, Cromwell proposed to alter the landscape over which a battle would be fought, so as to match the advantage the enemy had in interior lines.[15]

To that end, Cromwell ordered the construction of a pontoon bridge across the Severn just to the north of its junction with the Teme. Not only would this be of great value if the operations on 3 September ended in a siege but also in the short run it would provide the means by which troops could be passed from the east bank to the west, should the corps on the far side of the river experience any difficulty in crossing the Teme. This they would do not by directly providing reinforcements, as the bridge over the Severn was constructed to the north of the junction of the two rivers, but by striking the Scottish units defending the line of the Teme in the flank. At the same time, a similar bridge was to be thrown across the mouth of the river Teme. This would not be of great value in the event of a siege, but it would allow the force on the west bank to advance on Worcester bridge if the Scots were able to prevent it doing so at Powick or at Bransford further upstream. It would also have the potential to enable the forces on the west bank to support those on the east should the latter come under attack from the rest of the Scottish army. As a precaution, the western end of the Severn bridge and the northern end of the Teme bridge were to be no more than a pistol shot apart so that a single body of infantry could defend them both and be reinforced by one or both parts of the army if it came under attack.[16] This could, however, have led to congestion not only during the construction of the bridges but also as they came into use. Yet the fact that congestion is not mentioned in any of the accounts of the battle suggests that the bridgehead from the start was comparatively large, with infantry defending a perimeter beyond the flood plain of the Teme, presumably along the line of the hedge separating it from Wick field to the west.

IV

The course of the fighting on 3 September was reasonably straightforward. The corps advancing up the west bank of the Severn under the command of General Charles

---

15   The person who organised the operation was probably Major General Deane, who was at Upton with Lieutenant General Fleetwood. His previous post had been second-in-command of the New Model Army's artillery train.
16   Cary, *Memorials*, II, pp. 353 and 355.

Fleetwood encountered some opposition in Powick itself and much more when it tried to cross the Teme using the broken down bridge, which resulted in an impasse but within a couple of hours, the Scottish army's line of defence on the north bank of the Teme had been outflanked on both flanks and the defenders were falling back on Worcester bridge. When the king and his generals realised that their forces on the west bank of the Severn were giving way, they launched a vigorous attack on the New Model forces on the east bank. After some initial success, they were driven back by force of numbers, including almost certainly reinforcements from the west bank which used the pontoon bridge to cross the Severn. There followed a mass descent by the Cromwellian forces, both regulars and militia, on the south-east quarter of the city. The defenders of the outworks of Fort Royal, which was situated outside the walls on the Evesham road, were overrun; Sidbury gate was stormed; and fighting spread into the city, the last and bloodiest stage of the battle. At this point, the Scottish cavalry, which had seemingly played no part in the engagement on the east bank of the Severn, fled taking the king with them. They could make good progress through the open field country due north of Worcester but this came to an end within ten miles, and they found choke points in the enclosed country beyond defended by troops that Cromwell had stationed there in advance of the battle in preparation for such an eventuality. They therefore split up into smaller bodies and were hunted down one by one. Very few even of the senior officers on the best horses managed to escape, whilst possibly as many as 8,000 Scottish infantry surrendered in Worcester itself or its immediate surroundings before midnight.

V

It is now necessary to turn to the pontoon bridges, the process by which they were put in place and the part they played in the battle. First, they were not an innovation unlike the landing craft used to carry troops and horses across the Firth of Forth six week earlier. Bridges of that nature had been constructed on several occasions during the First Civil War to facilitate the investment of a large city situated on the banks of a river, as for example at York in 1644 and at Worcester in 1646. The pontoons were formed by boats deliberately sunk to rest on the river bed, which acted as supports for a roadway of planks, presumably with rails on either side to prevent accidental falls, and with ropes to hold everything together and to fix the construction securely to both banks. Military manuals show that boats to serve as pontoons, amongst other things, formed a normal part of a field army's supply train but these were not what Cromwell's engineers used at Worcester in 1651. The bridges over the Severn and the Teme required something more substantial, as did the topography of the place where they were to be constructed and it is not without reason that Cromwell described them as 'great boats'.[17]

---

17   Ibid., p. 357.

The illustrations in military manuals of boats used in bridging operations show them as being carried around the country on what look like purpose-built trollies.[18] They were also quite long and narrow, with sides no more than four feet high. As such, they could not have been used for the bridge over the Severn where the east bank was ten feet or more above the waterline. Instead, the pontoons were formed by boats which operated on the river and, given that twenty were apparently requisitioned for that purpose, they were probably barges used primarily for transporting coal and agricultural produce, rather than the larger trows which carried mixed cargoes as far along the coasts of the Bristol Channel as Bridgewater and Tenby and brought back mainly goods imported through Bristol as well as serge from the west country and anthracite from South Wales.[19] Moreover, if the normal type of army issue boats had been used, all the engineers would need to have done to get them to the bridging point on the east bank of the Severn was to hitch horses to the trollies and drag them overland a distance of two miles or so from the Pershore road close to where it now crosses the M5 Motorway. However, contemporary accounts show clearly that, although some of the bridging material was carried overland, it did not include boats.[20]

The timing of the bridges' construction is not a matter of dispute. They left Upton at dawn on the day of the battle pulled by gangs of men and arrived at the junction of the Teme and the Severn at about 2.00 pm. I do not want to belittle the achievement of getting boats to the right place in a relatively short time but to emphasise the effort involved gives a somewhat false picture, as it ignores the fact that dragging such boats up the river Severn was not a labour of Hercules but an everyday occurrence. From the late Middle Ages, bulky commodities in particular were transported wherever possible by water. It was cheaper, quicker and safer than carriage by road or across country. Moreover, the number of boats operating on the river had increased massively from the 1580s onwards, with the development of coal carrying from the mines at Broseley and Madeley in East Shropshire to the Severn-side ports as far south as Gloucester. The increase in traffic had caused a towpath to be created free of such obstacles as hedges without gates, which ran along the east bank of the Severn.

One contemporary account, however, implies that the barges for constructing the bridge over the river Teme were indeed dragged up the west bank.[21] This seems improbable but the wording is such that the passage can be read as indicating that the whole of the operation was under the control of General Fleetwood. He commanded

18   See for example K. Roberts, *Cromwell's War Machine* (Barnsley, Pen & Sword: 2005), pp. 75 and 77 for bridging trains in transit.
19   Atkin, *Cromwell's Crowning Mercy*, p. 77. I have been unable to locate Atkin's source but the number seems excessively large. Possibly more were seized than was strictly necessary in case of mishaps on the way or accidental sinkings when the boats were being manoeuvred into position.
20   T. Monkhouse, ed., *State Papers Collected by Edward, Earl of Clarendon* (3 vols, Oxford: 1767-86), II, p. 561. This is the only contemporary royalist account of the battle.
21   Cary, *Memorials*, II, p. 362.

the brigades stationed at Upton from 28 August onwards, which included not only those that marched up the west bank on 3 September but also the units guarding the convoy making its way up the towpath on the east bank, both of which started from Upton at about the same hour of the day.[22]

Accounts of the operation suggest strongly that the bridges were constructed almost simultaneously, which means that both sets of boats must have arrived at about the same time but if those intended for the Teme had followed the west bank, they would have been significantly slower due to the absence of a tow path. Also, there would have been no problem in getting the pontoons into the mouth of the Teme if they had been dragged up the east bank rather than the west. Having anchored their barges at a point slightly below the intersection of the two rivers all the bow-haulers had to do was use a rowing boat to transport themselves and their cables from the east bank to the west bank of the Severn and then to pull the barges into the mouth of the Teme.

Putting the pontoons in position thereafter would have been difficult, especially if the flow in either or both rivers had been too strong or too weak but there is nothing to suggest that this was the case. None of the contemporary accounts mentions exceptional rainfall whilst the two armies were making their way south or in the days between the capture of Upton bridge and the battle itself. However, if there had been a shortage of water in the river it would have been more easily fordable at Upton on 28 August but the bridging operation five days later could not have taken place. Malcolm Atkin, whilst mentioning the problem of water flow, adds that fighting going on all around the men who had the task of constructing the pontoon bridges would have made the task even more difficult but it is my contention that incoming fire would have made the task impossible. Instead I am convinced that the work was carried out unhindered by any form of military activity that would endanger life.

Finally, it is highly improbable that Cromwell's commanders did not use experts on the spot rather than soldiers to supervise, if not to perform in full, the task of dragging the boats upriver. In the Severn-side towns under the New Model Army's control – Gloucester, Tewkesbury and Upton – there were gangs of experienced bow-haulers who earned their living by manhandling boats along the short stretch between their town and the nearest one upriver. It is most likely that much if not all of the labour required would have been provided by such men, who would also have been familiar with the quirks of the boats they were required to pull. Moreover, they were experienced in dealing with convoys of boats as the pattern of bi-monthly spring tides, which allowed boats to pass out of the Severn estuary into the river, invariably caused a bunching of upriver traffic.[23]

22   Whitelock, *Memorials*, p. 507.
23   For the working of the Severn navigation see D. Hussey, *Coastal and River Trade in Pre-Industrial England* (Exeter, University of Exeter Press: 2001); B. Trinder, *Barges and Bargemen* (Chichester, Phillimore: 2005).

VI

There remains the question of how the plan was executed and for this a measure of Inherent Military Probability, a concept devised by Lieutenant Colonel Burne in the mid-twentieth century, needs to be applied to flesh out what little is to be found in contemporary sources.[24] The boats being dragged up the Severn from Upton would have been accompanied by an escort of horse and foot to prevent enemy interference with their progress but it proved to be an unnecessary precaution. More problematic was how the enemy would react when their observers on top of the tower of Worcester Cathedral saw them. In fact, it seems likely that the royalists either did not see them or mistook their purpose, the evidence for which will be discussed below. However, Cromwell was not to know this. If the enemy had correctly interpreted what was going when they saw the boats approaching the junction of the Severn and the Teme, they could have prevented the bridges being built. The bridgehead on the east bank would be too close to the parliamentary army for an attack on it not to have been followed by a counterattack in overwhelming force. However, all King Charles had to do was to move troops from Worcester to the north bank of the Teme where it joined the Severn and there was nothing Cromwell could do about it. From this perspective, it looks as if Cromwell was taking an uncharacteristic gamble but almost certainly a piece is missing from the jigsaw of considerations which gave him the confidence to allow the operation to proceed. In my opinion, he reduced the odds by ensuring that he had a large enough force securing both bridgeheads for the Severn bridge before the pontoons arrived, with artillery in place on the east bank to give them support, and as will be shown below, there is some evidence of this in one of the accounts of the battle.

Meanwhile, the brigades of the New Model Army under Fleetwood's command marching towards the west end of Worcester bridge from Upton were not making their way laboriously along the river bank. They had no reason to do so as they were not required to escort a convoy of boats. Instead they used the road until they ran into opposition in Powick village, at which point they fanned out so as to cover the south bank of the river as far as its junction with the Severn.

The ensuing firefight, not sight of the convoy of boats, was the first that the Scottish generals at Worcester knew of the enemy's approach. They then rushed in reinforcements which were sufficient to prevent further progress along the Upton road towards the bridge at Worcester. This and a threat to the crossing of the Teme to the west at Bransford were sufficient to occupy the whole of the attention of the Scots defending the river line. There is no evidence that they saw anything untoward happening to the east, and this is odd. Their view of traffic passing upriver would have been impeded by the rise of land immediately to the south and east of Powick whilst fighting was taking place in the village but when they fell back to Powick bridge, what was going on at the

---

24   A. H. Burne, *Battlefields of England* (London, Methuen: 1950) and A. H. Burne, *More Battlefields of England* (London, Methuen: 1952).

junction of the two rivers would have been easily visible. All I can suggest is that the smoke caused by the black powder used in contemporary muskets obscured the view.

As the convoy of boats neared its destination, a force of 1,000 foot escorting carts carrying planks, poles and some artillery pieces emerged from the Cromwellian army forces drawn up on the high ground to the southeast of Worcester and headed for the place where the eastern end of the bridge was to be fixed. This was noticed by the king and the Scottish commanders but they did nothing to impede what they clearly saw as the first stage in building a bridge across the Severn preparatory to a siege, although with materials that would suggest that it was to be no more than a foot bridge.[25]

What is more surprising is that there is no mention in the royalist account of the convoy of boats. The masts of twenty vessels must have been as clearly visible from the tower of Worcester Cathedral and there was nothing the bow-haulers could do to prevent their being seen. Admittedly, masts were hinged so that they could be lowered to allow boats to pass under bridges but they could not otherwise be lowered until the boats reached their destination. Masts carried sails so that they could take advantage of the wind if it was in the right direction but for the upriver leg of a voyage they had another important purpose that was no less than crucial. It was essential that tow ropes were attached to the top of the masts. If attached to the bows, boats would collide with the bank once the dragging operation got underway. It is, of course, possible that observers on the cathedral tower saw the convoy of boats as part of the normal traffic on the river but this seems highly improbable given the fact that the convoy was not merely in a war zone but approaching what was no-man's-land between two armies. The only suggestion I can make is that the boats were seen by the observers as being collected below the city in preparation for a siege, the intention being to build the bridge much closer to the fortifications, as in 1646 when the bridge had been built at St. John-in-Bedwardine, and that the prospect of them being used there and then did not enter their minds.[26]

Work on the bridge over the Teme appears to have proceeded simultaneously with that over the Severn. Once it was finished, Fleetwood's men that were not engaged at Powick were able to combine with Cromwell's in the bridgehead and to fight their way westwards, thus fatally undermining the Scots' position defending the line of the Teme. At the same time, New Model Army cavalry were striking east and north threatening to cut them off from Worcester bridge. This was the result of some excellent work by Fleetwood's dragoons, who had managed to secure what was left of Bransford bridge a mile upstream from Powick and presumably put some planks in place to enable infantry to cross.[27] The Scots therefore fell back whilst they could

25   Monkhouse, *Clarendon State Papers*, II, p. 561.
26   P. Hughes and A. Leech, *The Story of Worcester* (Almeley, Logaston Press: 2011), p. 87.
27   The dragoons were armed with short flintlock muskets or carbines, which gave them greater firepower than cavalry, which only had pistols, and greater flexibility than the conventional musketeers burdened by heavier weapons and coils of match.

through the small enclosures on the north bank of the Teme into the open fields of the village of Wick, where the engagement had taken place nine years before, and then into what are now the southwestern suburbs of Worcester. However, to the New Model Army's surprise, when they reached the bridge they crossed into the city rather than trying to escape to the north and west. Whilst this was going on, Cromwell led several regiments back across the bridge over the Severn to hit the Scots in the rear as they retreated towards the city having been worsted in the fighting with the forces on the east bank.

The thinking that lies behind this interpretation of the bridge-building operation came initially from applying Burne's concept of Inherent Military Probability but having re-read the primary sources several times over whilst preparing the final version, a practice I recommended in my protocols writing battle narratives,[28] I realised that there was what appeared to be a partial confirmation of the order of events at the time of the bridges' construction in a letter written by Robert Stapleton on the day of the battle:

> Having cleared our passages with a forlorn (hope) we laid a bridge over the Severn and another over the Teme ... The fight began on the other (west) side of the Severn and our foot from this (east) side began it, they clearing the way for the rest to come over after them.[29]

VII

Worcester was not purely a New Model Army victory. As at Preston, forces from the English counties also played their part. Contemporary accounts of the battle give full credit to the militia regiments, most particularly for their contribution towards victory in the fighting on the east bank of the Severn, though two regiments at least were with Fleetwood on the west bank.[30] They also reminded me of research I had undertaken many years earlier on the Cheshire soldiers who had fought with the New Model Army at Worcester.

Described as a brigade rather than a regiment, the Cheshire men were in the front line when the Scots sallied out of Worcester and attacked the forces on the east side of the city. They managed to beat off the attack and participated in the assault on Sidbury gate and the fighting in the town.[31] This is well known but it is worth remarking

28 Wanklyn, *Decisive Battles*, pp. 31-2.
29 Whitelock, *Memorials*, p. 507
30 Atkin gives an order of battle for Fleetwood's corps army in *Cromwell's Crowning Mercy*, p. 174. Four of the regiments he tentatively identifies as militia, Colonel Matthew's, Colonel Marsh's, Colonel Haynes's and Lord Grey's, were indeed militia from Essex, Hertfordshire, Dorset and Leicestershire respectively: *CSPD*, 1650, pp. 504, 506 and 510.
31 They are singled out for praise in one of the accounts of the battle: Cary, *Memorials*, II, p. 351.

that the Cheshire militia which fought at Worcester was particularly strong in that it comprised four regiments each consisting of nine companies of foot. The officers' names recorded in the county's maimed soldier petitions are pretty much a roll call of the commanders who had fought under Sir William Brereton in the First Civil War in Cheshire. Of the colonels two, Robert Duckenfield and Henry Brooke, had been colonels under Brereton. Another, Thomas Croxton had been Brereton's lieutenant colonel of foot. The fourth, Henry Bradshaw, who had been Duckenfield's major, was the brother of John Bradshaw who presided over the trial of King Charles I.[32]

During the engagement, Cheshire sources show that the county's regiments sustained heavy casualties. The Quarter Sessions Files for the years 1651-9 contain the names of 25 men who were so seriously wounded that they were incapable thereafter of earning enough money on which to live. They therefore petitioned the county court for annual pensions. There were also 13 widows of men slain at Worcester. Of those men who petitioned for pensions, nine had served in the ranks in the First or the Second Civil War. This case study is probably typical of the other militia regiments who fought at Worcester. Certainly quite a number of the militia officers commissioned in the period 1649-51 in other English counties had fought in the New Model or in its predecessors commanded by the earl of Manchester and Sir William Waller.[33] Sadly, the information as to the number of common soldiers with previous experience in parliament's armies who fought in the militias of other counties is not yet available and may never be. However, my inclination is to see the fine performance of the militia regiments at Worcester as due to the leaven of veterans in their ranks.

Conclusion

A number of observations should be made about the battle of Worcester's contribution towards an assessment of Oliver Cromwell's generalship. First, Cromwell has been downplayed in the hierarchy of generals because of the small size of the armies he commanded.[34] However, at Worcester he may have had as many as 30,000 men under his command either directly on the battlefield itself or indirectly blocking the Scots' possible escape routes. Second, although Worcester was in one sense the easiest of Cromwell's major battles in overall army command in that, unlike at Preston and Dunbar, his forces outnumbered the enemy by a considerable margin, it should not be forgotten that it was fought across an awkward military landscape and the enemy, though demoralised, were desperate. However, as at Dunbar, it is impossible to fault his tactical plan, especially if it was flexible enough to serve as a necessary stage in

---

32   For brief accounts of their military experience in the First Civil War, see R. N. Dore, ed., *The Letter Books of Sir William Brereton* (2 vols, Lancashire and Cheshire Record Society: 1984 and 1990), *passim.*
33   *CSPD*, 1650, pp. 504-12.
34   A. Woolrych, 'Cromwell as soldier', in J. Morrill, ed., *Oliver Cromwell and the English Revolution* (Harlow, Longman: 1990), pp. 93-118, at p. 117.

the preparations for a siege or as a stratagem for fighting a battle on two fronts. What also needs to be emphasised is the fact that all three of the battles in which Cromwell was in sole charge were primarily infantry battles and yet he was a commander who had built up his reputation as a leader and trainer of cavalry. The fact that he was not tempted to use the arm with which he was most familiar when he became army commander is yet another measure of his greatness.

Part II

Theory and Practice

3

The legacy of the Fighting Veres in the English Civil War

Dr Ismini Pells

In 1566, the seventeen provinces of the Netherlands revolted against the rule of Philip II of Spain. By 1581, only the seven northern, largely Protestant, provinces continued their fight for independence, whilst the ten southern, largely Catholic, provinces remained loyal to Spain. The northern provinces formed the Dutch Republic under the leadership of William the Silent, Prince of Orange.[1] Following William's assassination in 1584, the Dutch offered sovereignty over their republic to Elizabeth I of England. The offer was riddled with risks and the naturally risk-averse Elizabeth declined. However, instead she signed the Treaty of Nonsuch in 1585, which committed her to providing the Dutch with troops at her own expense. As security, Elizabeth was to have possession of Flushing and Brill – the so-called 'Cautionary Towns' – until the war was over and/or the money that had been spent by the English Crown in this venture repaid.[2] By 1588, there were additional English garrisons throughout the Netherlands in Dutch pay.[3] In 1616, James I's ever-increasing debts prompted him into agreeing to relinquish the Cautionary Towns in return for £200,000.[4] Most of the soldiers from the Cautionary Town garrisons were amalgamated into one

---

1   See J. Israel, *The Dutch Republic: Its Rise, Greatness and Fall 1477-1806* (Oxford, Clarendon Press: 1995), pp. 129-230.
2   The National Archives [hereafter TNA], SP 84/71/125, fol. 301 (State Papers Foreign, Holland c.1560-1780: State of the Cautionary Towns, 1615); Anon., *An Historical Account of the British Regiments Employed since the Reign of Queen Elizabeth and James I in the Formation and Defence of the Dutch Republic* (London: 1794), p. 3; E. Grimstone, *A Generall Historie of the Netherlands* (London: 1627), p. 1349; Israel, *Dutch Republic*, p. 228; G. Parker, *The Army of Flanders and the Spanish Road* (Cambridge, Cambridge University Press: 2004), p. 206.
3   Israel, *Dutch Republic*, p. 238.
4   *Calendar of State Papers, Domestic Series* [hereafter, *CSPD*], 1611-1618, p. 364; *Calendar of State Papers Relating To English Affairs in the Archives of Venice* [hereafter, *CSPV*], 1615-1617, p. 226.

regiment, which joined the three other English regiments dispersed throughout the Netherlands already in Dutch pay.[5] The war continued until Spain finally recognised Dutch independence in the Peace of Munster in 1648.[6]

The most celebrated commanders of the English forces in the Netherlands were Sir Francis Vere, from 1589 to 1604, and his brother, Sir Horace Vere, between 1605 and 1632. Francis (c. 1560–1609) and Horace (1565–1635) were the second and fourth sons, respectively, of Geoffrey Vere and Elizabeth Harkyns. Geoffrey Vere, whose seat was at Crepping Hall in Wakes Colne, Essex, was the fourth son of John de Vere, fifteenth earl of Oxford.[7] As David Trim noted, Francis Vere became famous in his home country during his exploits in the Netherlands. His ability at light infantry warfare has been praised by Dutch historians but he was also a good cavalry general and demonstrated mastery of siege warfare. In addition, he showed a talent for military administration, reorganising the English army in the Netherlands in the 1590s. Although Trim conceded that 'Vere's talents were those of an excellent corps commander and/or a staff officer, rather than of an army commander', he argued that the English troops under Francis's command 'played a crucial part in the operations of the 1590s by which the future of the Dutch republic was secured'.[8] Nevertheless, Trim also observed that the English involvement in the Netherlands in the late Tudor and early Stuart periods only begun to receive any scholarly attention towards the end of the twentieth century. Although Francis is probably the best known English military commander of the late sixteenth and early seventeenth centuries, most early modern English military commanders before the duke of Marlborough have been

---

5   *CSPV*, 1615-1617, p. 197; *CSPD*, 1611-1618, pp. 368 and 370; D. Carleton, *Letters from and to Sir Dudley Carleton, Knt: during his embassy in Holland, from January 1615/16, to December 1620*, ed. P. Yorke (London: 1775), p. 31; Nationaal Archief, 1.01.02: Archief van de Staten-Generaal (Archives of the States-General), No. 5886, Ingekomen ordinaris brieven en stukken van vorstelijke personen, gezanten, enz. betreffende Engeland, 1614-1639 (Letters and Documents received from royalty, ambassadors, etc. on England, 1614-39), unpag.; Nationaal Archief, 1.01.02: Archief van de Staten-Generaal (Archives of the States-General), No. 12589 – De Loketkas en de Secrete kas van de Staten-Generaal: Secrete kas Engeland (The cabinets and secret coffers of the States-General: Secret coffer for England), packet 31.

6   P. Wilson, *Europe's Tragedy: A New History of the Thirty Years War* (London, Penguin: 2010), pp. 735-6.

7   For an analysis of the Vere brothers' lives and careers, see D. J. B. Trim, 'Vere , Sir Francis (1560/61–1609)', *Oxford Dictionary of National Biography* (Oxford, Oxford University Press: 2008), online edn, http://www.oxforddnb.com/view/article/28209, accessed 16 September 2015; D. J. B. Trim, 'Vere, Horace, Baron Vere of Tilbury (1565–1635)', *Oxford Dictionary of National Biography* (Oxford, Oxford University Press: 2009), online edn, http://www.oxforddnb.com/view/article/28211, accessed 16 September 2015. See also C. R. Markham, *The fighting Veres* (London, Sampson Low: 1888).

8   D. J. B. Trim, 'Vere , Sir Francis (1560/61–1609)', *Oxford Dictionary of National Biography* (Oxford, Oxford University Press: 2008), online edn, http://www.oxforddnb.com/view/article/28209, accessed 29 January 2016.

largely ignored (other than Oliver Cromwell). This is especially true of Horace, who has attracted much less attention than his brother. Much of this can be put down to the fact that Francis came first and commanded in a period of more dazzling success for the Dutch Republic, as well as being 'a gifted self-publicist'. Francis ensured he attracted the attentions of historians through his *Commentaries*, which ostensibly are frank memoirs but actually serve to vindicate his reputation. However, Trim maintained that the quieter, more modest Horace was certainly as able a soldier and arguably more influential in the long term.[9]

The Veres' reputation encouraged many Englishmen to join the Dutch cause. The Veres were particularly successful in instilling an *esprit de corps* amongst their men, which rested upon honour and tradition and created a feeling of continuity from the celebrated Elizabethan campaigners through to the early Stuarts.[10] Those who were discontented by James I's and Charles I's reluctance to intervene on behalf of the international Protestant cause during the Thirty Years' War in Europe could alleviate their frustration by volunteering their services to Horace Vere. Moreover, this opportunity ensured that the art of war did not become forgotten in England during the prolonged periods of peace between 1604 and 1639.[11] The Veres were the teachers and patrons of a whole generation of soldiers and became synonymous with the development of English military professionalism.[12] Under their command, the English regiments in the Netherlands became, in Mark Fissel's words, 'reservoirs of military talent that might be deployed wherever English strategic interests were threatened'.[13] For example, men from these regiments were loaned for the expedition to the Palatinate led by Horace Vere in aid of James I's daughter Elizabeth of Bohemia in 1620, the force sent by Charles I under Sir Charles Morgan to support Christian IV of Denmark's Thirty Years' War campaigns in 1627-9 and Charles I's ill-fated attempt to raid Cadiz in 1625.[14] Moreover, veterans from the Veres' campaigns formed the nucleus of both

9   D. J. B. Trim, 'Vere, Horace, Baron Vere of Tilbury (1565–1635)', *Oxford Dictionary of National Biography* (Oxford, Oxford University Press: 2009), online edn, http://www.oxforddnb.com/view/article/28211, accessed 29 January 2016.

10   Markham, *Fighting Veres*, p. 456.

11   D. J. B. Trim, 'Vere, Horace, Baron Vere of Tilbury (1565–1635)', *Oxford Dictionary of National Biography* (Oxford, Oxford University Press: 2009), online edn, http://www.oxforddnb.com/view/article/28211, accessed 29 January 2016.

12   Ibid; Markham, *fighting Veres*, p. 455.

13   M. C. Fissel, *English Warfare, 1511-1642* (London, Routledge: 2001), p. 154.

14   S. L. Adams, 'Spain or the Netherlands? The dilemmas of early Stuart foreign policy', in H. Tomlinson, ed., *Before the English Civil War: Essays on Early Stuart Politics and Government* (London, Macmillan: 1983), pp. 79-102, at p. 85; TNA, SP 84/95/94, fol. 275 (State Papers Foreign, Holland c.1560-1780: Letter from Sir Horace Vere to Sir Dudley Carleton, 21 June 1620); Statens Arkiver, Tyske Kancelli Udenrigske Afdeling [German Chancellory's Foreign Department], England: Breve fra huset Stuart 1602-1714 [England: Letters from the House of Stuart, 1602-1714], Breve fra Karl I til Christian IV 1625-26 [Letters from Charles I to Christian IV, 1625-26], unpag. (Letter from Charles I to Christian IV, 11 October 1626); *CSPV*, 1625-1626, pp. 548 and 588; Nationaal

the royalist and parliamentarian armies in the English Civil War. The time that these men had spent under the Veres not only influenced their ability to fight but also the way in which they fought. This paper will identify some of the Veres' protégés that fought in the Civil War and examine how their actions in this conflict may have been influenced by their experiences in the Netherlands, especially how they established working relationships with those within their own armies and those in the armies of their adversaries.

The first battle of the Civil War was, in reality, the struggle for men and resources. As both sides sought to gain control of local magazines and fortifications, they faced the simultaneous problem of raising sufficient personnel to actually fight a war. It is a common enough fact that there was no standing army as such at the time in England. There was, of course, the militia – the 'Trained Bands' – and both parliament and the king attempted to secure their services under the Militia Ordinance and the Commission of Array respectively.[15] The Trained Bands have invariably received a bad press over the years: 'ill disciplined, ill equipped, ill trained' being the general consensus.[16] Despite attempts to rehabilitate their reputation, the perception that 'the trained bands of the county were anything trained', which 'served better as a vehicle for honourable display by the county elite than as a fighting force', is one that has persisted.[17] This is not the place to enter into this particular argument but suffice to say, the Trained Bands on their own were not a suitable force on which to base an army. Their use depended upon the compliance of Lords Lieutenant and enthusiasm of local activists and was complicated by the proviso that they were not, at least in theory, supposed to serve outside their shire.[18] Therefore, both sides turned to raising additional forces, in which process previous experience was held at a premium.

Archief, 1.01.02 – Archief van de Staten-Generaal [Archives of the States-General], No. 5889 – Ingekomen ordinaris brieven en stukken van vorstelijke personen, gezanten, enz. betreffende Engeland, 1614-1639 [Letters and Documents received from royalty, ambassadors, etc. on England, 1614-39], fol. 119 (List of ships and their commanders for the Cadiz expedition, 1625); TNA, SP 16/522/18 fols 27-8 and SP 16/522/19 fols 29-31 (State Papers Domestic, Charles I: Lists of officers in the Netherlands competent to take command in the Cadiz expedition, two copies, 18 October 1625 and 19 October 1625).

15   G. Davies, 'The Parliamentary Army under the Earl of Essex, 1642-45', *The English Historical Review*, 49 (1934), pp. 32-54, at pp. 32-3; M. J. Braddick, *God's Fury, England's Fire* (London, Penguin: 2009), p. 210.

16   Davies, 'Parliamentary Army under the Earl of Essex', p. 32.

17   H. Langelüddecke, 'The Chiefest Strength and Glory of This Kingdom': Arming and Training the 'Perfect Militia' in the 1630s', *The English Historical Review*, 118:479 (2003), pp. 1264-1303; P. E. J. Hammer, *Elizabeth's Wars: War, Government and Society in Tudor England, 1544-1604* (Basingstoke, Palgrave Macmillan: 2003), pp. 7-8; A. Woolrych, *Battles of the Civil War* (New York, Phoenix Press: 1961), p. 36; Braddick, *God's Fury*, p. 218.

18   Ibid., p. 214; Davies, 'Parliamentary Army under the Earl of Essex', p. 32.

On 12 July 1642, parliament resolved to raise a field army under the command of Robert Devereux, third earl of Essex.[19] According to his commission:

> having had long Experience and certain Knowledge that Robert Earl of Essex is, every Way, qualified for a Trust of so high a Nature and Concernment, in regard of the Nobility of his Birth, his great Judgment in Martial Affairs, approved Integrity and Sufficiency in divers Honourable Employments and Commands in the said Public Service of this State.[20]

Indeed, Essex was, as Michael Braddick has put it, 'an assiduous parliamentarian, often associated with anti-court positions' but most importantly, he was the highest-ranking peer with any extensive military experience.[21] Much of this experience had been gained under the Veres' tutelage. In many ways, Essex had always been destined for military pursuits. The third earl's father, the doomed Elizabethan favourite, fought alongside a young Francis Vere in the initial campaigns in the Netherlands in 1585 and presided over the raid on Cadiz in 1596, where Francis took charge of the land operations and Horace won his spurs.[22] His mother was the widow of the poet Sir Philip Sidney, whose death from wounds sustained in the Dutch cause at Zutphen fuelled 'one of the core values of English martial culture [that] was there was no hero quite as admirable as a dead hero'.[23] As a young man, Essex duly followed in his forebears' footsteps and headed for the Netherlands, where 'He at first trayled a Pike', which apparently 'did much indeere him to the Soundiers'.[24]

Purchase of the highest ranks was not uncommon in the Netherlands but when it came to recruitment and promotion amongst their junior officers, the English colonels did not generally prefer 'young men vpon letters and commends' but had 'an eye to old Souldiers of merit, service and experience'.[25] Therefore, even those from the highest echelons of society served amongst the ranks before being given a command. These

19 C. H. Firth and R. S. Rait, eds, *Acts and Ordinances of the Interregnum, 1642-1660* (London, Stationary Office: 1911) [hereafter *A&O*], I, pp. 14-16; *Journal of the House of Commons* [hereafter *JHC*], II, p. 668; *Journal of the House of Lords* [hereafter *JHL*], V, p. 208.
20 *A&O*, I, p. 14.
21 Braddick, *God's Fury*, p. 210.
22 R. Codrington, *The Life and Death of the Illustrious Robert, Earl of Essex, &c.* (London: 1646), p. 1; Markham, *Fighting Veres*, pp. 78, 228 and 233.
23 Codrington, *Earl of Essex*, p. 2; R. B. Manning, *Swordsmen: The Martial Ethos in the Three Kingdoms* (Oxford, Oxford University Press: 2003), p. 64.
24 Codrington, *Earl of Essex*, p. 8.
25 R. B. Manning, *An Apprenticeship in Arms: The Origins of the British Army, 1585-1702* (Oxford, Oxford University Press: 2006), p. viii; H. Hexham, *A Tongue-Combat Lately Happening Betvveene tvvo English Souldiers in the Tilt-boat of Grauesend, the one going to serue the King of Spaine, the other to serue the States Generall of the Vnited Provinces* (The Hague: 1623), p. 104.

men engaged as 'gentlemen volunteers', who received no pay but were not expected to pass musters or perform any specific duties.[26] Their main role was to stiffen the resolve of the ranks by demonstrating obedience to superior commanders, as well as setting an example in maintaining their arms, personal appearance and religious and moral discipline.[27] Most gentlemen volunteers served as pikemen because edged weapons enabled face-to-face combat, which was considered more honourable, unlike missile weapons that fired from a distance and thus considered rather unsporting.[28] Essex went on to be appointed one of the officers for Horace Vere's expedition to the Palatinate in 1620, between 1621 and 1623 he fought for the Dutch in Cleves and Arnhem and he served again under Vere at the siege of Breda in 1624-5 as colonel of one of the 'new' regiments raised for this venture.[29]

It is perhaps unsurprising that many of the men Essex selected to form the basis of his officer corps in the new parliamentary field army had too gained military experience on the Continent, including several who had served directly alongside the earl himself under Horace Vere.[30] Amongst these, Charles Essex had been the earl of Essex's page in the Low Countries until the earl obtained a captaincy for him in the English regiments in the Netherlands. According to the earl of Clarendon, Charles Essex 'thought his gratitude obliged him to run the fortune of his patron, and out of pure kindness to the person of the earl, as many other gentlemen did, engaged himself against the King, without any malice or rebellion in his heart towards the Crown'. During his time in the Netherlands, Charles Essex had apparently 'lived with very good reputation, and preserved the reputation of his decayed family'.[31] He was one of those seconded from the English regiments to Sir Charles Morgan's army, which, between 1627 and 1629, was sent by Charles I to assist his uncle, Christian IV of Denmark, in the Thirty Years' War.[32] His later career in the Netherlands is difficult

---

26 Manning, *Swordsmen*, p. 129.
27 H. Hexham, *The Principles of the Art Militarie Practiced in the Warres of the United Provinces* (London: 1637), pp. 6-7.
28 Manning, *Swordsmen*, p. 28; BL, Harleian MS 3638, fol. 156 (Sir Edward Cecil, Lord Wimbledon, 'The Duty of a Private Soldier).
29 TNA, SP 81/17/105, fol. 105 (State Papers Foreign, German States, 1577-1784: Officer list for Sir Horace Vere's expedition to the Palatinate, 1 July 1620); Codrington, *Earl of Essex*, pp. 8-10; A. Wilson, *The History of Great Britain, being the Life and Reign of King James the First, Relating To what passed from his first Access to the Crown, till his Death* (London: 1653), pp. 135-6, 138 and 280; G. Markham, *Honour in his Perfection* (London: 1624), p. [iv]; V. F. Snow, *Essex the Rebel: The Life of Robert Devereux, Third Earl of Essex, 1591-1646* (Lincoln, Nebraska, University of Nebraska Press: 1970), pp. 98 and 111-14.
30 Snow, *Essex the Rebel*, pp. 309 and 314. For a list of the successive senior officers in Essex's army, see Davies, 'Parliamentary Army under the Earl of Essex', pp. 47-8.
31 E. Hyde, Earl of Clarendon, *The History of the Rebellion and Civil Wars in Ireland begun in the year 1641*, ed. W. D. Macray, (Oxford, Clarendon Press: 1888), II, p. 369.
32 TNA, SP 75/8/468, fol. 468 (State Papers foreign, Denmark 1577-1780: List of captains and regiments under Sir Charles Morgan, c. 1627); TNA, SP 75/9/142, fol. 142 (State Papers foreign, Denmark 1577-1780: Muster of English Regiments at Zwolle, 17 May

to distinguish from that of his younger brother, Thomas Essex, who also served in the English regiments there. A 'Mr Essex' fought in Horace Vere's 'first company Coronell of Dort' at the siege of 's-Hertogenbosch in 1629 and a 'Captain Essex' was present at the siege of Maastricht in 1632.[33] Whilst these could be either brother, it is known for certain that in 1637, 'Lieutenant Coronell Thomas Essex' participated in the siege of Breda.[34]

Sir John Meyrick had also served under Horace Vere alongside the earl of Essex. Meyrick was a lieutenant to Essex in the Palatinate and then a captain in Essex's regiment at Breda, before continuing to serve under Vere at the sieges of 's-Hertogenbosch and Maastricht.[35] At the outbreak of the Civil War, Meyrick was appointed sergeant-major-general of Essex's infantry. When, in November 1642, parliament decided by their own 'absolute power' to replace Meyrick with another of Vere's veterans, Philip Skippon, Essex was apparently somewhat peeved, although Meyrick was made general of the ordnance.[36] Skippon had probably come under Horace's wing as a sixteen-year-old boy around 1615 and had risen through the ranks in Dutch service from a common soldier to a captain. He went with Horace to the Palatinate and served under him at the 1624-5 siege of Breda and the sieges of 's-Hertogenbosch and Maastricht. It is also likely that he went with Morgan to Christian IV of Denmark's aid and he eventually retired from Dutch service after being badly wounded at the siege of Breda in 1637.[37] Skippon also seems to have identified with the legacy of Francis Vere, as he owned a copy of Francis's *Commentaries*. The *Commentaries* had remained in manuscript for many years, circulating between and copied by those connected to the Veres, but it was from a corrected transcription of Skippon's copy that the work was finally published in 1657.[38] Despite starting their

1628); TNA, SP 75/9/335, fol. 335 (State Papers foreign, Denmark 1577-1780: Petition of English Captains in Glückstadt, 10 December 1628.

33   H. Hexham, *A Historicall Relation Of the Famous Siege of the Busse, And the suprising of Wesell* (Delft: 1630), p. [24]; H. Hexham, *A Iournall, Of the taking in of Venlo, Roermont, Strale, the memorable Seige of Mastricht, the Towne & Castle of Limburch vnder the able, and wise Conduct of his Excie: the Prince of Orange, Anno 1632* (London: 1633), p. [8]. See also TNA, SP 84/148/22, fol. 68 (State Papers Foreign, Holland, c.1560-1780: List of the English Regiments serving in the Netherlands, 11 March 1634) and British Library [hereafter BL], Kings MS 265, fol. 27v (List of English Regiments in Dutch Service, 1630).

34   H. Hexham, *A True and Briefe Relation of the Famous Seige of Breda* (Delft: 1637), p. [40].

35   TNA, E 101/612/73 (Exchequer Records: Accounts of pay issued to the troops serving for the defence of the Palatinate 1621); TNA, SP 84/121/88, fol. 255 (State Papers Foreign, Holland, c.1560-1780: List of officers for English Troops in Dutch Service, 1624); Hexham, *Historicall Relation Of the Famous Siege of the Busse*, p. [44]; Hexham, *Iournall, Of the taking in of Venlo*, p. 40.

36   Clarendon, *History of the Rebellion*, III, p. 16.

37   I. Pells, 'The military career, religious and political thought of Philip Skippon, c. 1598-1660', (Ph.D. thesis, University of Cambridge, 2014), pp. 33-70.

38   M. J. D. Cockle, *A Bibliography of English Military Books up to 1642 and of Contemporary Foreign Works* (London, Simpkin, Marshall, Hamilton, Kent & Co: 1900), p. 129; F. Vere,

professional relationship on the wrong foot, Essex and Skippon soon forged a strong partnership and the way in which the army they commanded fought was largely modelled by the Dutch mould.[39]

Charles I too sought to raise a field army and as with parliament, many of the commissions he issued went to men who had learnt the military ropes under the Veres. Whilst Charles retained nominal command of his army, he appointed as his Lieutenant-General Robert Bertie, earl of Lindsey.[40] As the grandson of John de Vere, earl of Oxford, Lindsey was the Vere brothers' cousin.[41] His early biographer, David Lloyd, claimed that as an eighteen-year-old man, the then plain Robert Bertie had played a heroic role in Francis Vere's great victory at Nieuwpoort in July 1600. Lloyd alleged that Bertie led several attacks in person, without injury, despite being unhorsed three times.[42] More certainly, Bertie went on (as Lord Willoughby) to be appointed, alongside the earl of Essex, colonel of another of the 'new' regiments raised to join Horace Vere's forces in the relief of Breda in 1624-5.[43]

Like Lindsey, Sir Jacob Astley, who was appointed sergeant-major-general of the royalist infantry, had also probably fought with Francis Vere at Nieuwpoort and had been given a commission shortly afterwards.[44] He continued to hold command under Horace Vere, eventually rising to the rank of sergeant-major-general of the English regiments.[45] Astley's portrait was one of twelve full-length representations of Horace's 'Officers and Captaines' that hung in the younger Vere's residence of Kirby

The Commentaries of Sir Francis Vere, ed. W. Dillingham (Cambridge: 1657), in Firth, C. H., ed., *Stuart Tracts, 1603-1693* (London, Constable: 1903), pp. 83-210, at p. 86; J. Eales, 'Anne and Thomas Fairfax, and the Vere Connection', in A. Hopper and P. Major, eds, *England's Fortress: New Perspectives on Thomas, 3rd Lord Fairfax* (Farnham, Ashgate: 2014), pp. 145-68, at p. 153.

39   For some discussion of this, see: I. Pells, "'this little Judgement which I have through my industry obtained unto, In Forraigne Countries': Philip Skippon and the lessons learnt from Continental conflicts in the English Civil War', *Cromwelliana*, Ser. III, no. 4 (July 2015), pp. 94-116.

40   P. Newman, *Royalist Officers in England and Wales, 1642-1660: A Biographical Dictionary* (New York, Garland: 1981), pp. xiii-xiv.

41   Ibid., p. 27.

42   D. Lloyd, *Memoires of the Lives, Actions, Sufferings & Deaths of those Noble, Reverend and Excellent Personages that Suffered by Death, Sequestration, Decimation, Or Otherwise, for the Protestant Religion* (London: 1668), p. 39. For the unreliability of this source, see A. Thrush, 'Bertie, Robert, first earl of Lindsey (1582–1642)', *Oxford Dictionary of National Biography*, (Oxford, Oxford University Press: 2007); online edn, http://www.oxforddnb. com/view/article/2277, accessed 19 November 2015.

43   Markham, *Honour in his Perfection*, p. [iv].

44   I. Roy, 'Astley, Jacob, first Baron Astley of Reading (1579–1652)', *Oxford Dictionary of National Biography* (Oxford, Oxford University Press: 2004), online edn, http://www. oxforddnb.com/view/article/817, accessed 19 August 2015.

45   TNA, State Papers, SP 84/71/131 (State Papers Foreign, Holland c.1560-1780: List of English and Scottish Captains, 1615), fol. 312; Hexham, *Seige of Breda*, p. 3.

Hall, Essex.[46] Astley had also participated in Horace's expedition to the Palatinate and was part of the force seconded to Christian IV of Denmark.[47] Astley was a favourite of Elizabeth of Bohemia, who called him her 'little Monkie'.[48] It was even said that he also gave military instruction to her son, Prince Rupert, at a young age and Elizabeth certainly commended Astley for being 'so diligent about in waiting on my sonns' at the siege of Breda in 1637.[49] Both future royalist cavalry commanders, Rupert and Maurice, had fought alongside the English Regiments at the siege and Rupert had even allegedly accompanied the Prince of Orange[50] into the field as a thirteen-year-old in 1633.[51] Other royalist officers who had fought under the Veres included the governor of York, Sir Thomas Glemham, who served at 's-Hertogen-bosch and Sir Nicholas Byron, who commanded one of the three infantry brigades in the royalist army in autumn 1642, who had risen to the rank of captain in the Netherlands by 1633.[52]

Many men came directly from the English regiments still serving in the Netherlands to fight for the royalist cause, including several veteran officers recruited by George Goring.[53] Goring, in the best traditions of the archetypal cavalier, had been a hand-some, witty and dashing young man, who (as handsome, witty and dashing young men do) ended up broke. Having worked his way through his wife's dowry, his unamused father-in-law, the earl of Cork, agreed to purchase him the command of Horace Vere's own regiment, following the latter's retirement.[54] Goring served as Colonel of this regiment from 1633 until the siege of Breda in 1637, where he was wounded in the ankle.[55] He was given an honourable retirement and returned to England, where he was made governor of Portsmouth. At the outbreak of the Civil War, Goring's loyalties were uncertain. He eventually declared for the king but was forced to surrender

46   Eales, 'Anne and Thomas Fairfax', pp. 156-7.
47   TNA, E 101/612/73 (Exchequer Records: Accounts of pay issued to the troops serving for the defence of the Palatinate 1621); TNA, SP 81/34/236 (State Papers Foreign, German States, 1577-1784: Muster Roll of Four Regiments Under General Morgan), fol. 236.
48   N. Akkerman, ed., *The Correspondence of Elizabeth Stuart, Queen of Bohemia* (2 vols, Oxford, Oxford University Press: 2011-15), II, p. 108.
49   R. W., Ketton-Cremer, *Norfolk in the Civil War* (London, Faber: 1969), p. 163; Akkerman, *Correspondence of Elizabeth Stuart*, II, p. 650.
50   The Prince of Orange and commander-in-chief of the Dutch army at this time was William the Silent's son, Maurice of Nassau.
51   Akkerman, *Correspondence of Elizabeth Stuart*, II, pp. 621, 622n and 262n.
52   Clarendon, *History of the Rebellion*, II, pp. 286 and 347-8; Hexham, *Historicall Relation Of the Famous Siege of the Busse*, p. [43]; BL, Kings MS 265, fol. 27 (List of English Regiments in Dutch Service, 1630).
53   *CSPV*, 1642-1643, p. 131.
54   R. Hutton, 'Goring, George, Baron Goring (1608–1657)', *Oxford Dictionary of National Biography* (Oxford, Oxford University Press: 2004), online edn, http://www.oxforddnb.com/view/article/111000, accessed 26 August 2015.
55   BL, Kings MS 265, fol. 27v (List of English Regiments in Dutch Service, 1630); Hexham, *Seige of Breda*, pp. 21-2; Clarendon, *History of the Rebellion*, II, p. 269n.

Portsmouth after a brief siege. Under the terms of surrender, he was allowed to leave the country for France, from whence he travelled into the Netherlands.[56] He returned to Newcastle from Amsterdam at the end of December, bringing with him several officers from the English regiments in the Netherlands and money that had been raised there.[57] A delighted Charles I rewarded him by appointing him Lieutenant-General of the horse in the northern army under the earl of Newcastle.[58]

In addition to the men recruited from the English regiments, both sides engaged the services of foreign soldiers, many of whom originated from the Protestant heartlands of the Netherlands and Germany where the Veres' veterans had plied their military trade. Mark Stoyle identified 105 foreign army officers, of which 59 fought in royalist armies, 40 fought in parliamentarian armies and six fought first for parliament and then the king.[59] How far those who employed the expertise of these men had actually served directly alongside them on the Continent is unclear but what is certain is that both sides were cautious in their use of mercenaries. The Marquis of Worcester opposed letting Lord Ruthven fight for the king on the basis that he was 'a soldier of fortune' who was 'here today and God knows where tomorrow', whilst the parliamentarian Lord Brooke proclaimed that he would rather have 'a thousand honest citizens who can handle their arms, whose hearts go with their hands, than thousands of mercenary soldiers that boast of foreign experience'.[60] Escalating distrust of foreign officers amongst the parliamentarian alliance meant that few were commissioned into the New Model Army.[61] Furthermore, public opinion often lumped Englishmen who had served for pay in overseas armies and foreign mercenaries together and the former 'developed reputations for inflated self-regard, swearing, drinking, reveling, and importing frightful continental practices into English military life'.[62] Both were regarded with suspicion, not least as they were viewed as the most likely candidates for side-changing.[63] This appeared to be a stereotype not without substance when these men were amongst the most prominent defectors from the parliamentary cause in 1643, as the prospects of regular pay and military success seemed increasingly unlikely. Many civilians questioned the ideological commitment of career soldiers to the cause, believing that they only fought for pay and that they prolonged the war for their own enrichment.[64] Parliament was forced to issue a declaration clearing Meyrick

56   Ibid., I, p. 554-5 and II, pp. 315 and 315n; *CSPV*, 1642-1643, p. 155.
57   Ibid., 1642-1643, p. 223.
58   Clarendon, *History of the Rebellion*, II, p. 466.
59   A. Hopper, *Turncoats and Renegadoes: Changing Sides during the English Civil Wars* (Oxford, Oxford University Press: 2012), p. 69.
60   C. Carlton, *Going to the Wars: The Experience of the English Civil Wars, 1638-1651* (London, Routledge: 1992), pp. 20-1.
61   Hopper, *Turncoats and Renegadoes*, p. 70.
62   Ibid., pp. 61-2.
63   Ibid., p. 61.
64   Ibid., p. 67.

of suspicions of infidelity to their cause in December 1642, whilst in February 1643 Thomas Essex was arrested on charges of planning to betray Bristol to the royalists, despite slim evidence.[65]

No doubt the unsavoury reputation of mercenaries and English soldiers who had served abroad rested a good deal on the English contempt for Johnny Foreigner. As the Venetian Ambassador had remarked, 'the English nation in war and in other things claims to be superior to all other nations, and is by no means disposed to yield this claim'.[66] Nevertheless, the stigma attached to 'mercenaries' and 'soldiers of fortune' was widely held in early-modern Europe and it was commonly believed that, in comparison to native soldiers, 'strangers are covetous, and consequently corruptible'.[67] The English perception of the unprincipled mercenary was, in part, derived from reports of the Thirty Years' War, where soldiers who served under contract for pay were (in theory) free to choose a new army at the expiration of that contract and many moved between armies without compunction.[68] However, not all those who were paid to fight merely sold themselves to the highest bidder. The commitment to Calvinist beliefs and the principle of defending these on an international scale that was so prevalent amongst the Englishmen who fought in Continental armies meant that most Englishmen only served in the armies of Protestant powers.[69] Henry Hexham, who had begun his military career as Francis Vere's page before rising to become quartermaster of Horace Vere's own regiment and whose published accounts provide one of the best sources for the activities of the English regiments in the Netherlands, insisted that the English were so well-affected to the Netherlands' cause that the Dutch used them not as mercenaries but 'nobly, freely, and bountifully as Natives'.[70] He accepted that the English soldiers took pay but it was out of sheer necessity, as who could have afforded not to? Of course 'the modester and better sort' were 'mixt with bad deseruers' but that was not to deny many fought 'freely, not with respect to the money, but love of the Cause and Country'.[71] Likewise, despite high profile defections, there seems to have been a correspondingly high level of constancy to their respective causes amongst the foreigners and those with previous military experience in the Civil War.[72]

65 Ibid., pp. 66-7.
66 *CSPV*, 1615-1617, pp. 431-2.
67 Manning, *Swordsmen*, p. 21; L. Roberts, *VVarrefare Epitomized, In a Century, of Military Observations: Confirming by Antient Principles The Moderne practise of Armes* (London: 1640), p. 14.
68 Hopper, *Turncoats and Renegadoes*, pp. 62-3; C. V. Wedgwood, *The Thirty Years War* (London, J. Cape: 1938), p. 87.
69 Hopper, *Turncoats and Renegadoes*, p. 63; D. Trim, 'Calvinist Internationalism and the English Officer Corps, 1562–1642', *History Compass*, 4/6 (2006), pp.1024–48.
70 Markham, *Fighting Veres*, pp. 318 and 318n; Hexham, *Tongue-Combat*, p. 104. Hexham remained quartermaster of Vere's regiment after Goring purchased the command in 1632.
71 Ibid., pp. 64 and 104.
72 Hopper, *Turncoats and Renegadoes*, pp. 72 and 76-7.

The legacy of the Fighting Veres in the Civil War was not simply one of manpower. The way in the Veres' protégés managed their armies in this conflict was also influenced by their time in the Netherlands. The royalist officer Sir Richard Grenville had learnt the profession of a soldier in the Netherlands, apparently in Horace Vere's own regiment, where 'he was looked upon as a man of courage, and diligent officer, in the quality of a captain, to which he attained after a few years' service'.[73] He followed Vere to the Palatinate and at the unhappy conclusion to that conflict, returned with his commander to the Netherlands. He afterwards served in the expedition to Cadiz, the voyage to the Ile de Rhé and in the Swedish army in Germany.[74] Grenville had been fighting the Irish rebels when Civil War broke out in England but when the king ordered the Cessation of Arms in September 1643, he volunteered his services for parliament and was made lieutenant-general of the horse in Sir William Waller's army. However, as he rode to join Waller's forces at Basing House, he made a dramatic defection to the king at Oxford and was dispatched to the royalist forces in the West.[75] When, in 1645, Grenville was appointed field marshal of the royalist army in the West, he declared that 'he neither would nor could command men who were not paid'.[76] Ian Roy argued that Grenville's experiences on the Continent and in Ireland had taught him that regular pay was vital to maintain discipline and morale.[77] During his campaigning in Devon and Cornwall the previous year, Grenville had made himself 'odious to both counties' by raising what money he pleased for his army and imprisoning those who refused to pay, along with the constables who would not make them. Yet, he kept his men 'from committing any disorder or offering the least prejudice to any man', which 'raised him much credit amongst the country people'.[78]

If Grenville's previous experiences had indeed taught him that plunder and indiscipline could be prevented through regular pay, then his time in the English regiments under the Veres certainly provides at least some of the substance to Roy's claim. Unlike many of the armies fighting in the various theatres of the Thirty Years' War, the Dutch had introduced a regular pay system into their army to prevent their soldiers from plundering their way across the countryside. This was very important when, like in the English Civil War, much of the fighting took place within their own borders and they did not wish to alienate their people from their cause.[79] The Dutch prided themselves

---

73   Clarendon, *History of the Rebellion*, III, p. 418.
74   G. Granville, Lord Lansdowne, *The Genuine Works in Verse and Prose, Of the Right Honourable George Granville, Lord Lansdowne* (London: 1736), II, pp. 231 and 234.
75   Clarendon, *History of the Rebellion*, III, pp. 421-3.
76   Ibid., IV, p. 61.
77   I. Roy, 'Grenville, Sir Richard, baronet (bap. 1600, d. 1659)', *Oxford Dictionary of National Biography* (Oxford, Oxford University Press: 2004), online edn, http://www.oxforddnb.com/view/article/11494, accessed 10 November 2015.
78   Ibid., IV, pp. 58-9.
79   Israel, *Dutch Republic*, p. 268.

on their prompt and regular payment of their forces. Allegedly, 'nobody's pay is delivered [late] even for an hour'.[80] There were also benefits in clothing and provisions and an established system for kit exchange.[81] That said, there was no denying that the monthly wages were small. Moreover, the month was calculated at 40 days.[82] Those offered to a common foot soldier were similar to that which seven-year-old children could earn in Norwich by knitting stockings.[83] Skippon acknowledged that 'Captaines in these Countries [the Netherlands] serve in a most uncomfortable and unhappy condition, who by the ill payment, are forced to live theeves or dye beggars, or spend their owne meanes'.[84] Clarendon noted that though Glemham 'was a gentleman of a noble extraction, and a fair fortune', he had 'much impaired' his inheritance through spending 'many years in armies, beyond the seas', as well as later in the king's army.[85] Nevertheless, meagre though the Dutch wages were, neither side in the Civil War managed to emulate the regularity of their pay system. By honouring their promise to pay their soldiers' wages, the Dutch maintained cohesion and sustained loyalty in their army, despite periodic defeats.[86] The impact of £3,000,000 worth of arrears of pay on the New Model Army in 1647 is well known.[87] It is curious to speculate how many other veterans of the Veres' campaigns, who were forced to contain an increasingly vocal and demanding soldiery throughout the later 1640s and the 1650s may have shared General George Monck's nostalgia for the Netherlands, 'Where soldiers received and obeyed commands, but gave none'.[88]

According to Clarendon, Monck 'was a gentleman of a very good extraction, of a very ancient family in Devonshire' but 'Being a younger brother he entered early into the life and condition of a soldier, upon that stage where all Europe then acted, between the Spaniard and the Dutch'.[89] In fact, Monck's military career had actually begun much earlier, as his chaplain and biographer Thomas Gumble recorded. When Monck was 'very young, not arrived at the seventeenth year of his age' he was entrusted into the care of Richard Grenville (who happened to be Monck's cousin) for 'that Voyage into *Spain*', which has been presumed to be the bungled attempted

80   M. Glozier, 'Scots in the French and Dutch Armies during the Thirty Years' War', in S. Murdoch, ed., *Scotland and the Thirty Years' War, 1618-1648* (Leiden, Brill: 2001), pp. 117-41, at p. 131.
81   *CSPV*, 1615-1617, p. 157.
82   Hexham, *Principles of the Art Militarie*, p. 19.
83   J. R. Hale, *War and Society in Renaissance Europe* (New York, Fontana: 1985), p. 110.
84   P. Skippon, *The Christian Centurians Observations, Advices, and Resolutions: Containing Matters Divine and Morall* (London: 1645), p. 267.
85   Clarendon, *History of the Rebellion*, II, p. 286.
86   Wilson, *Europe's Tragedy*, p. 145.
87   I. Gentles, 'The Arrears of Pay of the Parliamentary Army at the End of the First Civil War', *Bulletin of the Institute of Historical Research*, 48 (1975), pp. 52-63, at p. 62.
88   C. H. Firth, ed., *The Clarke Papers* (4 vols, London, Camden Society: 1891-1901), IV, p. 22.
89   Clarendon, *History of the Rebellion*, VI, p. 152.

on Cadiz in 1625.[90] Mark Stoyle has argued that there is little other evidence for Monck's involvement in that campaign but although Stoyle's research has proven that Gumble has confused his chronology and certainly the part Monck played in it is unclear, Monck would certainly have been just shy of his seventeenth birthday in 1625.[91] Nevertheless, it is possible to relate the circumstances surrounding Monck's subsequent military career with more confidence. Monck's family 'though of great Revenues, by their great Hospitality, and other generous ways of Expence, had much weakened and engaged their estate'.[92] When his father was arrested for debt, Monck, his elder brother and an ally tracked down the under-sheriff responsible for the arrest in an Exeter tavern and 'gave him a due Chastisement (as well he deserved)'.[93] What Gumble's rather sanitised version of events obscures is that fact that the wretched sheriff later died from the repeated cudgelling and stab wounds inflicted by the sword of the younger Monck.[94] With bleak financial prospects and now wanted for murder, Monck ran away to war and joined Charles I's voyage for the relief of La Rochelle in 1627. In this expedition 'he carried Colours under that valiant and old Commander *Sir John Burroughs*', who won fame as the gallant commander of Vere's forces in the garrison of Frankenthal during the Palatinate expedition.[95]

It was only after this, with 'all being peace in *England*, and he having espoused himself to his Sword', that Monck resolved to go to the 'School of War in the United Provinces'. Apparently, Monck 'learned Obedience to his Superiors, and to exact Discipline of those under his Command' in the Netherlands, 'where so many brave Spirits of the *English* Nation have gathered Lawrels; who there learned, and taught the Arts of War, and were alwayes reckoned in the List of our Worthies, as the *Veers, Norrises, Morgans,* and many others'.[96] He was originally assigned to the regiment of the earl of Oxford, which must have been sometime prior to the siege of Maastricht, as the earl perished in that encounter.[97] Monk subsequently transferred to Horace Vere's own regiment, where he was serving when Goring took over the reins and by which time he had gained 'the reputation of a very good foot-officer'.[98] He also distinguished himself at the siege of Breda in 1637, when at the pivotal moment, after the English

90   T. Gumble, *The Life of General Monck, Duke of Albermarle, &c.* (London: 1671), p. 4.
91   M. Stoyle, 'An Early Incident in the Life of General George Monck', *Devon and Cornwall Notes and Queries*, 37:1 (1992), pp. 7-14, at pp. 10-11; R. Hutton, 'Monck , George, first duke of Albemarle (1608–1670)', *Oxford Dictionary of National Biography* (Oxford, Oxford University Press: 2012), online edn, http://www.oxforddnb.com/view/article/18939, accessed 29 January 2016.
92   Gumble, *Life of General Monck*, p. 1.
93   Ibid., p. 3.
94   Stoyle, 'An Early Incident', pp. 9-10.
95   Gumble, *Life of General Monck*, p. 4; Anon., *More Nevves From the Palatinate* (London: 1622), p. 18.
96   Gumble, *Life of General Monck*, p. 5.
97   Ibid., p. 5; Hexham, *Iournall, Of the taking in of Venlo*, p. 35.
98   Clarendon, *History of the Rebellion*, VI, p. 152; Gumble, *Life of General Monck*, p. 7.

regiments had sprung their mine on the enemy's hornwork, 'The first Officer then of the English, which was to fall vp the Breach, and to enter it was Captaine Monke, Coronell Gorings Captaine, with 20 musketteirs, and 10 Pikes'. Monck and his men, 'ere the smoake was vanished', fell 'pell mell' upon the waiting enemy until reinforcements seized upon the advantage Monck had gained and their adversaries were 'slaine, drownd and wholly routed'.[99] He returned to England shortly afterwards, in 1638.[100]

Despite Monck's later gripes, throughout the Civil War parliament did attempt, like the Dutch, to ensure regular pay for their troops to improve discipline, as well as aid recruitment. A series of measures were passed to raise the necessary funds for this: the ordinance for the weekly assessment on 24 February 1643 levied a direct taxation on all the counties of England and Wales; the sequestration ordinance of 27 March confiscated royalists' estates, from which revenues could be raised; and the excise ordinance of 22 July imposed a purchase tax on many everyday commodities.[101] However, these measures were hindered by problems in their implementation. For example, although 87% of the gross amount due on the Monthly Assessment for the New Model Army between February 1645 and October 1646 was actually collected – a 'strikingly high return by the standards of the time' – money was slow to reach the treasurers at war in Guildhall.[102] Taxation is seldom ever popular, not least in the Civil War when the amounts levied were unprecedented and those who lived in contested areas often ended up paying contributions to both sides.[103] Resistance to taxation increased as the war dragged on. Not a penny of the renewed monthly assessment passed in March 1647 was paid by December and the effect this had on the morale of the soldiery has been alluded to above.[104] Throughout the Civil War, mutinies amongst parliamentary armies caused by the dire straits resulting from lack of pay were not uncommon and there is plenty of evidence for plunder and free quarter.[105] That said, the parliamentary ordinances at least represented an attempt to impose a systematic orderliness on their fiscal demands. Royalist armies were forced to resort to informal exactions of the sort levied by Grenville more frequently than their parliamentary counterparts.[106] To those who were financially eligible to contribute, such *ad hoc* collections must have seemed little better than the plunder they were supposed to prevent.[107]

99   Hexham, *Seige of Breda*, p. 3.
100 R. Hutton, 'Monck , George, first duke of Albemarle (1608–1670)', *Oxford Dictionary of National Biography* (Oxford, Oxford University Press: 2012), online edn, http://www.oxforddnb.com/view/article/18939, accessed 29 January 2016.
101 *A&O*, I, pp. 85-100, 106-17 and 202-14.
102 I. Gentles, *The New Model Army in England, Ireland and Scotland, 1645-1653* (Oxford, Blackwell: 1992), p. 29.
103 Braddick, *God's Fury*, pp. 396-7.
104 Gentles, *New Model Army*, p. 30.
105 Braddick, *God's Fury*, p. 397.
106 Ibid., p. 397.
107 Carlton, *Going to the Wars*, p. 282.

In fact, even in the English regiments under the Veres, regular pay was not enough on its own to prevent plunder. As Machiavelli recognised, discipline had to be reinforced by fear of harsh punishment.[108] The Dutch army was subject to a series of *Lawes and Ordinances*, which had been issued by the States-General (the ruling assembly of the Dutch Republic) in 1590. All those in Dutch service, including the English serving under the Veres, would have had to swear to obey these and the officers were expected to enforce them.[109] It is noticeable that whilst many of the directives concerned purely military offences (such as mutiny, corresponding with the enemy, sleeping on watch and refusing orders), these only came after the commands regulating civilian interactions (such as murder, rape, adultery, setting fire to houses, thieving, violence and threatening women), which were themselves only secondary to the decrees concerned with blasphemy and deriding God's word or the ministers of the Church.[110] The punishments for breaking these ordinances were severe. Punishments included boring through the tongue, whipping and, in many instances, death.[111] When it came to enforcing punishment, if, as Machiavelli argued, it was 'better to be feared than loved', then it was here the Vere brothers differed.[112] Although Horace was a strict disciplinarian, he was less stern than his brother and had a reputation for modesty and ruling men by kindness, rather than severity. It was said that soldiers were in awe of Francis but loved Horace.[113]

Misdemeanours undoubtedly occurred in the Netherlands, as after all, the *Lawes and Ordinances* were instituted for a reason. One English soldier, Thomas Raymond, noted that whilst campaigning in the southern Netherlands around Maastricht and Liège, the soldiers upset the locals by stealing and plundering. The soldiers' behaviour no doubt was influenced by the fact that they were campaigning outside of the Dutch Republic, where the local Catholic populace was particularly 'exasperated' by the soldiers breaking down religious images and bringing them back to camp to make sport of them.[114] Although Raymond blamed 'most of the mischeife' on the 'hangers on of the army', such behaviour was detrimental to the Prince of Orange's[115] attempts at that time to win over the southern provinces and encourage them to revolt against

---

108 F. Gilbert, 'Machiavelli: The Renaissance of the Art of War', in P. Paret, ed., *Makers of Modern Strategy from Machiavelli to the Nuclear Age* (Princeton, Princeton University Press: 1986), pp. 11-31, at p. 25.

109 United Provinces of the Netherlands Staten Generaal, *Lawes and Ordinances touching military discipline* (The Hague: 1631), p. [1].

110 Ibid., pp. [1]-[6].

111 Ibid., p. [1].

112 Gilbert, 'Machiavelli', p. 25.

113 Markham, *Fighting Veres*, p. 365.

114 T. Raymond, *Autobiography of Thomas Raymond and Memoirs of the Family of Guise in Elmore, Gloucestershire*, ed. G. Davies (London, Camden Society: 1917), p. 42.

115 Maurice of Nassau had been succeeded by his half-brother, Frederick-Henry, as Prince of Orange and commander-in-chief of the Dutch army on the former's death in 1625.

Spanish rule.[116] Yet, the military hierarchy in the Dutch army seems to have taken moral discipline seriously. The *Lawes and Ordinances* were read out at the head of every regiment at the start of the campaigning season.[117] Punishments were enforced. For example, two soldiers and a drummer were hanged at Maastricht for robbing peasants who brought in provisions for the army.[118] The enforcement of moral discipline must have been at least reasonably successful, as the Venetian Ambassador noted with surprise that Dutch citizens thought nothing of leaving their wives and daughters alone with troops. Some towns even applied to have troops quartered on them because they were so well behaved and there were economic benefits to hosting the soldiers, 'who spend twice so much as the States allow them'.[119]

During the Civil War, both sides issued sets of military directives similar to those used in the Dutch army. In September 1642, parliament issued their own *Lawes and Ordinances* in response to complaints of disorderly conduct in Essex's army.[120] These *Lawes and Ordinances* were revised in 1643 and reissued in 1646 for the New Model Army under Sir Thomas Fairfax.[121] The royalists too had their own *Military Orders and Articles*, which went through various revisions over the course of the war.[122] In fact, 'contrary to expectations', the royalists actually outdid the parliamentarians in the number of ordinances they issued governing morality and religion.[123] Henry Hexham, who remained in Dutch service throughout the Civil War, heard of the 'pillagins, plundrings, and insolences, committed by some of the Melitia on both sides

116 Raymond, *Autobiography*, pp. 40 and 43-4; *CSPV*, 1629-1632, pp. 629 and 636; TNA, State Papers, SP 84/145/4, fols 12-14 (State Papers foreign, Holland 1560-1780: Declarations of the States-General to the Provinces under Spanish rule, 22 May 1632 and 12 September 1632).

117 Israel, *Dutch Republic*, p. 268; Hexham, *Iournall, Of the taking in of Venlo*, p. 1.

118 Ibid., p. 6.

119 G. Oestreich, *Neostoicism and the Early Modern State* (Cambridge, Cambridge University Press: 1982), p. 79; W. Brereton, *Travels in Holland the United Provinces England Scotland and Ireland M.DC.XXXIV-M.DC.XXXV*, ed. E. Hawkis (Manchester, The Chetham Society: 1844), p. 70.

120 *JHL*, V, p. 343; England and Wales Army, *Lawes and Ordinances of Warre Established for the better Conduct of the Army by His Excellency the Earle of Essex* (London: 1642).

121 England and Wales Army, *Lawes and Ordinances of Warre, Established for the better Conduct of the Army, by His Excellency the Earl of Essex* (London: 1643); England and Wales Army, *Lawes and Ordinances of Warre, Established for the better Conduct of the Army, by His Excellency the Earl of Essex* (London: 1646).

122 England and Wales Sovereign (1625-1649: Charles I), *Military Orders and Articles Established by His Majestie, For the better Ordering and Government of His Maiesties Army* (York: 1642); England and Wales Sovereign (1625-1649: Charles I), *Military Orders and Articles Established by His Maiestie for the better ordering and government of His Maiesties Armie* (Oxford: 1643). See also England and Wales Sovereign (1625-1649: Charles I), *Orders and Institvtions Of VVar, Made and ordained by His Maiesty, And by Him delivered to His Generall His Excellence The Earle of Nevvcastle* (London: 1642).

123 B. Donagan, *War in England 1642-1649* (Oxford, Oxford University Press: 2008), pp. 153-4.

in my native Countrie', which he complained 'grieves mee at the very heart, to think upon yt'. He acknowledged that 'his sacred Majesty by his Generalls, as likewise the Parliament by theirs, have made, and proclaimed good, and wholesome Lawes and Articles, for the keeping and observing of Marshall discipline, & the restraint of insolences in their Armies' but he maintained that:

> it will not be amisse, to transport into England, that our Chiefs & Commandeurs there, maye see the Lawes, Articles, Placcards, and Proclamations, touching Marschall discipline, by which our ould, and conquering armie here is governed in the service of the high and mighty Lords the States Generall.

Hexham therefore published a translation of the Dutch *Lawes and Ordinances* in January 1643 as a corollary to his *Principles of the Art Militarie*, in which he had sought to explain the drill movements practised in the Dutch army to an English audience in three instalments printed between 1637 and 1640.[124]

It must be said that the regulations issued by both sides in the Civil War were also influenced by other European military orders, such as *The Svvedish Discipline*, and previous English directives that had been issued for the war against Scotland in 1639-40, whilst they also varied according to the differing ideological and practical preoccupations of each side at the time of publication.[125] Moreover, the implementation of these regulations was entirely down to the initiative of the commanding officer of a regiment and it should not be assumed that previous service in the Netherlands was a guarantor of good behaviour. However, there are numerous cases of Vereronian veterans who, like Grenville, were moral disciplinarians. Even Goring, who Clarendon (with his characteristic cattiness) claimed was so fond of the bottle that he was not able to resist the temptation even when he was in the middle of his enemies and who allowed his horse to commit 'horrid outrages and barbarities', has undergone a character revision.[126] Ronald Hutton pointed out that Clarendon originally wrote this section of his *History* as a defence against criticisms levelled at him by Goring and Greville and thus must be treated with the utmost caution.[127] Whilst not denying that Goring's men were undisciplined, Hutton has shown that they were forced to subsist on free quarter

124 H. Hexham, *An Appendix Of the Lavves, Articles, & Ordinances, established for Marshall Discipline, in the service of the Lords the States Generall of the united Provinces, under the Commaund of his Highnesse the Prince of Orange* (The Hague: 1643), p. [i].
125 W. Watts, *The Svvedish Discipline* (London: 1632); England and Wales Army, *Laws and Ordinances Of Warre, For the better Government of His Maiesties Army Royall, in the present Expedition for the Northern parts, and safety of the Kingdome* (London: 1639); England and Wales Army, Lawes and Ordinances of Warre, Established for the better conduct of the Service in the Northern parts (London: 1640); Donagan, *War in England*, pp. 147-56.
126 Clarendon, *History of the Rebellion*, III, p. 444, and IV, p. 10.
127 R. Hutton, 'Clarendon's History of the Rebellion', *The English Historical Review*, 97: 382 (1982), pp. 70-88, at p. 79.

due to a lack of pay. Goring attempted to minimalise the impact of this by meeting the local gentry and agreeing a fixed sum per man for his soldiers' support, which would be deducted from the rate levied to pay local troops. He asked for daily accounts and promised that infringements of the arrangement by his soldiers would be punished with death.[128] As Hutton concludes, 'How well this scheme worked is unknown, but it certainly represented the most enlightened possible approach to the problem'.[129]

On the parliamentarian side, Skippon published three books, based upon material that he had penned whilst serving under Horace Vere in the Netherlands, for the religious and moral edification of his soldiers.[130] In the second of these, *True Treasure*, Skippon exhorted his men to 'oppose and punish wicked men and wickednesse by all meanes he can'.[131] Fairfax had plunders, mutineers had deserters shot, he punished swearing, drunkenness and whoring and he enforced the punishment of boring through the tongue for blasphemy.[132] Fairfax was, in many ways, the spiritual heir of the Veres, not least through his marriage to Horace's daughter Anne.[133] The connection between the Veres and the Fairfaxes stretched back over three generations. The parliamentary general's grandfather, Thomas, first Lord Fairfax, had fought alongside Francis in the 1580s. His great uncle (the first Lord's brother), Sir Charles Fairfax, had rallied the English troops at Nieuwpoort, acted as a hostage at the siege of Ostend in 1602 and commanded his regiment in the diversionary capture of nearby Sluys in 1604, before being killed in action in the final days of the siege in 1604. Sir Charles was not the only Fairfax fatality in the Protestant cause on the Continent. Sir Thomas's uncles, William and John, had died at the siege of Frankenthal under Horace's command in 1621. Sir Thomas himself had fought as a seventeen-year-old in the trenches at 's-Hertogenbosch in Horace's 'first company Coronell of Dort' and went on to marry his old commander's daughter at Hackney church on 20 June 1637.[134]

---

128 Ibid., pp. 81-2
129 Ibid., p. 82.
130 P. Skippon, *A Salve For Every Sore, or, A Collection of Promises out of the whole Book of God, and is The Christian Centurion's Infallible ground of Confidence* (London: 1643), p. [xviii]; P. Skippon, *True Treasure, or Thirtie holy Vowes, Containing The brief sum of all that concerns the Christian Centurion's conscionable walking with God* (London: 1644), pp. [i]-[ii]; P. Skippon, *The Christian Centurians Observations, Advices, and Resolutions: Containing Matters Divine and Morall* (London: 1645), p. 233.
131 Skippon, *True Treasure*, p. 45.
132 Gentles, *New Model Army*, pp. 106-7.
133 Markham, *Fighting Veres*, p. 460; Eales, 'Anne and Thomas Fairfax', p. 152.
134 Ibid., pp. 147-8; Markham, *Fighting Veres*, p. 452; D. J. B. Trim, 'Fairfax, Sir Charles (d. 1604)', *Oxford Dictionary of National Biography* (Oxford, Oxford University Press: 2008), online edn, http://www.oxforddnb.com/view/article/9077, accessed 23 December 2015; TNA, SP 81/17/105, fol. 105 (State Papers Foreign, German States, 1577-1784: Officer list for Sir Horace Vere's expedition to the Palatinate, 1 July 1620); Hexham, *Historicall Relation Of the Famous Siege of the Busse*, p. [42].

The influence of the Veres' legacy over the Civil War extended beyond the internal relations by which armies were administered to external relations between adversaries. The assumption in early modern Europe that one could only win honour in battle when engaged against a worthy enemy had led to the belief that there was a European brotherhood of arms, sharing the same values.[135] Barbara Donagan demonstrated how traditional chivalric concepts merged into a code of military professionalism, in which the importance of a soldier's reputation in honouring his word was crucial to relations between opponents at a time when infrastructure and sanctions were inadequate to enforce treaties, surrenders, safe conducts and paroles.[136] This led to the establishment of pre-agreed conventions, which it was assumed would be honoured, such as the articles between Spain and the Netherlands that agreed fixed rates of ransom for officers and soldiers.[137] Much of this code was based on a sense of reciprocity – a need to do as one would be done by – rather than high theory. Honorific rituals were not based on a desire to cling to an obsolete, aristocratic doctrine but a crucial aspect in the development of military professionalism.[138] Furthermore, civilians could not help but get caught up in military actions and so their needs had to be considered too. Therefore, soldiers' honour combined civilian codes within their military codes and their sense of honour developed from common moral and cultural traditions, as well as from common professional standards.[139]

As Donagan argued, the siege warfare that Horace Vere's men experienced during the Dutch offensive from 1629 onwards provides the perfect opportunity to view the code of honour in action.[140] During the negotiations for the surrender of both 's-Hertogenbosch and Maastricht, hostages were exchanged as a guarantee of each side would honour the ceasefire and the final articles of surrender reflected a respect for the valour with which the towns had defended themselves. The garrison was given the honour of marching out with the horse parading with trumpets sounding, cornets displayed and armed with pistols in hands; whilst the foot paraded with drums beating, colours flying, matches lighted and bullets in their mouths. All the sick and wounded were permitted to remain until they had recovered.[141] Separate articles were made with the clergy and magistracy to reflect the

---

135 Manning, *Swordsmen*, p. 36.
136 Donagan, *War in England*, p. 167.
137 H. Hexham, *An appendix of the lavves, articles, & ordinances, established for marshall discipline, in the service of the Lords the States Generall of the united provinces, under the commaund of his highnesse the Prince of Orange* (The Hague: 1643), p. 13.
138 Donagan, *War in England*, p. 129.
139 B. Donagan, 'The Web of Honour: Soldiers, Christians and Gentlemen in the English Civil War', *The Historical Journal*, 44:2 (2001), pp. 365-89, at pp. 367 and 389.
140 D. Maland, *Europe at War 1600-1650* (London, Macmillan: 1980), p. 137; Donagan, *War in England*, pp. 11 and 293.
141 Hexham, *Historicall Relation Of the Famous Siege of the Busse*, pp. 31-[32]; Hexham, *Iournall, Of the taking in of Venlo*, pp. 41-2.

civil needs of the towns.[142] At 's-Hertogenbosch, the Prince of Orange insisted on saluting the governor's wife, a compliment returned by the governor himself when he saluted Elizabeth of Bohemia (who was present with her husband Frederick at the siege) as he marched out of the town.[143] During the siege of Maastricht, a parley was organised so that the defenders could come and collect the body of one of their ensigns, who had been slain during a sally out of the city and when the garrison sent trumpeters to demand the exchange of prisoners, they commended the Prince of Orange's 'clemencie, and mercye, that they were not all put to the sword'.[144]

Certainly in the early stages of the Civil War, the manner in which many of the campaigns were conducted was clearly influenced by these experiences. In fact, the role of honour was particularly important to participants in a civil war, who, by nature, inhabited the same geographical space, spoke the same language and shared the same psychological space.[145] Fellow Englishmen could not be viewed as barbarous 'others', outside the protections of humanity, so a prevalent view in the Civil War was 'that enemies might be mistaken honourable men rather than dishonourable traitors'.[146] A good example of this is provided by the siege of Reading in 1643. The earl of Essex followed the honourable protocol of summoning the governor, Sir Arthur Aston, (who had himself seen foreign military service in the armies of Russia, Poland and Sweden) to yield Reading upon quarter. When Aston refused, Essex unsuccessfully attempted to persuade him to send the women and children out of the town, which, by the rules of warfare, would now be subject to a storm.[147] However, Essex's council of war favoured starving the town into submission instead.[148] Ultimately, Reading was forced into surrender by bad morale in the royalist garrison, caused by a near-fatal head wound to Aston from falling masonry (though he lived to tell the tale, only to be battered to death with his own wooden leg whilst defending Drogheda in 1649).[149] Aston's replacement, Richard Feilding, requested a parley and honourably refused to

142 Hexham, *Historicall Relation Of the Famous Siege of the Busse*, pp. [36]-[41]; Hexham, *Iournall, Of the taking in of Venlo*, pp. 43-6.
143 Hexham, *Historicall Relation Of the Famous Siege of the Busse*, p. [42].
144 Hexham, *Iournall, Of the taking in of Venlo*, pp. 9 and 13.
145 Donagan, *War in England*, p. 65.
146 Donagan, 'Web of Honour', pp. 388-9.
147 Clarendon, *History of the Rebellion*, III, p. 13; *A Continvation Of certain Speciall and Remarkable passages*, No. 41 (13-20 April 1643), p. 3; Codrington, *Earl of Essex*, p. 25; Snow, *Essex the Rebel*, p. 359; B. Morgan, 'Aston, Sir Arthur (1590x93–1649)', *Oxford Dictionary of National Biography* (Oxford, Oxford University Press: 2004), online edn, http://www.oxforddnb.com/view/article/823, accessed 20 August 2015.
148 *CSPV*, 1642-1643, p. 268; M. Wanklyn, *The Warrior Generals: Winning the British Civil Wars 1642-1652* (New Haven, Yale University Press: 2010), p. 50.
149 I. Gentles, *The English Revolution and the Wars in the Three Kingdoms, 1638-1652* (Harlow, Routledge: 2007), p. 170; Codrington, *Earl of Essex*, p. 26; Clarendon, *History of the Rebellion*, III, p. 17; *A Continvation Of certain Speciall and Remarkable passages*, No. 42 (20-27 April 1643), p. [5]; *The Kingdomes VVeekly Intelligencer: sent abroad To prevent mis-information*, No. 17 (25 April-2 May 1643), p. 130; B. Morgan, 'Aston, Sir Arthur (1590x93–1649)', *Oxford*

break off negotiations, even though he had received word via Sir Lewis Dyve's servant (who had swum across the Thames to the garrison) that Rupert was on his way with a relief force.[150] In a public vindication of their honour, the royalist garrison were given the privilege of marching out of Reading with their arms, ammunition and baggage and with their colours flying and free to join the rest of the royalist army at Oxford or Wallingford. Carriages were provided for the sick and injured, whilst civilians who had accidentally got trapped in the town were given liberty to leave without hindrance and the inhabitants to be free from plundering or imprisonment.[151]

That said, not all the proceedings were the epitome of gentlemanly conduct and many of the rules were broken. Despite the fact that Essex had paid his men twelve shillings each in lieu of plunder and that he had provided a guard for the exiting garrison, there was little he could do to stop his men plundering the royalist wagons as they rolled out of Reading. At this breach of faith, the royalists, quite understandably, took great offence.[152] It also meant that when the boot was on the other foot a year later at Fowey, the victorious royalists did not hesitate to fall upon the vanquished parliamentarians.[153] Furthermore, whilst the London public considered the terms of surrender at Reading extraordinarily generous, Charles ordered Feilding to be court-martialled.[154] The king was particularly incensed that soldiers in the Reading garrison who had defected from parliament were exempted from the articles of surrender and executed.[155] It was perfectly acceptable under martial law to execute defectors.[156] However, Charles had declared Essex and his commanders rebels and told the parliamentarian soldiers that they were being beguiled into treason. In these circumstances the king was of the opinion that the recognised codes of conduct that existed between

Dictionary of National Biography (Oxford, Oxford University Press: 2004), online edn, http://www.oxforddnb.com/view/article/823, accessed 20 August 2015.

150 *A Continuation Of certain Speciall and Remarkable passages*, No. 42 (20-27 April 1643), p. [5]; *The Kingdomes VVeekly Intelligencer: sent abroad To prevent mis-information*, No. 17 (25 April-2 May 1643), pp. 129-30 and 134; P. Young and W. Emberton, *Sieges of the Great Civil War 1642-1646* (London, Bell and Hyman: 1978), pp. 22-3.

151 Clarendon, *History of the Rebellion*, III, p. 24.

152 B. Donagan, 'Codes and Conduct in the English Civil War', *Past and Present*, 118 (1994), pp. 65-95, at p. 91; Donagan, *War in England*, p. 239; Clarendon, *History of the Rebellion*, III, pp. 24-5 *The Kingdomes VVeekly Intelligencer: sent abroad To prevent mis-information*, No. 17 (25 April-2 May 1643), p. 132.

153 *The Kingdomes VVeekly Intelligencer: sent abroad To prevent mis-information*, No. 72 (10-17 September 1644), p. 576; R. Symonds, *Richard Symonds's Diary of the Marches of the Royal Army*, ed. C. E. Long and I. Roy (Cambridge, Cambridge University Press: 1997), p. 66.

154 Wanklyn, *Warrior Generals*, p. 52; *The Kingdomes VVeekly Intelligencer: sent abroad To prevent mis-information*, No. 17 (25 April-2 May 1643), p. 134; Clarendon, *History of the Rebellion*, III, p. 27.

155 Clarendon, *History of the Rebellion*, III, p. 27; *The Kingdomes VVeekly Intelligencer: sent abroad To prevent mis-information*, No. 17 (25 April-2 May 1643), p. 138.

156 Donagan, *War in England*, p. 243.

two equal sides did not apply. Nevertheless, according to the Venetian Ambassador, even Charles's supporters did not agree with this.[157]

So what conclusions is it possible to draw about the legacy of the Fighting Veres in the English Civil War? Firstly and most obviously, it is clear that veterans from the Veres' campaigns provided both many of the men and much of the mentality for the Civil War. By the start of the war, both sides were well aware of the array of military talent available to them and eagerly sought their services, several of whom had fought directly alongside each other on the Continent. Personal relationships were no doubt vital to the recruitment process. However, it is also important to note that the Veres' veterans were not always well received. Officers who had returned from overseas service were often satirised in the popular press.[158] The earl of Warwick faced a protest from the Essex Trained Bands when he attempted to parachute in veterans from the Dutch wars, in place of the local officers who the men knew and trusted.[159] This suspicion did not solely rest on the traditional English admiration for themselves and their institutions measured by a contempt and dislike for foreigners.[160] The presence of several officers who had formerly fought on the Continent amongst the high profile side-changers of 1643 did nothing to enhance the reputation of the experienced men.

Besides, previous experience did not necessarily translate into tactical ingenuity when applied to the peculiarities of fighting in England. As John Twentyman, the Newark memoirist reminisced, those who had served in foreign wars 'were so renowned that they were thought able to do wonders among us in the beginning of our unhappy Discords'.[161] Yet, the campaigns in the Netherlands had been long and drawn-out affairs, which lacked the decisive battles of, for example, the Swedish campaigns of the Thirty Years' War. The veterans of the Dutch wars who fought under the Veres therefore have been compared unfavourably to their colleagues who had seen service in Sweden and accused of too much caution and a corresponding lack of imagination.[162]

---

157 *CSPV*, 1642-1643, p. 268; Donagan, *War in England*, p. 130.
158 Hopper, *Turncoats and Renegadoes*, p. 62.
159 Captain Farres, *A Speech Spoken vnto his Excellence the Earle of Warwicke, By Captaine Farres, in the behalfe of the whole County of Essex* (London: 1642), pp. 3-6.
160 G. Parrinder, *The Routledge Dictionary of Religious and Spiritual Quotations* (London, Routledge: 2000), p. 287.
161 Hopper, *Turncoats and Renegadoes*, p. 65.
162 W. B. Devereux, *Lives and Letters of the Devereux, Earls of Essex, in the Reigns of Elizabeth, James I., and Charles I. 1540-1646* (London, J. Murray: 1853), II, p. 458; Woolrych, *Battles*, pp. 13-14; A. H. Burne, and P. Young, *The Great Civil War: A Military History of the First Civil War, 1642-1646* (London, Eyre: 1959), p. 227; Wanklyn, *Warrior Generals*, p. 41; K. Roberts, *Cromwell's War Machine: The New Model Army 1645-1660* (Barnsley, Pen & Sword: 2005), p. 27.

Likewise, previous service under the Veres did not automatically make men military moralists who enforced good behaviour amongst those under their command. Outrages were committed by both sides during the Civil War and not even the most assiduous officer could attempt to prevent this through emulating the Dutch system of regular pay if he was not provided with the money to do so by the administrators of his side's war machine. Whilst the Civil War may not have seen the same wilful destruction as, for example, that in Germany during the Thirty Years' War, this was little comfort to those who fell victim to marauding soldiers.[163] Moreover, the code of honour did not always work as well in practice as it did in theory. The established conventions were placed under severe strain as time wore on, especially in the midst of the sense of betrayal surrounding the re-opening of hostilities in 1648.[164]

Nevertheless, what the Veres had created was a school of war, which gave their pupils the confidence and a degree of competence to meet the challenges presented by the English Civil War. Like all pupils, the quality naturally varied: some had learnt their lessons and some had not. Indeed, some lessons were useful and some were not. Yet, between them all, perhaps what these men have once again reminded us is that the art of war in England in 1642 was not the dead dodo it was once thought to be.[165]

163 J. S. Morrill, *Revolt in the Provinces: The People of England and the Tragedies of War 1630-1648* (London, Longman: 1999), p. 193.
164 Donagan, *War in England*, pp. 293-4.
165 The argument that 'the profession of arms was alive and well in pre-war England' had been championed by Donagan in *War in England*, pp. 33-64. See also B. Donagan, 'Halcyon Days and the Literature of War: England's Military Education Before 1642', *Past and Present*, 147 (1995) pp. 65-100; M. C. Fissel, ed., *War and government in Britain, 1598-1650* (Manchester, MUP: 1991); M.C. Fissel, *English Warfare, 1511-1642* (London, Routledge: 2001); P. E. J. Hammer, *Elizabeth's Wars: War, Government and Society in Tudor England, 1544-1604* (Basingstoke, Palgrave Macmillan: 2003); P. E. J. Hammer, *Warfare in Early Modern Europe 1450-1660* (Aldershot, Ashgate: 2007); R. B. Manning, *Swordsmen: The Martial Ethos in the Three Kingdoms* (Oxford, Oxford University Press: 2003); Manning, R. B. *An Apprenticeship in Arms: The Origins of the British Army, 1585-1702* (Oxford, Oxford University Press: 2006).

4

William Rowley and Richard Baxter: An introduction to puritanism in seventeenth-century Shrewsbury and Shropshire

Prof. Tim Jenkins

Introduction

Protestantism became firmly established in Shrewsbury, the county town of Shropshire, during the sixteenth century. This subsequently provided an environment that allowed for the development of 'puritan' beliefs during the early Stuart period. Shropshire was also the birthplace of the immortal Richard Baxter and it was whilst visiting members of the godly community in Shrewsbury, such as William Rowley, that Baxter began to develop his religious convictions.

Consequently, Shropshire was more than a little responsible for the development of so-called puritan ideas during the period of the Civil War, which is somewhat ironic when one considers that the majority of the county remained largely loyal to Charles I. This chapter attempts to explore the role of the godly community within the context of a county town to more fully understand their influence in terms of societal and religious innovation.

Rowley's Mansion: Social & Economic Background of Shrewsbury

Shrewsbury suffered from significant economic stagnation in the early sixteenth century, primarily due to the decline of toll receipts relating to market activities during the middle and late fifteen hundreds. The economic decline, coupled with the impact of epidemics, inevitably led to a sharp fall in population. Nevertheless, population growth rapidly increased due to the economic impact of the trade in Welsh cloth and by the 1580s, Shrewsbury was at the pinnacle of a period of prosperity. By the mid-1630s, the population of the town had doubled to more than 6,000 from a figure of less than 3,000 in the 1560s.[1]

Consequently, the Shrewsbury Drapers' Company became both highly influential in the running of the town and the distribution of its associated wealth. Shrewsbury became the hub of a large organised business network whereby merchants brought cloth from the farmer-weavers for shearing and finishing before being transported for sale in London and beyond. However, by the mid-seventeenth century, the utilisation of the river for such trade had begun to decline. Malcolm Wanklyn observed that:

> Those towns on the banks of the river which still retained their traditional woollen cloth industries, such as Shrewsbury, Worcester, and Bridgnorth, rarely despatched their products by water after 1660. This was probably because their principal trading link was with London, in a different direction from that taken by the Severn navigation, rather than because overland carriage was seen as more suitable for the movement of textiles.[2]

However, the presence of the Council of the Welsh Marches in the town also enhanced the economy through the provision of services through other substantial trades.[3]

It was during the late sixteenth century that substantial infrastructure investment was committed by the corporation, particularly in the construction of the town grammar school. Between 1549 and 1592 the corporation acquired the leasehold of a substantial property in Rotten Lane, later Spring Gardens, and finally secured the freehold in 1576.[4] After numerous improvements to the site and curtilages, the current frontage was rebuilt between 1627 and 1630 in Grinshill stone. Nigel Baker reminds us of the significance of the educational establishment, stating:

> Within 80 years, the decayed mercantile tenement had been transformed into a towering mass of state-of-the-art Renaissance architecture, adverting the wealth, and the learning of the town to all approaching up Castle gates.[5]

The architectural style adopted for the redevelopment would thus support the interpretation that Stuart so-called 'court' culture, influenced by foreign fashions, was not exclusive to the royal court but had, in fact, infiltrated throughout the country.

---

1   N. Baker, *Shrewsbury: An Archaeological Assessment of an English Border Town* (Oxford, Oxbow: 2010), pp. 181-2.
2   M. Wanklyn, 'The Impact of Water Transport Facilities on the Economies of English River Ports, c.1660–c.1760', *Economic History Review*, 49:1 (1996), pp. 20-34, at p. 26.
3   M. Wanklyn, 'The Severn Navigation in the Seventeenth Century: Long-Distance Trade of Shrewsbury Boats', *Midland History*, 13 (1988), pp. 34-58, at pp.38-9.
4   Baker, *Shrewsbury*, p. 182.
5   Ibid., p. 182.

Figure 4.1 View of Rowley's House and Mansion. (Author's photograph)

The grammar school notwithstanding, Shrewsbury still possesses a wealth of surviving buildings from the late sixteenth and early seventeenth centuries which portray the affluence then prevalent. In a similar arrangement to the combined dwelling and shop arrangements that dominated the town centre during the period, certain areas of the suburbs were developed as purpose-built industrial areas combining commercial function with often opulent onsite accommodation. Of those surviving examples, Rowley's Mansion and House (Mansion constructed in brick and the House timber framed) remains the finest example of the combined dwelling and business function of the emerging middle classes. However, as Nikolaus Pevsner conceded, the current building is no longer in context and, alas, 'Shrewsbury has treated it cruelly.'[6]

Although no formal contract or primary source has yet come to light stating when and by whom the present structures, both Mansion and House, were constructed, it is likely that they were built by the Rowley family. The Rowleys are recorded as having significant properties in the vicinity of Barker Street and Knockin Street (Hill's Lane) by the late sixteenth century.[7] Hugh Owen made the following observations in 1808 in relation to the provenance of the buildings:

---

6   N. Pevsner, *The Buildings of England: Shropshire* (Harmondsworth, Penguin: 1974), p. 277.
7   R. Morris and P. Stamper, 'A Structural Survey & Documentary History of Rowley's House & Mansion, Shrewsbury', *Shropshire County Council Archaeology Service*, Report 69 (May 1995), p. 2.

> From the dates still remaining on the leaden pipes, it appears that this mansion was erected in the year 1618, and it is said to have been built by William Rowley, an eminent brewer of this town, a branch of trade which has long since ceased to exist in it, though known in other places to lead to great wealth, and though it formerly prevailed amongst us to a considerable extent; as indeed the building contiguous to the edifice now before us may alone serve to show.[8]

There is no shortage of irony that William Rowley accumulated so much of his wealth from brewing. One might be forgiven for contemplating that his puritan principles, particularly in opposition to popular pastimes, sporting and general revelry on Sundays, which no doubt included the consumption of a drop of ale, were ill matched to his means of income generation.[9]

Shrewsbury Puritanism and William Rowley:

The Rowley family originated from Worfield Parish, outside Bridgnorth, in southeast Shropshire and were first mentioned in the Shrewsbury Guild Merchant Roll of 1252. The family association with Shrewsbury was further cemented with the arrival of William, who was admitted a burgess of the town in 1594. Upon first moving to the town, William Rowley (1572-1645) lived in Shoplatch but in 1605 moved to Knockin Street, the current location of the House and Mansion attributed to him.[10]

    Although evidence remains incomplete, it would appear that Rowley was in business partnership with one Richard Cherwell. Upon Cherwell's death in 1605, Rowley acquired the majority of the estate and commodities. Although the business was predominantly centred on brewing, the partners also had interests in the Welsh cloth trade. Rowley became a member of the Drapers Company and had a factor in London where John, his brother, also traded as a merchant.[11] Hugh Owen also suggested that Rowley had wider commercial interests far beyond the town, and indeed the British Isles:

> This gentleman also appears to have embarked in the settlement of Barbados, a favourite speculation with the commercial men of the time, and is related [sic] to have planted Rowley's Islands in the Caribbean.[12]

---

8   H. Owen, *Some Account of the Ancient and Present State of Shrewsbury* (Shrewsbury, Sandford: 1808, Reprinted Didsbury, Morten: 1972), pp. 237-8.
9   B. Coward, *The Stuart Age: England 1603-1714* (London, Longman: 1994), pp.87-8.
10   Morris and Stamper, 'Structural Survey & Documentary History of Rowley's House', pp. 2-3.
11   Ibid., pp. 2-3.
12   Owen, *Some Account*, p. 538.

There can be no doubt that William Rowley was indeed a skilled entrepreneur and innovator as defined by the emerging middle classes of the early Stuart age. Christopher Hill's interpretation of puritanism still adequately describes the merchants and entrepreneurs of the time:

> Some have seen a 'holy pretence', a Machiavellian double-talk, in much of the Puritans' use of the Bible. I think this is to attribute too conscious motives to troubled men trying to find guides to living in a world rapidly changing but hag-ridden by authority; where innovation, novelty, were dirty words. Traditional authorities had to be found for the untraditional actions forced on men. The Machiavellianism, if any, was unconscious; at worst a utilitarianism, an adaptation of norms to the demands of the environment.[13]

Rowley's reputation in the town continued to grow and he served as a bailiff in 1628 and was amongst the first aldermen appointed to the newly established Charter of Incorporation granted to the town in 1638.[14] However, despite financial success, his religious persuasions ultimately threatened his entire commercial empire.

By the early 1620s, there was a sizeable godly community established in Shrewsbury, which remained active up until the outbreak of the Civil War. Rowley was prominent among their number. One area in which this community proved particularly successful was the infiltration of godly preachers into numerous curacies around the town. This was evident in the installation of Richard Lee at St Julian's in 1641 and Julines Herring at St Alkmund's the following year.[15] Isabel Calder observed of Herring that:

> At St. Alkmond's he preached on Tuesday morning and on the Sabbath at one o'clock in order not to interfere with the regular services, repeating his sermon before supper in the evening at the house of a friend. He was loyal to the king but scrupulous in matters of ceremony and, after the time of the feoffees, was finally suspended.[16]

Herring was appointed by the Corporation in 1618 until he was eventually forced out by Archbishop William Laud and his supporters on 14 April 1635.[17] Notwithstanding

---

13   C. Hill, "Reason' and 'Reasonableness' in Seventeenth-Century England', *The British Journal of Sociology*, 20:3 (1969), pp. 235-252, at p. 243.
14   Owen, *Some Account*, pp. 538-539.
15   W. Champion and A. Thacker, eds, *A History of Shropshire Vol. VI, Part I: Shrewsbury General History & Topography* (London, Boydell & Brewer: 2014), pp. 180-1.
16   I. Calder, 'A Seventeenth Century Attempt to Purify the Anglican Church', *The American Historical Review*, 53:4 (1948), pp. 760-75, at pp. 769-70.
17   T. Bracher and R. Emmett, *Shropshire in the Civil War*, (Shrewsbury, Shropshire Books: 2000), p.8.

religious differences, many local clergy, such as Peter Studley the vicar of St. Chad's, resented the increasing use of lecturers. Whilst they disliked this trend in terms of salary, they especially opposed the religious doctrine of the lecturers and exploited any opportunity to denounce so-called puritanism and champion the High Church Laudian reforms.[18]

One such opportunity arose in 1633, when after a day working in the fields Enoch ap Evan came home to his house in Clun and murdered both his brother and mother with an axe. Evan claimed that the murders were the result of an argument over the necessity of kneeling to receive the communion. Studley, after visiting Evan in prison, became convinced that puritan dogma had unhinged his mind and caused him to commit the killings.

The incident persuaded Studley of a puritan plot to undermine the social order and compelled him to write a pamphlet in 1634 entitled *Through the Looking Glass of Schism: Wherein a Brief and True Narration of the Execrable Murders done by Enoch ap Evan, a Down-Right Separatist, on the Bodies of his Mother and Brother, with the Cause Moving him Thereunto.* The work importantly highlighted the growth of non-conformity in Shrewsbury in the early seventeenth century:

> Unto this town of ours, diverse Gentleman from many parts of the kingdom, have within these last twelve years resorted: Residing here to plant themselves for fixed habitation, and expecting to enjoy with impunity the vain toys and schismatical [sic] conceits they brought hither with them. But my truth is, under God, and the sacred and royal majesty of our king, that the reverend bishop will either in short time reform their irregularities, or cause them to return to the places of their former abode.[19]

Studley clearly believed that puritanism had become a serious threat to both society and the civic institution of the Church in Shrewsbury. However, of further interest is that he actually listed those he suspected of causing such schism by their occupation:

> Here also have flocked mechanical fellows of many artifices and professionals, masons, carpenters, brick-layers, corsers, weavers, stone-gravers, and what not. And being in their persons of worthless quality, and receiving countenance of men of better rank, they have presented our town with disobedience and schism.

Studley's pamphlet is almost three hundred pages long and although one must be careful in regard to his motives, there can be little doubt that genuine concern is

18   Ibid., p. 8.
19   P. Studley, *Through the Looking Glass of Schism: Wherein a Brief and True Narration of the Execrable Murders done by Enoch ap Eva, a Down-Right Separatist, on the bodies of his Mother and Brother, with the Cause Moving him Thereunto* (London: 1634), pp. 178-9.

expressed amongst the polemic. His reference to dissenters receiving tolerance from men of rank undoubtedly displays a dismay at the lack of stronger controls, particularly as the town Corporation, which included Rowley, were responsible for facilitating more liberal expressions of opinion.

However, although Hill argued that puritanism and trades were intrinsically linked, it is difficult to prove any direct correlation.[20] In reality, what is without doubt is that the increase in Shrewsbury's population during in the early part of the sixteenth century meant that the town required additional construction work. This was likely to have been far more influential upon the influx of tradesman to Shrewsbury than the presence of 'puritanism'. Studley, it would appear, was not just protesting against non-conformist activities but also the population explosion in an early Stuart period in an outburst of snobbish nimbyism.

The response from the godly community to the murders committed by Enoch ap Evan was to simply declare that he was suffering from insanity.[21] However, prominent puritans of the town regularly crop up in diocesan visitation records, in which William Rowley became a regular feature in the 1620s and 1630s. In 1620 he was presented for not receiving communion, 1626 for not attending his parish church and in 1633 for not bowing at the name of Jesus.[22]

It is also worth noting that Studley and Rowley were by no means strangers. As curate of St Chad's, Studley named both William Rowley and fellow draper George Wright as people who admitted puritans to their houses and allowed them to sing both psalms and prayers most Sunday evenings of the year.[23] However, despite Studley's protestations, it would appear that Shrewsbury enjoyed a particular religious tolerance prior to the 1630s whereby Herring, and other public preachers before him, let the Drapers' Hall as his residence whilst in employment of the Corporation. Indeed, even the diocesan authorities were inclined to allow some lenience towards puritanism and allowed Herring to preach at St. Alkmund's every Tuesday morning and even on the Sabbath as long as such sermons did not clash with any others taking place in the town.[24]

Nevertheless, despite evidence of tolerance, the religious factions became more polarised during the 1630s. By 1642 and the onset of the Civil War, Rowley began to lose all social influence and was named on a list of 13 members of the town council declared delinquents and barred from meetings until they cleared themselves.[25]

20   C. Hill, 'Puritans and the Poor', *Past & Present*, 2 (1952), pp. 32-50, at p. 38.
21   P. Lake, 'Puritanism, Arminianism and a Shropshire Axe-Murder', *Midland History*, 15 (1990), pp. 38-64, at pp. 38-40.
22   Bracher and Emmett, *Shropshire in the Civil War*, pp. 7-8.
23   B. Coulton, 'Rivalry & Religion: The Borough of Shrewsbury', *Midland History*, 28 (2003), pp. 28-50, at pp. 38-9.
24   Ibid., pp. 38-9.
25   Bracher and Emmett, *Shropshire in the Civil War*, p. 21.

Rowley died in 1645 before having the opportunity to clear his name and, not without some irony, was buried at St. Chad's church.

Richard Baxter (1615–1691)

The relationship between Rowley and Baxter deserves exploration, not only because of their Salopian heritage, but also because they were instrumental in cultivating each other's religious beliefs. Baxter was born in Rowton, Shropshire, christened at High Ercall, and spent his early life in Eaton Constantine. His father was a reformed gambler who later embraced puritanism which doubtless contributed significantly to his future religious convictions.

During his early education Baxter despaired of the earthliness of the local clergy and eventually attended the endowed school at Wroxeter, before moving to the Royal Courts of Ludlow and then London. However, he soon realised that he was not best suited to the life of court culture and moved back to Eaton Constantine, where he began teaching at Wroxeter. Following the death of his mother, he began to seriously contemplate a career in the church under the direction of Reverend Francis Garbet.

Once into his early twenties, Baxter became friendly with notable nonconformists, such as Walter Craddock and William Rowley, who held regular meetings in Shrewsbury. Although he did not entirely agree with their doctrines, it was the persecution of such friends by the ecclesiastical establishment that encouraged him to oppose Laudian reforms. Frederick Powicke argued that:

> Practically he had always been a conformist. He had never known any, even among so-called puritans, who were not until about 20 years of age he became acquainted with some very zealous godly nonconformists in Shrewsbury who, for certain departures from the prescribed order of worship, were prosecuted by the bishops. It was the fact of such men being so treated for a fault of no great consequence that created much prejudice in him against their troubles.[26]

It is probably during this period that Baxter became acquainted with Rowley and referred to him as a 'very dear friend.' In 1641, for example, Rowley lent Baxter some books on the government of the church and on the controversy about the proper position of the altar, which helped to convince Baxter of the corrupt nature of the diocesan system.[27]

---

26   F. J. Powicke, *A Life of the Reverend Richard Baxter: 1662-1691* (Weston Rhyn, Qunita Press: 2009), p. 21.

27   R. Baxter, 'The Life of Richard Baxter: Written By Himself for the Sake of His Children', *Transactions of the Shropshire Archaeological and Natural History Society*, Fourth Series, 9:1 (1924), pp. 127-40, at p. 133.

Baxter was ordained in 1638 and took up the position of headmaster at the endowed school in Dudley, where he once again was drawn to the friendship of nonconformists, although his own religious persuasions remained unclear. Whilst he was not opposed to either bishops or the liturgy, he disliked wearing the surplice and dissented against the use of the cross in baptism. His beliefs gradually developed and whilst holding a position at Bridgnorth in 1640, he formally rejected the Laudian oath which he believed 'sort to bind clergy to episcopacy and Arminian theology'.[28] The following year, a committee of the parish of Kidderminster asked Baxter to take up the position of lecturer, an appointment that he energetically undertook and transformed the parish into a godly community within two years. When war was finally declared, his disenchantment with the Caroline Church of England ensured that his support was firmly declared for parliament.

Baxter fled Kidderminster and joined various parliamentary garrisons, before returning briefly to Shropshire in 1643 following an invitation of Humphrey Mackworth and Thomas Hunt to join them at Wem. Although he stayed for little more than two weeks, he successfully managed to secure the release of his father from the royalist garrison at Lilleshall.[29] Powicke mainatined that there were few events in which Baxter rejoiced during the Civil War but the royalist capture of Shrewsbury was indeed a highlight:

> He rejoiced not only because it was a victory for the parliament but also because it was gained without loss of blood and ensured the safety of his father as well as that of many old and dear friends.[30]

Shrewsbury during the Civil War

In many ways, Shrewsbury was somewhat of an oasis, particularly in regard to its obvious puritan sympathies, to the often quoted broad definition that support for the king was predominately situated in the west, whilst parliamentary support was largely to be found in the east. Thomas Auden observed that:

> Shropshire as a whole sympathised with the royal cause, and Shrewsbury shared this sympathy. A few years before – in 1638 – Charles had expressed his sense of the loyalty of the town by granting them a new charter, and when war broke out, it is clear that the king calculated on the town taking his side.[31]

28   Bracher and Emmett, *Shropshire in the Civil War*, p. 5.
29   Powicke, *Life of Reverend Richard Baxter*, p. 60.
30   Ibid., p. 61.
31   Auden, *Shrewsbury*, p. 160.

Nevertheless, despite the royal charter, it is worth noting that in the same year the number of town councillors almost doubled and contained strong puritan representation.[32]

Charles arrived in Shrewsbury on 20 September 1642, having spent the previous night in Wellington, and took up his quarters at the Council House. However, it would be wrong to assume that Shrewsbury or Shropshire was wholeheartedly dedicated to the royalist cause. An intended speech of 1642 by the mayor of Shrewsbury, John Studley, brother of Peter Studley, was reported in an 1879 volume of the *Transactions of the Shropshire Archaeological and Natural History Society*. It was originally intended to be delivered to Charles I on his visit to Shrewsbury and declare the support of the town but appears not to have been conveyed:

> May it please your Majesty,
> I here present you with the keys of the town of Shrewsbury, with the sword, and the mace, emblems of authority I exercise under your majesty over the people of this place; who, are all surprised with an ecstasy of joy, to behold your noble presence within their walls that the air rings with the echo of it. The heartily desire your journey hither, may be accompanied with as much prosperity and contentment as your royal heart can wish and the height of your calling does deserve.[33]

It is difficult to believe that the mayor's speech was a representative consensus of views by members of the town council, particularly considering that thirteen of its members were declared delinquents immediately following the arrival of the king.[34]

The king obviously felt it necessary to appoint a staunch supporter of the Crown to the position of governor of Shrewsbury and Sir Francis Ottley was selected in 1642, a position which he held until 1644. Despite the relative harmony, Ottley found it necessary to extract a declaration of loyalty, on pain of death, from the inhabitants.[35] Charles also considered that there was enough dissent in the county to give a proclamation at Bridgnorth on 14 October 1642 warning against opposition to royalist occupation:

> Since we came to this County, we have found by very probable information, that although the greatest number of our subjects have with much alacrity expressed their duties and affections to us, yet some persons of good quality in this County either maliciously affected against our good person and government, or ignorantly misled and seduced with the wicked and traitorous persuasions of others,

---

32   Ibid., p. 160.
33   W. A. Leighton, 'The Mayor of Shrewsbury's Intended Speech 1642', *Transactions of the Shropshire Archaeological and Natural History Society*, 2:3 (1879), pp. 398-9, at p. 398.
34   Bracher and Emmett, *Shropshire in the Civil War*, p. 21.
35   W. Phillips, 'The Ottley Papers Relating to the Civil War', *Transactions of the Shropshire Archaeological and Natural History Society*, Second Series, 8:2 (1896), pp. 199-280, at p. 200.

have been very busy in raising uttering or dispersing of scandalous and seditious speeches, tending to the slander of our person and government, of purpose to alienate the affections of our subjects against us, and unnaturally and traitorously to stir up war and rebellion against us in this our Kingdom.[36]

The principle agitators mentioned in the proclamation were Thomas Nicholls and Humphrey Mackworth, both Shrewsbury men, and Thomas Hunt. However, there was also evidence of dissent amongst the clergy and before the king reached Shrewsbury, Samuel Fisher, a puritan clergyman of Upton Magna Parish, exerted all his powers to persuade Richard Newport, of High Ercall, to champion the parliamentarian cause.[37]

Nevertheless, Shrewsbury remained in royal occupation for the duration of the conflict until 1645. However, despite the royalist persuasion of the town, the inhabitants were suffering from an impoverished condition by 1644. This was partly due to the continued demand of money, materials and labour made by both Lord Capel and Prince Rupert in succession but also because trade largely ceased once parliamentarian forces became active in the environs of the town, producing a state of siege. William Phillips summarised the situation thus:

It is no matter of surprise that a sullen spirit of discontent pervaded the minds of many, and made them long for at least a change of masters, in the hope of some relief, and led a year later to the betrayal of the town.[38]

The demands on the inhabitants to serve their king began almost immediately after his arrival, when he gave a speech on Michaelmas Eve 1642 announcing that a mint would be established in the town:

I have sent hither for a mint, and will melt down all my own plate, and expose my land to fail or mortgage, that if it be possible to bring the least pressure upon you. In the meantime I have summoned you hither to invite you to do that for me and yourselves, for the maintenance of your religion, the law of the land (by which you enjoy all you have) which other men do against us.[39]

---

36 'A Proclamation for the Better Peace and Quiet of our County of Salop', *Transactions of the Shropshire Archaeological and Natural History Society*, Fourth Series, 10:2 (1926), pp. XXVI-XXVII, at p. XXVI.

37 J. E. Auden, 'Ecclesiastical History of Shropshire during the Civil War, Commonwealth & Restoration' *Transactions of the Shropshire Archaeological and Natural History Society*, Third Series, 7:2 (1907), pp. 241-307, at p. 249.

38 W. Phillips, 'Shrewsbury During the Civil War of Charles I', *Transactions of the Shropshire Archaeological and Natural History Society*, Second Series, 10:2 (1898), pp. 157-72, at p. 157.

39 England and Wales. Sovereign (1625-1649: Charles I), *His Majesty's Speech: At Shrewsbury on Michaelmas Eve Last, to the Gentry and Commons of the County of Salop there Assembled*

The reference to religion is an insight into the depth of the societal machinations of the conflict. However, regardless of religious persuasion, it would have been difficult to deny such a request from a reigning monarch and it was a major factor in the suffering experienced by the residents of the town prior to parliamentary victory.

The nature of the religious control imposed in Shrewsbury during the royalist occupation can be glimpsed from a sermon preached in the town by Edward Symmons, chaplain to the Life Guard of the prince of Wales. Symmond gave his address on 19 May 1644, which was based largely upon Proverbs 17.11. This passage decreed that 'an evil man seeketh only rebellion, therefore a cruel messenger shall be sent against him' and he proceeded to explain the threat to society:

> A rebel is an evil or wicked man; for such a one is he, that seeks rebellion: sure then rebellion itself must needs be a wicked work, or a work of wickedness, because it is that which is the judgement of God's spirit, wicked men only search for, or thirst after: there is your doctrine.[40]

However, despite the proclamation, discontentment in the town had grown to such an extent that even passages from the bible could no longer justify or placate the trials of occupation.

The town was finally captured on the night of 21/22 February 1645. Parliamentarian forces from the garrison at Wem, led by Colonel Reinking and Colonel Mytton, reached the Castle Foregate undetected with assistance from the townsfolk in accessing the Watergate, later known as Traitors Gate. After a brief skirmish, the town was successfully secured for parliament by dawn.[41] Despite the capture of both the town and castle, there is evidence that relationships were not entirely harmonious between the two senior parliamentary officers responsible for the victory. Dispute immediately broke out with regard to who should be appointed governor. Both Mytton and Reinking claimed the honour and attempted to gain support via the Speaker of the House of Commons and both published pamphlets.[42]

A copy of Mytton's account was published soon after, which clearly highlighted his attempts to secure the position of governor and embellished the gratefulness of the inhabitants for being freed of occupation:

(London: 1642).

40   E. Symmonds, *A Military Sermon: Wherein by the Word of God, the Nature & Disposition of a Rebel is Discouraged, and the King's True Soldier Described and Characterised* (Oxford: 1644), p. 3.

41   Auden, *Shrewsbury*, pp. 170-1.

42   J. E. Auden, 'Lieutenant Colonel Reinking in Shropshire', *Transactions of the Shropshire Archaeological and Natural History Society*, 47:1 (1933), pp. 33-47, at pp. 40-1.

The whole County are glad of this, the well affected part thereof, and desire that Colonel Mytton may be governor thereof; who is an honest, cordial, well affected man, and of true integrity.[43]

Reinking, unhappy with previous accounts, later published his own which finished 'this account, though tedious, imports the substance of the passage. And the substance hereof is as true as tedious.'[44] However, despite their efforts, it was decided that the appointment should be decided by the Committee of Shropshire, who subsequently selected Humphrey Mackworth to the office on 26 March 1645.[45]

The Restoration Period and Conclusions

The two most notable non-conformist incumbents of Shrewsbury churches during this period were John Bryan and Francis Tallents. Bryan was first the minister of the Abbey and afterwards of St Chad's; Tallents was the minister of St Mary's. Both men were close friends of Baxter 'and not only men of ability, but men of moderate and tolerant views forwards those who differed from them.'[46] Following the Act of Uniformity in 1662, they shared the ministership of a chapel in the High Street, which was originally erected as a Presbyterian place of worship but later became Unitarian and is where Charles Darwin worshiped as a boy.[47] However, puritanism rapidly declined from 1660 when General Monk declared for the king and the direction of both social and religious life in Shrewsbury returned to more traditional ways. Even Baxter supported the Restoration and wrote the following passage in *A Treatise of Self Denial*, published in the same year as Charles II came to the throne:

> How long have some been longing, and praying, and moving and labouring for peace among the professed sons of piety and peace in England? And all (for ought I see) almost in vain: unless to the condemnation of a selfish unpeaceable generation.[48]

It was clear that Baxter had in fact concluded that the return to monarchy was the only way of obtaining peace, which supports to a degree the interpretation that many

---

43   W. Brereton, *Shrewsbury taken. A copy of Sir William Brereton's letter to the Parliament: and the copy of a letter from the Committee of Shropshire: with a full relation of the manner of the taking of Shrewsbury, by Colonel Mitton and Colonel Bowyer, with Sir William Brereton's and Colonel Mitton's forces, on Saturday last, February 22* (London: 1645), p. 11.
44   W. Reinking, *A More Exact & Particular Relation of the taking of Shrewsbury than hath hitherto been Published* (London: 1645), p. 6.
45   Ibid., p. 6.
46   Auden, *Shrewsbury*, p. 177.
47   Pevsner, *Buildings of England: Shropshire*, p. 277.
48   R. Baxter, *A Treatise of Self Denial* (London: 1660), p. 5.

puritans were in essence deeply conservative. Baxter's decision ultimately protected, rather than threatened, the status quo.

In Shrewsbury, upon the Restoration of the monarchy, the offer of Royal Pardon was issued on 14 April 1660 and it was not long before residents of Shrewsbury and its environs submitted applications. Once again, this would suggest that once the immediate threat, either real or perceived, of popish plots and catholic influence had subsided, the majority of ordinary residents were happy to return to the old ways in the knowledge that the conservative and protestant hierarchy of the town was secured.

All the declarations were heard before the mayor of Shrewsbury between 6 and 9 June and totalled 87 in number. The declarations predominantly represented citizens with puritan sympathies and is an interesting indicator as to the social status of those whom were most influenced. Auden carried out an initial examination of the material and concluded:

> An analysis of the trades and professions mentioned, shows that the number embraced 5 esquires, 17 gentlemen, and 3 clergy; but far the larger part were engaged in some form of business, ranging from glovers and drapers down to handicraftsmen. To these must be added a small country contingent, consisting of 4 yeoman and 3 husbandmen: and lastly, a few soldiers.[49]

The evidence would suggest that the core of the puritan support lay in the societal middle class and Auden highlighted that 73 of the declarants 'were sufficiently educated to write their name.'[50] One of the most prominent declarants was Francis Tallents, who had become vicar of St Mary's in 1653. Tallents was formally reappointed in the Restoration period but decided to give up his cure in 1662 rather than apply for episcopal ordination, before joining with Bryan to minister to the nonconformists of Shrewsbury.[51] It would appear that the religious tolerance prevalent in the early Stuart period had returned to Shrewsbury, allowing for the exploration of religious diversity but strictly in accordance with predominantly protestant doctrine.

49   T. Auden, 'Acceptances of the Royal Pardon at the Restoration 1660', *Transactions of the Shropshire Archaeological and Natural History Society*, Second Series, 2:1, (1889-90), pp. 141-158, at p. 146.
50   Ibid., p. 146.
51   Ibid., p. 155.

5

Organised Chaos: Applying seventeenth-century military manuals to conflict archaeology

Warwick Louth BA MLitt

Introduction

Historians and enthusiasts have all made use of drill manuals to represent organised development of military manoeuvre, through a growth in psychological and techno-logical innovation. Yet their ability to dictate artefact recovery has not been exploited archaeologically until recently. The Duke of Wellington, talking about Waterloo, described it as 'one may well try to tell the story of a battle as of a ball'.[1] In this sense, he might have been talking about the chaos of battle but he might equally have been talking about the level of drill choreography. Yet, the reality of being able to complete such movements under enemy fire is another matter entirely. While we can create predictive modelling measuring the uniformity presented through these manuals, what is to say they represent the reality of military manoeuvre, rather than the ideal, their enactment on the battlefield truncated and simplified according to the situation and time constraint? Indeed, the ability to perform the 128 individual movements and orders required in drill book fashion to load a musket and then engage with the enemy would test even the most hardened veteran. Likewise, the movement in perfect unison of 5,000 men at once within a single formation is unlikely to be undertaken with rela-tive ease. Therefore, in order to highlight the means of tracking and characterising these theories, modelling has to be broken down into personal and tactical; the former consisting of actions undertaken by the individual, which can be witnessed through evidence of markings identified through use wear analysis, the latter looking at spatial distribution of artefacts to find common arrangements that mirror the forma-tions used. In a wider perspective, by directly identifying sites relevant to conflict on

1   A. Barbero, *The Battle: A New History of the Battle of Waterloo* (London, Atlantic Books: 2006), p. v.

historic battlefields, heritage boundaries may be tightened, allowing economic agreement with local development.

This chapter will address these issues by creating a series of rules and trends by which the representation of personal and grand tactical characterisation may be undertaken. This will be done by highlighting the range, nature, use and identification of manual trends and examining how they might be tested, before testing their validity against battlefield studies carried out at Edgehill, Cheriton and Naseby. Through this, it is hoped to expand the potential of conflict archaeology to create moving landscapes where we can track troop bodies, individuals and thus provide relevance for protection and further exploration. What this chapter intends to be is an exploration of the evidence presented through contemporary military manuals and its application within an archaeological methodology to create conflict landscapes, rather than a treatise and exploration of the reality and use of tactical science on the battlefield.

Hypothesis

Military drill came about through standardised parade ground choreography, allowing a commander to move his troops around a battlefield with ease, combining the skills and manoeuvrability of infantry, cavalry and artillery to meet particular tactical situations. With the growth of combined arms warfare in the wake of the wars of the Protestant reformation, individual discipline was paramount in the success of utilising an army's strengths. Whether they formed deep blocks of marching infantry, thinly spread lines of cavalry or indeed a small peppering of independent skirmishers, it is likely that each one of these forms is likely to have lost or dropped items, leaving their mark on the localised archaeological record. This can consist of the humblest hobnail, coin or button lost in general day-to-day campaign life and marching, to items mislaid or destroyed in the chaos of battle, such as musket balls and furniture to individual weapons and armour. If such a pattern of movements was adhered to at all levels in a uniform fashion, artefact scatters should lead to site formation patterning which mirrors the drills identified in these documents completely, their characterisation highlighted through correlations of artefacts within metal detecting surveys in the localised reconstructed landscape, directly associated or indeed laid out in a pattern suggesting drill characterisation. Should such a model exist, dependent upon contemporary trends and individuals, this ought to create boundaries within which a battlefield influence might be applied, which is based around individual scale of conflict and army composition and dictates the frequency of investigation rationale. The model could be applied both to previously investigated sites and sites waiting to be investigated. This has the ability to directly truncate the possible area an archaeological team is required to actively survey within the local landscape, effectively utilising and limiting resources to gain the maximum yield, while at the same time eliminating outstanding anomalies just outside the main correlation of the battlefield zone, providing focus for more intensive research elsewhere. If such levels of choreography are visible, higher frequency analysis of the character and materiel of artefact assemblages could discern how much contemporary drill manuals were adhered to and where we can see them enacted, or not as the case may prove. However, in any investigation it is important to understand that the localised level of preservation is going to vary and differ constantly between sites. What is presented here in this research rationale is merely a theoretical approach and the actual historical reality of tactical science enacted within a battle may not necessarily be represented within our study.

Limitations

For an investigation of this size to be able to make the best possible yield of this hypothesis, a series of limitations, truncations and omissions have to be addressed. The prime study area addressed shall be the First Civil War in Britain and Ireland in 1642-6. At this time, the major artistic mathematical, philosophical, scientific and technological changes being realised as a result of the Renaissance were implemented into the widespread contemporary religious wars under the guise of the 'military revolution'.[2] This allowed the implementation of wider gunpowder technology and mathematical understanding to be implemented into the best use of firepower and hand-to-hand fighting, as well as the effective movement and logistics of armies. These all harked back to previous military thinkers to allow for a multi-facetted armed force that could bring multiple offensive and defensive capabilities to bear upon each other.[3] The medieval manner of feudalistic indenture, raiding warfare and localised skirmishing was over. Therefore, this study will exclude the late medieval period, despite the birth of such manuals during this time period, as their early realisation often only covered the poetic ideals of the knightly soldier, rather than the reality of campaign life.[4]

A common method, recently pioneered by Martin Marix-Evans, is the theory that initial generalised orientation can be garnered through aerial photography. This can identify clear evidence of plough lines and ridge and furrow field systems, a factor that increasingly influenced early modern warfare as commanders sought the best use of cavalry, without clear cut tripping hazards, as well as easier movement of artillery vertically rather than laterally.[5] Metal detectors, on the other hand, only have limited range and the naturally surrounding geology and land use may affect the total yield

---

2 J. R. Hale, *The Art of War and Renaissance England* (Washington, The Folger Shakespeare Library: 1961), p. 1.

3 M. Knox and W. Murray, *The dynamics of military revolution, 1300-2050* (Cambridge, Cambridge University Press: 2001), p. 12, in John Carman and Patricia Carman, *Bloody Meadows: Investigating Landscapes of Battle* (Stroud, Sutton Publishing: 2006), p. 148.

4 C. Allmand, 'The Fifteenth-Century English Version of Vegetius' De Re Militari', in M. Strickland, ed., *Armies, Chivalry and Warfare in Medieval Britain and France: Proceedings of the 1995 Harlaxton Symposium*, Harlaxton Medieval Studies VII (Stamford, Paul Watkins: 1998), pp. 30-45.

5 Personal communication with Phil Steele, 'Plough lines on battlefields', 2014.

and model created. Deep ploughing has the ability to move surface artefacts later-ally downwards away from any possible survey signal, while heavy mineralised soils and increased use of agrochemicals provide differing signals obstructing the arte-fact signature.[6] Even differing equipment, formatting and surveying techniques can often damage a survey's yield, clearly seen at Edgehill and Naseby, as well as Marston Moor.[7] It is also possible to create models surrounding military hierarchies, conflicts and forces incorporating clan, militia or ethnic groups, such as those encountered with Montrose's forces during the War of the Three Kingdoms. However, due to their ideo-logical allegiance, incorporating backwards, archaic methods, these are not currently incorporated by military science and thus will also not be studied here. Neither have siege or artillery manuals been included; a lack of mathematical, engineering and design skills throwing them beyond the scope of this chapter. However, battle-maps and plans have been included, as they are used for the training of officer cadets at modern staff colleges. The representation of plans in profile, rather than schemati-cally, showing their attempt to illustrate military science in action, was a factor that was quickly incorporated and exploited by many sixteenth- and seventeenth-century manuals.

Theory and Method

To undertake a clear analysis of the source material presented, we must incorporate historiographical—topographical analysis, to prevent assumptions and misdemean-ours from being created. While Alfred Burne's rule of Inherent Military Probability (IMP) might be tantamount to the investigation, it is important to account for changes in thought processes and localised terrain to use it to its potential. Archaeologists and historians have often relied too heavily upon outdated, subjective source material at face value, forcing setbacks within battlefield studies. This can be seen through Peter Newman's siting of the final position of the Marquis of Newcastle's Whitecoats at the battle of Marston Moor within White Syke Close based purely on assumption and the misreading of primary source material (in itself not necessarily providing a complete view of the battlefield space) without a shred of archaeological, landscape, or tactical evidence.[8]

In order to move away from this, John Carman maintained that we are required to break down types and terrain battles are fought over, into their component types.[9]

---

6   G. Foard, *Naseby: The Decisive Campaign* (Barnsley, Pen and Sword Military: 2004), p. 20.
7   Ibid., p. 20.
8   G. Foard, *Battlefield Archaeology of the English Civil War*, BAR British Series 570 (Oxford, Archaeopress: 2012), p. 9; G. Foard, 'English Battlefields 991-1685: A Review of Problems and Potentials', in D. Scott, L. Babits and C. Haecker, eds, *Fields of Conflict: Battlefield Archaeology from the Roman Empire to the Korean War* (Dulles, Potomac Books: 2009), p. 141.
9   Carman and Carman, *Bloody Meadows*, p. 17.

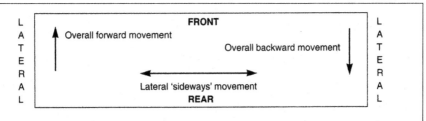

Notes to interpretation
1. In general, armies drawn up for battle occupy more space laterally than in depth.
2. In general, armies move towards each other to contact, rather than edging sideways, and retreat in the opposite direction.
3. Any turning movements in battle – whether of one army or of both – will tend to distort the overall shape of the battlespace, but the general lines of movement within the space will remain discernible.

Figure 5.1 Bounding the battlefield space. By calculating lateral movement, we create a field of influence that dictates the amount of space relevant to the investigation and thus dictate the numbers and manoeuvres necessary to fill and move in the designated space. (Carman and Carman, *Bloody Meadows*, p.135).

Taking an anthropological stance, conflict types highlight the needs of primitive versus true war, ritual versus real war, showing that while one is based far more on the general economy, control of resources and governing body, the other is far more inherent, sporadic and less governed by rationale, thus governing the space, scale and nature of general defence implemented.[10] To record the various inputs upon the landscape, geographical regression is essential in order to measure our assumptions.[11] This questions what we mean by battlefield space, whether it simply incorporates the area where direct military assault occurs or whether we can incorporate the bureaucratic, economic and social existence of an army into this space as well.[12] Carman has argued that it is the space in which lateral movement by a military force is possible, in some cases directly overlapping the spaces where habitation occurs, which allows a model to be created. This shows the ultimate lack of a possible unified image within such a conflict, while also creating an output whereby collateral damage is factored into conflict aims.[13]

Thus we must take a post-processual approach when looking at a battlefield, looking at the engagement with the landscape through human experience and events. By looking at how people and military organisations work, John C. Barrett agreed that

---

10   H. H. Turney-High, *Primitive Warfare: Its Practice and Concepts* (Columbia, University of South Carolina Press: 1949), in Carman and Carman, *Bloody Meadows*, p. 18.
11   Ibid., pp. 19-22.
12   Carman and Carman, *Bloody Meadows* p. 26; G. Foard and R. Morris, *The Archaeology of English Battlefields: Conflict in the Pre-Industrial Landscape* (York, CBA: 2012), p. 9.
13   Ibid., p. 9.

for the distinctions [between people] to have operated...it was necessary for people to *move* between regions; to enter and leave each other's presence, to observe passively or to act, to lead processions or to follow. The practice of social life is thus...performed.

This has the effect of making war a game that can be followed easily.[14] However, war defies common action and thus it is only by looking through IMP for dysfunctional behaviour within our normal understanding that we can compare and contrast differences between time periods and the reality of historical military drill.[15] Thus, where little archaeological evidence is available, we can apply historical source material to predict the quantity and distribution of archaeological material. We also have to be wary of the complete lack of secondary analysis to build upon and the dangers of building upon assumptions.[16] We have to mitigate for changes within technological innovation, practice and thought through the spread of the industrial, ideological and social Renaissance, as seen in Spain, Holland and Sweden, the major powers of the period.[17] In that sense, when looking for general tactical and strategic trends undertaken by the likes of Sir William Waller, Ralph Hopton, Prince Rupert and other general officers, where first-hand accounts and archaeological data remains elusive, the researcher may use their previous military conduct, connected with possible innovations they picked up during their service on the continent. However, it could make understanding more difficult. Through the eighteenth and early nineteenth century, common practice was for general drill to follow state-sanctioned regulations and military specialist-produced light infantry drill. However, should neither of the above have the effectiveness, speed and innovation required on the battlefield then commanding officers often instituted their own regulations.[18] These were dependent on unit scale from platoon to brigade, as witnessed by Robert Monro's regulations for the Scots Brigade in Dutch service during the 1680s, meaning that drill manuals were often never uniformly imposed.[19]

Thus, to create archaeological characterisation, we must integrate historiography, using records and knowledge of army composition, order of battle, formation and rules for overall space occupied. At the same time, we can also fill gaps in our

14   J. C. Barrett, *Fragments from Antiquity: an archaeology of social life in Britain 2900-1200 BC* (Oxford, Blackwells: 1994), pp. 4-6, in Carman and Carman, *Bloody Meadows*, p. 23.

15   L. H. Keeley, *War before Civilization. The Myth of the Peaceful Savage* (Oxford and New York, OUP: 1996), pp. 62-3, in Carman and Carman, *Bloody Meadows*, pp. 23 and 26; Foard, *Battlefield Archaeology*, p. 9; D. D. Scott, R. A. Fox, M. A. Connor and R. Harnon, *Archaeological Perspectives of the Battle of the Little Bighorn* (Oklahoma, University of Oklahoma Press: 1989) pp. 146-7.

16   Foard, *Battlefield Archaeology*, p. 8.

17   Ibid., p. 18.

18   A. Blake, *Re-creating the Drill of the 95th Rifles*, http://www.95th-rifles.co.uk/research/drill/, accessed 2 April 2014.

19   Ibid.

historical knowledge through further archaeological research, to produce a realised three dimensional regression back to the contemporary day of battle.[20] Incorporating associated limitations as algorithms within our work, such as fatigue and visibility, we gain an anchor as to why formations or assemblages provide the character they do, along with walking surveys to understand the landscape limitations forcing the boundary of areas of archaeological interest. A clear example can be seen at Towton, where the presumed Yorkist battle line is bound by the villages of Towton and Saxton on a plateau with a ridge to the North, while further being enclosed by a Marsh to the East.[21] Therefore, while we can rely upon basic IMP linked to assemblage characterisation, the ability to misrepresent the tactical landscape and the way people move through it is clear. Only through gradual understanding of the facets upon which a battlefield is experienced, physically and metaphysically through remembrance and historical recording, may processual, informed use of source material and military manuals be used to effectively position the extent of conflict.

What is a military manual?

The 'military revolution' of the sixteenth century required the systematic choreography of different troop types within particular tactical arrangements. This often referred back to classical works (such as Vegetius's *De Re Militari* or *The Tactics of Aelian* by Aelian Aelianus) or memoirs and orations (such as those provided by Caesar, Tacitus and Thucydides). The strategy and philosophy of these works were used as means of empire building, whilst their practical use of tactics on the battlefield were adapted to suit modern technology. That said, in many cases this proved to be a steep learning curve, as tactical innovation was often copied to the letter and evidence of differing ancient Greek styles of counter march, for example, merely confused the common soldier.[22] As early as 1408, manuscript evidence for the siege of Aberystwyth makes references to classical texts teaching Sir Thomas Berkeley the ideal way to take the fortress, a sure sign of the growth of abstract thinking over chivalric ideal.[23] However, with no localised national conflict or military academies and with many soldiers lacking schooling to understand abstraction, it was felt that the best way to diffuse military strategy and planning was through the adaptation and translation of existing military manuals to accommodate modern fashion. This was achieved through

---

20 Foard and Morris, *English Battlefields*, p. 21; Foard, 'Problems and Potentials', pp. 140.
21 Foard and Morris, *English Battlefields*, p. 18.
22 D. Bornstein, 'Military Manuals in Fifteenth-Century England', *Medieval Studies*, 37, (1975), pp. 469-477, at p. 469; J. R. Hale, *Renaissance War Studies* (London, The Hambledon Press: 1983) p. 232; H. Kleinschmidt, 'Using the Gun: Manual Drill and the Proliferation of Portable Firearms', *The Journal of Military History*, 63:3 (1999), pp. 601-29, at p. 603; D. R. Lawrence, *The Complete Soldier: Military Books and Military Culture in Early Stuart England 1603-45* (Danvers, BRILL: 2009), pp.138 and 226.
23 Bornstein, 'Fifteenth-Century England', pp. 469.

converting archaic weaponry and terms and making them work for the technological limits and needs of musketry (for example, the 1614 edition of Caesar's *Annals* included an appendix explaining the rudiments of Maurician tactics), along with the widespread publication of new manuals, with drill broken down step by step through pictorial, schematic and written sources describing and explaining the correct handling and management of an army on campaign (see Figure 5.2).[24]

The creation of military manuals institutionalised and unified military action. No longer were individuals required to train for years to master the longbow, saving the commander money, as well as providing him with a cheap asset that would develop and grow according to the level of conflict enacted.[25] With the spate of military manuals available of varying quality and the duty of any gentlemen to be informed with latest military tradition and technology, the officer class were far from elite, a factor reflected in many of the contemporary books and manuals.[26] These were disseminated by the likes of the Honourable Artillery Company, veterans and mercenaries

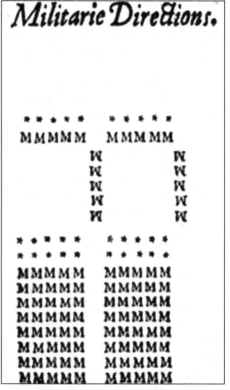

Figure 5.2 Diagram extract from Davies's *The Art of War* detailing the movement from column of march to firing line, showing the ability of increased use of simple diagrams to diffuse abstract military science into layman's terms, providing a wider military skill base. (Lawrence, *Complete Soldier*, Fig. 12/207)

returning from wars on the Continent, or occasionally state-sanctioned systematic drill (see Figures 5 and 6). That said, the level these were disseminated is not clear, due to a wish to leave a modicum of anonymity with a nation's armed forces.[27] Particularly effective drill, experienced by the likes of Prince Maurice of Nassau or Gustavus

24   Lawrence, *Complete Soldier*, p. 119.
25   Kleinschmidt, 'Using the Gun', p. 615.
26   S. Porter, *Destruction in the English Civil Wars* (Stroud, Alan Sutton Publishing: 1994), p. 14; Hale, *Renaissance War Studies*, p. 233; J. Raymond, *Henry VIII's Military Revolution: The Armies of Sixteenth-Century Britain and Europe* (London, Tauris Academic Studies: 2007), p. 9.
27   Hale, *Renaissance War Studies*, p. 254.

Adolphus, was disseminated and felt to be the ideal, as attested through examples like Sir Thomas Audley's *A booke of orders for the warre both by sea and land*, Jacques de Gheyn's engravings, or Robert Monro's 1637 *His Expedition With The Worthy Scots Regiment: An Abridgement of Exercise for the Young Souldier*, although this could prove to be merely spreading tactical knowledge to understand enemies' weaknesses.[28]

The success of such books must be attributed to their accessibility to all ranks of education and soldiery, taking abstract theories and movements and breaking them down into individual stages, based upon duties, skills, command structures, signals, postures, methods of training, formation movements and tactical situations, all at various scales from platoon to army scale tertio, from pike to shot, to individual weapons, thus being applicable from sergeants to generals.[29] This standardised the level of learning surrounding basic regimental sciences and allowed mathematical theorem to become common knowledge, meaning that square roots could be used to achieve optimal movement and use of a military force's numbers and thus create uniformity of impact.[30] The ability to impart generalisation and truncated orders through the increased use of annotated images allowed maximum detail to be conveyed to even the lowliest private, as seen with the works of Jacques de Gheyn.[31] Moreover, the ease of transport of these manuals meant that certain military codes and practices could become commonly known maxims, such as the five vowels of military practice or oft-quoted rhymes. This broke down the need for large scale drill, as realised by the Honourable Artillery Company between 1614 and 1619, after which drill was increasingly published as broadsheets and pamphlets.[32]

However, we must remember when looking at pictorial evidence for the running of a military unit that what is presented is an ideal and occasionally not workable (such as Gervase Markham's Wheel, which required 5,000 men to pivot on the spot; or the mathematical application of wedges, saws and pincer movements, which simply cannot be formed in sequence).[33] Indeed, C. H. Firth argued that we should approach all manuals with caution, due to the limited scale of resources and degrees of separation and realisation between Continental wars and those fought in Britain, many examples being suffused with dramatic romanticism.[34] Charles Carlton maintained that 90% of the available literary output of the military revolution is unreliable, the

---

28   C. Carlton, *Going To The Wars: The Experience of the British Civil Wars 1638-51* (London, Routledge: 1992), p. 261; Lawrence, *Complete Soldier*, pp. 141, 175 and 226.
29   Carlton, *Going To The Wars*, pp. 71 and 255-8.
30   Lawrence, *Complete Soldier*, p. 43.
31   Ibid., p. 141.
32   Ibid., pp. 163, 165 and 189-90; D. R. Lawrence, 'The Evolution of the English Drill Manual: Soldiers, Printers and Military Culture in Jacobean England', in P. Langman, ed., *Negotiating the Jacobean Printed Book* (Farnham, Ashgate Publishing: 2011), pp. 117-36, at p. 119.
33   Hale, *Renaissance War Studies*, p. 260.
34   Carlton, *Going To The Wars*, pp. 72-3.

number of books representing the lucrative popularity of such texts rather than socio-technological emancipation. This is seen through the lack of agreement between different texts on the amount of correct drills required to use a pike or musket.[35] That said, it does not assuage the success and popularity of such texts, with 90 manuals published within Britain between 1590 and 1642.[36] Indeed, in March 1642, Colonel Edward Harley spent £2 10s on eleven manuals. The complete reliance of officers on these documents for their education and their continued use as far as the battle-field is shown by the copy of Thomas Styward's *The Pathwaie to Martiall Discipline* now held in the Bodleian Library, which is covered in blood after its owner, Sir John Gell, was shot whilst the book was in his pocket at the battle of Hopton Heath.[37] If anything, military manuals represent the physical manifestation of the coming of age of the military revolution and the emancipation of abstract thought, science and mathematics, to allow a unified force to be achieved and understood at all levels of the military establishment. They provide an archaeological map, should they prove accurate, which provides meaning and movement to a blank landscape.

Yet, at the same time as the military manual was coming to fruition, the military map was also being developed. Often drawn up as the official account of landscape reconstruction and troop movement on the day of battle, the battle map transformed from a three dimensional depiction of events and drill movements in the sixteenth to seventeenth centuries to a schematic depiction in the eighteenth century.[38] However, as these maps are often created from the viewpoint of the winning commander, coupled with the limits of space or rectification of tactical mistakes and assumptions, an analysis needs to be undertaken to ascertain the subjectivity of the cartographer.[39] Clear examples of this can be seen indicated on maps of the battles of Culloden (1746) and Killiecrankie (1689), the former showing James Wolfe's Regiment completely covering the Culwhiniac enclosures, dismissing threats to the government lines, while in the latter, the alteration of the position of General Hugh Mackay shows him as a more aggressive commander than the evidence declares.[40]

Despite this, such maps provide a model, integrating contemporary landscape boundaries with working tactical forms, providing focus to our archaeological study of the battlefield and its environs.[41] Starting with the likes of Pannett's map of the battle of Pinkie (1547), the rudimentary features of the military map exist but individual minute

35   Ibid., pp. 72-3.
36   Ibid., p. 1.
37   Ibid., p. 71; Lawrence, *Complete Soldier*, p. 196.
38   R. C. Woosnam-Savage, "To Gather an Image Whole': Some Early Maps and Plans of the Battle of Culloden', in T. Pollard, ed., *Culloden: The History and Archaeology of the Last Clan Battle* (Barnsley, Pen and Sword Military: 2009), p. 164.
39   Ibid., p. 164.
40   Ibid., p. 49.
41   T. Pollard, 'Mapping Mayhem: Scottish Battle Maps and their Role in Archaeological Research', *Scottish Geographical Journal*, 125:1, (2009), pp. 25-43, at p. 26.

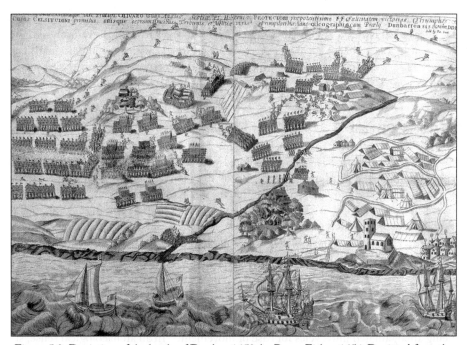

Figure 5.3 Depiction of the battle of Dunbar, 1650, by Payne Fisher, 1654. Depicted from the east, such a map highlights the issues surrounding limited space on maps. The royalist army on the far ridge of hills is completely truncated by the Brox Burn on the left. Rather than show the whole battle, it inadvertently recreates a moment in time, creating a fantasy that never occurred. (WA.Suth.C.3.293.1 Peter Stent (Publisher), 'The Victory at Dunbar' Image © Ashmolean Museum, University of Oxford).

representation of unit numbers and types, along with an idealistic representation of the surrounding landscape and English subjectivity, mean that more questions about the subsequent space is created than solved.[42] Certainly by the time of Lützen (1632) (See Figure 5.7), Naseby (1645) (See Figure 5.19) and Dunbar (1650) (See Figure 5.3), fully represented images of orders of battle, landscapes of tactical significance, firing lines, positions of individuals and tactical movement are fully realised and represented, albeit always subjectively.[43] That said, two main problems stand out. Firstly, all of these maps lack space on paper to fully realise spatial positioning, thus forcing major truncations of forces and landscapes, creating a reality which never truly existed. For example, the Scots flank on the map of Dunbar is represented far too close in formation due to the aesthetic representation of the Scots camp at Brox Burn (See Figure 5.3).[44]

42 Ibid., p. 26-30.
43 Ibid., p. 30-2.
44 Ibid., p. 31.

Equally, a map can merely represent a select point in time, thus creating an existence that was never realised nor understood on the day of the battle. However, through use of the available archaeological resources on a site, linked with regimental identifiers, we can use our current understanding to create anchor points within the localised landscape to actively pivot and restructure the tactical relevance and influence upon the battlefield area.

Artefactual Trends

So if tactical innovation is to be represented within the archaeological record, how is this to be manifested? Representation needs to take place on two levels. Firstly the personal level, the individual performing the drill who is likely to deposit particular artefacts, as well as circumstantial, under which the deposition takes place. Secondly, tactical representation, seen through spatial positioning mirroring the form of a tactical body of troops. Through the frequency of investigation, using historical accounts, linked with localised recorded orientation of associated finds, limited interpretation may be undertaken unique to that space, creating a multi-layered landscape. Weapons-handling drill varied greatly between system and manual, with 31-62 drills for musket, 15-65 for pike, 23 for marching and 20 for horseback (although these figures merely represent what should be performed on paper), many of these drills being amalgamated into cycles for ease of movement.[45] In an archaeological sense, six drills leave archaeological remains for musket, two for pike and eight for horse:

Musket[46]
- Place your rest – ability to lose musket furniture.[47]
- Take up your bandolier – ability for cartridge bottle or stopper to fall off.
- Open your pan – possibility of loose or broken powder flask nozzle falling off.
- Open your charge – ability for copper top to cartridge from bandolier falling off.
- Ram home your charge – impression of the scouring stick (ramrod) left imbedded in the surface of musket ball.[48] Evidence of gnawing associated with musket balls

---

45 W. Bariffe, *Military discipline, or The young artillery-man* (London: 1657), p. 2; J. Cruso, *Militarie Instructions For The Cavallrie* (Cambridge: 1632), pp. 39-41; J. de Gheyn and D. J. Blackmore, ed., *The Renaissance Drill Book* (London, Greenhill Books: 2003); C. Matthew, ed., *The Tactics of Aelian or On the Military Arrangements of the Greeks: A New Translation of the Manual that Influenced Warfare for Fifteen Centuries* (Barnsley, Pen & Sword Military: 2012); R. Ward, *Anima'dversions of warre; or, A militarie magazine of the truest rules, and ablest instructions, for the managing of warre* (London: 1639); S. Wright, *Militarie Disciplines For The Royalist Army of the Sealed Knot* (Southampton, The Sealed Knot: 2003).

46 de Gheyn and Blackmore, *Drill Book*, pp. 111, 127, 130, 141 and 149.

47 Bariffe, *Military discipline*, p. 2.

48 D. F. Harding, *Lead Shot of the English Civil Wars: A Radical Study* (Oxbow Books, Oxford: 2012), p. 67.

may equally represent issues with the commissariat and balls being provided of the wrong calibre.[49]

- Cock your match – an insecurely fastened serpentine (hammer) to the musket lock springing off.

Pike

- Charge your pike – represented through pike heads discovered in isolation.[50] Battles between forces using lances against pikes require further analysis of possible heads to differentiate between the two.[51] Accumulations of small finds represent fallen wounded.[52]
- Push of pike – taking soil samples to understand the level of compaction at a stratigraphic horizon to identify trampling.

Horse

- Order your hammer – serpentine springing off.
- Bend your cock – losing priming pan on lock.
- Lade with bullet – pistol balls with scouring stick impression, evidence of extensive sprue might represent loading through waxed paper cartouche.
- Gage your flask – loss of priming flask nozzle.
- Draw your Rammer – possible tinned scouring stick.
- Span your Pistol – brass pistol butt, wheellock spanner for lock.
- Present and give fire – fragments of iron pyrite (wheellock) and lost gun flints (flint/doglock)
- Close quarter fighting/engaging with the enemy – Any evidence of pierced or damaged armour due to inaccuracy of contemporary weapons. Also look for weapons impact inflicted upon armour for links to particular manuals and drill. The representation of horseshoes and nails, tack (bit, girth buckle, stirrup, spur etc.), fragments of armour, particularly from visor and articulated attachments to the shoulders, arms and upper legs are also possible signs of a force of cavalry, quantifying the levels of artefacts being necessary to gage their level of importance.[53] Additionally, sites where levels of horse-related paraphernalia are discovered might also be soil tested for a horizon of compression, although this might as likely be caused through pike/artillery positions.[54]

49   D. M. Sivilich, 'What the Musket Ball Can Tell Monmouth Battlefield State Park', in D. Scott, L. Babits and C Haecker, eds, *Fields of Conflict: Battlefield Archaeology from the Roman Empire to the Korean War* (Westport, Potomac Books, 2009), pp. 84-101, at p. 89.
50   de Gheyn and Blackmore, *Drill Book*, p. 211; Wright, *Sealed Knot*, pp. 14-5.
51   Cruso, *Militarie Instructions*, p. 34.
52   Wright, *Sealed Knot* p.15
53   Cruso, *Militarie Instructions*, p. 35.
54   Ibid., pp. 39-42.

Figures 5.4.1 and 5.4.2 Many of the items commonly associated with drill, all found at Edgehill. Original and experimentally fired musket balls, showing the effects of lack of wadding, allowing gases to expand around the bullet, the low melting point causing the projectile to expand and score the sides of the barrel. This is also typologically highlighted through the pitted texture to the lower hemisphere of the projectile, due to the bullet resting on the black powder charge. (Foard and Morris, *British Battlefields*, p.77)

Figure 5.4.3 Musket ball impacted against a hard surface, thus forming this mushroom typology. This is likely to be a pebble or stone, as experimental firing undertaken at The Centre for Battlefield Archaeology has proven that unless hitting bone, lead projectiles retain their morphology even after passing through a body. This probably represents raw troops firing too low. A similar morphology is created when doubleshotting a musket. (Foard and Morris, *British Battlefields*, p.77)

Figure 5.4.4 Slug bullet good for expanding power against armour. While it has previously been argued that this typology is based purely on ease of manufacture, experimental firing and corroboration of this type of shot in low frequency areas assumed to be where push of pike has taken place corroborates its role. (Foard and Morris, *British Battlefields*, p.77)

Figure 5.4.5 Powder flask nozzle. Often these are good indicators of individual firing positions, due to the difficulties inherent in loading from horseback. Clearly identified in quantities highlighting Sulby Hedges at Naseby, a clear progression for associating firing positions would be to eliminate hedge lines from OS readouts and focus metal detecting comparatively to see whether loading in isolation is deposited behind cover. (Foard and Morris, *British Battlefields*, p.124)

Figures 5.5.1, 5.5.2, 5.5.3 and 5.5.4 Typical Postures resulting in archaeological remains.
(J. de Gheyn, *Wapenhandlinghe*, The Hague: 1607)

Figures 5.6.1 and 5.6.2 Typical Postures resulting in archaeological remains.
(J. de Gheyn, *Wapenhandlinghe*, The Hague: 1607)

Figure 5.7.1 Cavalry postures resulting in
archaeological remains: Return your hammer.
(Cruso, *Militarie Instructions
For The Cavallrie*)

Figure 5.7.2 Cavalry postures resulting in
archaeological remains: Order your hammer.
(Cruso, *Militarie Instructions
For The Cavallrie*)

By identifying sub-divisions artefactually within the wider battlefield through use-wear analysis, linked to particular processes, the ability to orientate individuals within the wider armies, and therefore groups they were associated with, becomes apparent. However, only through looking at spatial orientation and layout of these particular finds is any meaning, facing and direction offered to battlefield events.

Military drill on the seventeenth-century battlefield was extremely formalised, particular models being instituted according to nation and school of thought. By quantifying available spatial schematic information from battle-plans, accounts, drill and known influences, our knowledge of individual generals can be modelled so that when investigating one of their unsurveyed battlefields, we can model expected deployment and manoeuvres associated with them over the current landscape. Here we shall cover the three main common deployment models associated with the period: the Dutch, Swedish and English models.

Instituted by Maurice of Nassau in 1593, the basic Dutch deployment was a pike block flanked by sleeves of musket, with cavalry flanking these units. The position of honour was in the vanguard on the right of the line, due to the necessity of deploying an army from march to order of battle.[55] This formation was based around the Roman triarii system of three lines (the last two acting in reserve to fill holes within the depleted front ranks), represented through a checkerboard profile with staggered alternating lines to feed troops into tactical development (see Figure 5.8).[56]

Firing was carried out by salvee or caracole, the front rank firing before retiring to the rear to reload, allowing rear ranks to advance and continue firing.[57] Thus, archaeologically, this should be represented at high frequency by alternating blocks of high density musket ball scatters, divided by areas with little ordinance. These scatters should show parallel linear associations of multiples of 6-32 ranks and 3-16 files (the contemporary depth of units), 38-100 artefacts representing identifiable unit scatters.[58] These scatters are likely to result in an artefact mean frequency of 1.5-3.3 feet (0.91metres), or 5 feet × 10 feet (1.52 × 3.04 metres) for cavalry, between artefact spread, showing likely ordered and close order spacing within a unit.[59] Thus, if the frequency extends above the listed range, the possibility of that particular unit being caught while standing or on the march can be quantified through source material.[60]

55   de Gheyn and Blackmore, *Drill Book*, p. 9; K. Roberts and J. Tincey, *Edgehill 1642: First Battle of the English Civil War* Campaign 82, (Oxford, Osprey Publishing: 2001) p. 24; K. Roberts, *Pike and Shot Tactics 1590-1660* (Oxford, Osprey Publishing: 2010), pp. 16-17.
56   Matthew, *Aelian*, p. 45; Roberts, *Tactics*, p. 5.
57   Roberts, *Tactics*, p. 11.
58   Bariffe, *Military discipline*, pp. 5, 7 and 9; de Gheyn and Blackmore, *Drill Book*, p.9; Matthew, *Aelian*, pp. 19-45; Ward, *Anima'dversions*, pp. 226-31; Wright, *Sealed Knot*, pp. 4-5.
59   Bariffe, *Military discipline*, p. 10; Cruso, *Militarie Instructions*, p. 45; Foard, *Battlefield Archaeology*, p. 125; Matthew, *Aelian*, p. 25; Wright, *Sealed Knot*, p. 5.
60   'Handy Hints from the Infantrie Garden', http://members.thesealedknot.org.uk/?page_id=2013, accessed 19 May 2013.

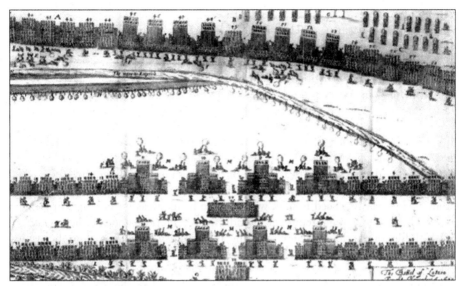

Figure 5.8 The battle of Lützen, 1632: Swedish troops in the foreground showing typical Swedish model deployment, compared with Imperialist troops at the top of the picture representing the typical Dutch deployment model.
(W. Watts, *The Swedish Intelligencer*, London: 1632)

Bariffe and Hexham show firing systems firing by block and then retiring to the sides, represented by parallel linear block profiles, either massed Swedish style or sporadically placed across the field like the Dutch. Unfired balls signify smaller blocks further back from the firing line made up of raw troops.[61] These unfired balls are equally important in identifying the possible localised fire position. Through the use of a quantifiable histogram, we can look for correlations in differing calibre of ball, identifying differing weapons systems used by either side.[62] Establishing the site of a unit, we can then work out the accuracy of battle-maps and accounts, as well as the modern position of contemporary heritage amenities, to provide meaningful archaeological protection. Thus we can accurately assume 300 metres between divisions, weapons divisions 4-150 metres and individual companies 20-100 metres, between lines consisting of about 20-70 metres, the rear line being the shortest at 700 metres, thus providing regimental/tactical influence designations within the battlescape.[63]

61   Roberts, *Tactics*, pp. 49-52; Wright, *Sealed Knot*, p. 18
62   Sivilich, 'Musket Ball', p. 87.
63   Cruso, *Militarie Instructions*, pp. 60-1; Ward, *Anima'dversions*, pp. 99 and 316; Wright, *Sealed Knot*, p. 12; A. Schurger, 'Die Schlacht von Lützen – Stumme Zeugen einer blutigen Schlacht', *Archäologie in Deutschland*, 1 (2009) pp. 22-5.

Therefore, a regiment's total frontage measures 700 x 300 feet, calibrated frontages for single division measuring 7392 metres2.[64] If there is a high concentration of cavalry represented in the vicinity, assemblages will be tightly compacted correlations, taking a circular grouping of mixed artefacts musket balls, represented (if we are following Bariffe's model) in alternating bands in multiples of four.[65]

A middle point between both forces should be represented through evidence of broken weaponry but largely devoid of ordinance-based evidence. This provides evidence of hand-to-hand combat, the reality of damaged weaponry such as dented trigger guards, buckles, weapons and pieces of armour highlighting them from the rest of the battlefield.[66] Such assemblages should have a wider frontage than other assemblages, due to the tactical need for a larger number of fighting men when engaging with the enemy, normally providing coverage of about twelve feet of doubled front.[67] However, we need to look within these blank areas for evidence of isolated musket balls. These might represent sporadic firing by forlorn hopes, either advancing through files of multiples of eight or acting as a skirmish line, directed on the armies' flanks or in front and anchored on hedge/wall lines/field boundaries for cover, in bodies spreading around 22 metres.[68] These would be identified through limited linear groupings, one end of the assemblage proving denser than the other, representing rapid advance and retiring according to the advance of the enemy. Flanking cavalry action should be characterised by small-scale linear correlations of small calibre pistol and carbine fire, or a mixed assemblage with no association, signifying firearms used during the melee of two bodies of horse. The possibility of small scale soil analysis might be undertaken to understand compaction and inclusions representing a small-scale horizon of large-scale trampling (see Figure 5.9).

This system might be complicated through the adoption of Gustavus Adolphus's Swedish deployment model, revolving around the demi-hearse. Sleeves of musket would advance and connect to form a firing line. Their volley fired, they disconnected and allowed the pike to advance. Thus, our model would be represented by a series of linear large-scale musket ball assemblages, accompanied by a large gap before they pick up again. Swedish-style deployment took an arrowhead formation, blocks of pike producing a composite centre, composite bodies of musket flanking them and also forming a reserve between lines, creating a composite sandwich (See Figure 5.8). Thus, as we can tell that a Swedish unit was supposed to hold 1,204 files, at a spacing of 50cm-1 metre2 the likely space it incorporated was 1,000-2,000 metres2,

---

64   Cruso, *Militarie Instructions*, p. 38; Ward, *Anima'dversions*, p. 70.
65   Bariffe, *Military discipline*, p. 127; Wright, *Sealed Knot*, p. 18; The Sealed Knot, 'Handy hints from the Infantrie Garden', *Orders of the Daye* (The Sealed Knot: 2002).
66   T. Pollard, 'Capturing the Moment: The Archaeology of Culloden Battlefield', in T. Pollard, *Culloden: The History and Archaeology of the Last Clan Battle* (Barnsley, Pen and Sword Military: 2009), pp. 130-162; Wright, *Sealed Knot*, p.26
67   Bariffe, *Military discipline*, p. 10.
68   Ibid., p. 87; Ward, *Anima'dversions*, p. 68.

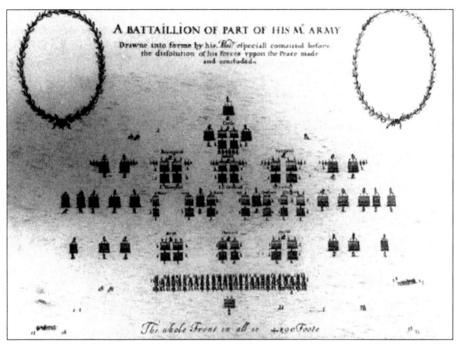

Figure 5.9 Tertio showing hybrid English model, combining the composite nature of the Swedish model with the linear combined arms Dutch model. This was used increasingly after the battle of Edgehill, as the need for fluidity of tactical movement reinforced recommendations from veterans of the Thirty Years War. (G. Adolf II, *Des Hochlöblichsten König zu Schweden Brigaden wie Hr solche Zu lest von 16 Compagnien vndt von Zweÿen Regimentern hat stellen woollen*, Stockholm: 1631, Fig. 53)

the distance between the horn battle and the main body being 10-20 metres.[69] The increasing use by Gustavus Adolphus of swine feathers (sharpened stakes used as a deterrent against artillery) might lead towards the identification of musket firing positions, better characterisation of drill manuals and artefact assemblages, through highlighting stratigraphic evidence of pits. Such methods of defence were commonly incorporated by veterans of the Continental wars and act as an indicator of patterns of where individuals were situated on the battlefield, such as Sergeant-Major-General Henry Tillier or Sir William Waller's Triple Firing System.[70] This is likely to be represented through large-scale musket ball assemblages situated on the peripheries of the field, the centre dominated by merely broken weaponry representing pike blocks.

69   Matthew, *Aelian*, pp. 27-35.
70   Bariffe, *Military discipline*, p. 127; Sealed Knot, *Infantrie Garden*.

Within Britain and Germany, at the conclusion of the Thirty Years War and the beginnings of the English Civil War, officers found these formations too static and adapted the two systems. These composed of Swedish formations organised at a Tertio level but using alternating Dutch style.

Using localised Viewshed analysis and landscape regression, the ability to presume firing orientation and direction, provides an anchor profile upon which to orientate battle accounts, identify units engaged and their position, which can be linked to historical personalities, with a higher than average level of accuracy.

Edgehill

Our first case study shall look at the battlefield of Edgehill in Warwickshire, the site of the initial major battle of the Civil War. Tactically distinct, with either side deploying in clear cut formations of parliamentarian Dutch versus royalist Swedish pattern models, it allows us to create three distinctive spheres of influence based on societal norms of precedence around two sleeves of cavalry with a composite infantry centre.[71] Using Sir Bernard de Gomme's battle map completed for Prince Rupert, corroborated with written accounts, we get the view that the royalist deployment area was on top of the Edgehill scarp, the extent restricted but anchored by a pre-enclosure series of hedges.[72]

Using this estimated location, we can apply Ward's law of frontages to understand the approximate area to which archaeological activity provides potential. Therefore, an average number for the royalist army of 14,000 (10,000 foot covering a collective space of 2.4 miles, 2,500 cavalry covering 2.6 miles and 800-1,000 dragoons over 30 feet) provides a five mile stretch over which the royalist army was deployed. The parliamentarian army, with similar numbers, occupied a similar sphere of influence at the foot of the hill, although all these measurements extending further due to gaps between units.[73] Therefore, using figures provided by the order of battle, taking an assemblage of 300 shot over 800 metres on the parliamentarian cavalry left, should by body create a distribution of 38 shot per 100 metres, represented through the fact that cavalry were likely to only fire one round before engaging or falling back. For a compact infantry centre with 530 bullets found within 100 metres, the proximity within one metre of approximately 41 musket balls shows the propensity for drawn-out volley firefights, rather than protracted skirmishing.[74] By undertaking landscape regression, using David Pannett's 1970s landscape survey, with Henry Beighton's 1726 battle map, we see the main action aligned along a north-south orientation, the gap between both forces a 1,000-metre gap, accounting for the short range, low rate

71   Foard, *Battlefield Archaeology*, p. 123.
72   Ibid., p. 124.
73   Ibid., p. 125.
74   Ibid., p. 170.

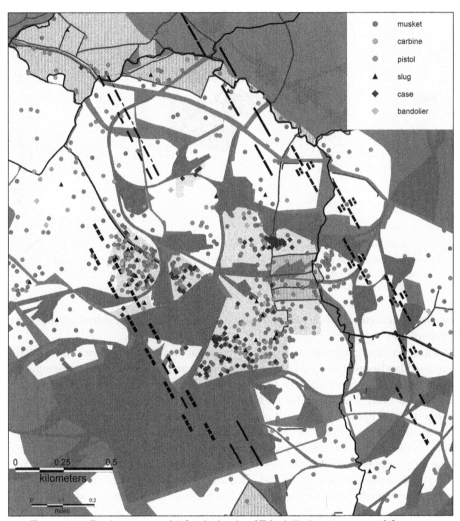

Figure 5.10 Deployment model for the battle of Edgehill, showing assumed frontages
(3 feet × 7 feet, 300 yards infantry; Horse 5 feet × 10 feet, 100 yards) and unit depths (8 ranks),
as well as obvious Dutch versus Swedish tactics before tactical innovation could come to play
during the early years of the Civil War. Reconstructed landscape and associated metal detector
finds are overlaid, showing high scale correlations being used as anchor points for varying troop
types within the landscape. (Foard, *Battlefield Archaeology*, p.125)

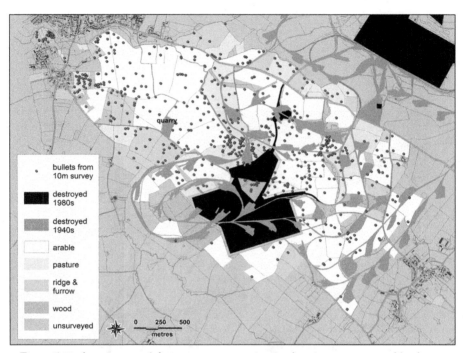

Figure 5.11 Associate metal detector survey, superimposed against reconstructed landscape and field boundaries. Red symbols = bullet finds; other symbols = other finds; blacked out areas represent modern RLC/MOD depot. (Foard, *Battlefield Archaeology*, p.122)

of fire and inaccuracy of the weapons of the period, as well as the initial psychological hesitation to engage.[75]

However, the calculated frontages of both surveys do not fit within a partially enclosed landscape, merely truncating and forcing armies into a linear grouping, thus misappropriating contemporary tactical innovation.[76] Using this model, the parliamentarian cavalry has been forced forward, further than is deemed necessary, on a steep inclined knoll, where it will play little influence on the passage of battle, while obstructing the movement of neighbouring units and truncating the parliamentarian line, making it immovable.[77] Glenn Foard has dismissed these shortfalls, arguing that disparagement and anomalies within contemporary drill manuals means that the contemporary order of battle and calculated frontage are not accurate and that the lack of topographic evidence within written accounts of the battle and even tactical

75   Ibid., pp. 135 and 137.
76   Ibid., pp. 135 and 137.
77   Ibid., pp. 135 and 137.

inexperience within the officer corps of the parliamentarian army prior to initial conflict might explain this anomaly.[78]

Moving on to the artefact assemblage represented, the differentiation between the weapons systems and firing lines of either side can be discerned through the proliferation of 28.5 bore parliamentarian and 12.5 bore royalist shot, suggesting that rather than proliferation of similar calibre weapons by either side for easier logistical use, a number of foreign or indeed older pattern firearms were in circulation to place as many soldiers in the firing line as possible.[79] However, similarities between the calibre of a number of carbine and musket balls means that it is often spatial analysis, referencing surviving accounts and plans that provides archaeological interpretation. In this instance a contested assemblage represents the parliamentarian baggage guard, due to the risk of a stray spark from other firearms.[80] Equally, the high proportion of non-regulation slug bullets represented within low density areas, identifying pike blocks, suggests a widespread break from manual tradition, experience forcing musketeers fighting against armoured troops to use such a projectile for its stopping and expansive force, like a modern dum-dum bullet.[81]

However, while we can differentiate troop types on a part of the battlefield according to weapon type, the low frequency of survey merely provides profile characterisation of the intensity of fighting, rather than highlighting individual units, their movements and events, musket volley scatters being equally mixed with hail shot.[82] Looking at such an assemblage, it is clear that either side of the central accumulation there are distinctive gaps, possibly representing sleeves of cavalry. Here, metal detector survey supports the drill book Swedish deployment and landscape analysis of existing pre-enclosure boundaries shows the extent such a unit spread, although the presence of a number of hedgerows rather than a clear plain supports de Gomme's view of integration of supporting dragoons.[83] However, the lack of pistol balls in these sectors of the battlefield suggests the accuracy of the written account: Prince Rupert abandoned drill manuals in favour of the charge, whilst parliament retained the Swedish caracole system, a suggestion of its use at Edgehill shown through a series of linear groupings to the southwest of these anomalies.[84] Looking at the central main infantry battle line, we can see a 300-yard gap between either line, the ultimate maximum range to which a soldier was likely to hit his opponent, although the assemblages spherical, rather than deformed, profile suggests many of the troops were inexperienced and thus prone to firing high and not hitting their target. A few musket balls mushroomed at 100 yards, possibly as a result of veteran

78   Ibid., pp. 125-35.
79   Ibid., p. 156.
80   Ibid., p. 157.
81   Ibid., pp. 162 and 165.
82   Ibid., pp. 156-7.
83   Ibid., p. 162.
84   Ibid., p. 162.

troops holding their fire and going by manual advice.[85] Identified royalist calibre shot start at a wider interval between 250 and 500 metres, uniformly suggesting the use of firing by salvee and providing a landscape area to which manoeuvre by horn battle might be represented.[86] A gap between the two lines suggests the engagement of push of pike, although the fragmentary nature of the site due to Ministry of Defence development and lack of correlation of investigation means that results need to be further examined. However, by and large, frontage depths for musket balls are represented in multiples of six to eight, mirroring contemporary calculations of unit depths that this early in the war were still adhered to.[87]

Obviously, as with the majority of sites on this study area, the artefact distribution always has to be objectively analysed for contamination from continued re-enactment on these sites but with the yield of ordinance based on evidence available, a number of conclusions can be made. Very rarely are the tactical systems used by either army so polarised and distinctive from one another, a major contributory factor to this investigation. Thus Edgehill provides a solid benchmark of how archaeology and drill manual analysis can be applied to one another.

Cheriton

The second site we shall look at is Cheriton, in Hampshire, the site of Sir William Waller's crowning victory in April 1644 that forced the War of the Three Kingdoms to centre upon the Home Counties. Although not easily accessible at time of writing, small-scale ongoing investigation of other Waller battlefields at Lansdown Hill and Roundway Down might be compared to see genuine model and artefact correlations associated with particular tactical styles. As with Edgehill, Cheriton proves that Marix-Evans's belief about effective use of cavalry through alignment along existing plough lines to provide battlefield orientation seems to bode true here.[88] Based on a southwest-northeast orientation, essential artefact differentiation between musket and pistol balls was essentially achieved, coupled with topographic map regression, which allowed for the demarcation of five isolated bodies of troops linked to field boundaries for cover.[89]

Focus was therefore based around large-scale correlations, allowing a higher frequency of interpretation of the individual soldiers' zone of influence and of the

85   Foard, *Battlefield Archaeology*, pp. 161 and 165; Schurger, 'Lützen', p. 24.
86   Foard, *Battlefield Archaeology*, p. 170.
87   Ibid., p. 170.
88   Ibid., p. 337; Battlefields Trust/English Heritage/National Monuments Record, *Cheriton*, http://www.battlefieldstrust.com/media/578.jpg, http://www.battlefieldstrust.com/media/579.jpg, http://www.battlefieldstrust.com/media/580.jpg, accessed 24 July 2014); P. Steele, 'Ploughlines and orientation'.
89   J. Bonsall, 'The Study of Small Finds at the 1644 Battle of Cheriton', *Journal of Conflict Archaeology*, 3:4 (2007), pp. 29-52, at p. 35.

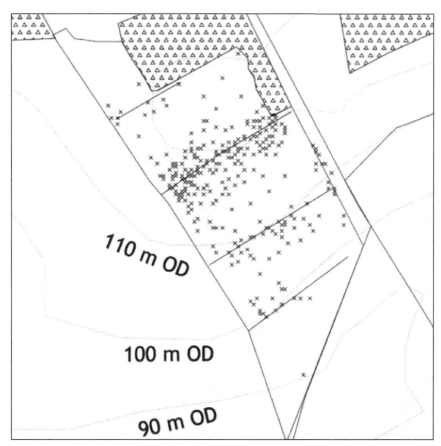

Figure 5.12 Metal detector survey of a section of Cheriton Battlefield. At this frequency and with little interpretation, the spatial results mean little. Only through further investigation highlighting correlations and spheres of influence may an explanation for this artefact patterning start to be realised, as here showing the breakdown into five phases. (Bonsall, 'Study of Small Finds', Fig. 3/37)

surrounding battlefield.[90] This can be understood through the psychological manifestation of particular boundaries and markers as a means by which soldiers may keep in formation and in their focus within the chaos of battle, as well as a morale booster, being used as a barricade to provide defensive enfilading fire against offensive cavalry as can be suggested through associated horse pendants and pauldron (shoulder) armour plates.[91]

90   Ibid., p. 37.
91   Ibid., p. 35.

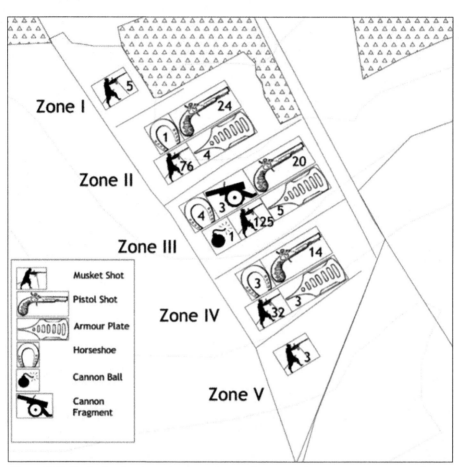

Figure 5.13 By further breaking these correlations down into their component types and uses, we can start to dictate the possible position of troop types and associated individuals upon the battlefield, as well as tactical trends, here represented through a English model Dutch deployment pattern. (Bonsall, 'Study of Small Finds', Fig. 4/39)

Thus we can provide effective, logical movement that can be linked to first-hand accounts of the battle and further broken down into tactical models.[92] In the metal detector survey we can see the parliamentarian line, situated to the north, start an advance along a south-west incline, the vertical wide spread of musket shot possibly representing the royalist fighting retreat towards the plateau and cover of Cheriton Wood between zones I-III.[93] A clear defined gap between the royalist firing line,

92   Ibid., p. 45.
93   Ibid., p. 46.

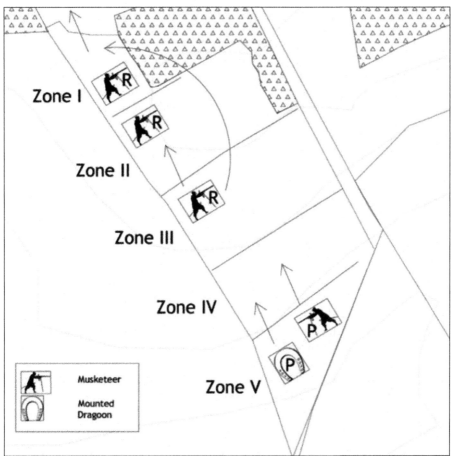

Figure 5.14 By further examining the artefact assemblage for characteristic abnormalities, forensically identifying individual weapon systems, we can start to track the movement of troops across the battlefield, as well as positively identify the historical events contributing to the archaeological record. (Bonsall, 'Study of Small Finds', Fig. 6/45)

represented through the linear block in Zone II-III and that of the parliamentarians in zones IV-V, possibly shows the site where re-evaluation may reveal more evidence for hand-to-hand fighting and push of pike.[94] An individual possible loading position of a musket block caught in a crossfire can be identified, its purpose identified through isolated apostle and powder flask nozzle recoveries.[95]

94   Ibid., p. 46.
95   Ibid., p. 38.

While the survey is too low a frequency to positively identify individual groups of troops, looking at identified associated groupings of musket balls, particularly those associated with zones III-IV, many of the depths of these associations occur in multiples of six, proving that tactical mathematics was often adhered to. Isolated groupings within this gap may relate to the breaking of Sir Henry Bard's regiment in square by Sir Arthur Haselrige's cuirassier cavalry: a number of localised impacted musket balls which possibly bounced off armour, three pieces of pauldron armour and the localised presence of cavalry being confirmed through the identification of the Gloucester 1644 keyhole typology of horseshoes of eight contemporary horseshoes.[96] Such evidence of heavy resistance, highlighted by a denser frequency of shot, may well indicate the site of Haselrige's attack by a forlorn hope of dragoons. A linear band of 58 small calibre musket shot (carbine) characterises the forlorn hope used to finally break up Bard's formation between Zones II-V, forcing the royalist line further back.[97] While it is difficult with such a low frequency to break down individual fighting units and their formations, the metal detector survey and style that James Bonsall has produced does provide the ability to quantify spatially the distribution of finds to an easily understandable standard. This enables us to make the generalisation that both armies were roughly forming an English model deployment, formed of individual Swedish composite bodies within a checkerboard pattern for flexibility of strategy. Equally, the possibility of broadly identifying two individual units involved, Bard's and Haselrige's, provides further potential for anchoring the boundaries of the battlefield. However, we must remember that this merely constitutes a small strip of the entire battlefield. Such an investigation provides the means to possibly predict archaeological potential throughout the rest of the site, while also providing a case study for archaeological movement to be measured against on other sites.

Naseby

Finally we shall look at the battlefield of Naseby, the decisive battle of the Wars of the Three Kingdoms and the battlefield that forced a turnaround in battlefield and historic landscape protection in Britain. Depictions of Naseby border the change in military cartography in two individual maps created after the battle. Firstly, we have de Gomme's depiction created for Prince Rupert many years after the battle. This uses the typical eighteenth-century method of depicting battlefields as schematics, with units depicted as blocks and with little evidence of movement or indeed terrain obstacles, which are merely represented through arrows.[98] However, the more famous depiction is Robert Streeter's map from Joshua Sprigge's history of the New Model

---

96   Bonsall, 'Cheriton', pp. 41 and 46; J. Adair, *Roundhead General: The Campaigns of Sir William Waller* (Stroud, Sutton Publishing: 1997), pp. 165-6.
97   Bonsall, 'Cheriton', pp. 39 and 46.
98   Foard, *Naseby*, p. 17.

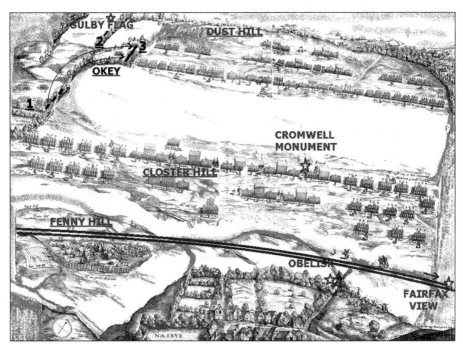

Figure 5.15 Robert Streeter's depiction of the battle of Naseby for *Anglia Redivia* (1647), with a large parliamentarian subjectivity. Major modern landmarks and focal points of fighting have been superimposed upon the image. (P. Steele, http://ecwbattles.files.wordpress.com/2009/07/streeters-naseby-adjusted.jpg, accessed 20 August 2014)

Army, *Anglia Rediviva,* published in 1647. This represents both armies in profile, with stylistic representation of the surrounding landscapes and taken from notes and forms of battle applied at the time by Sergeant-Major-General Phillip Skippon on 11 June 1645 and corresponding memoranda from his royalist counterpart Sir Jacob Astley.[99]

However with little to no representation of the actual terrain on the ground, idealised formations, erratic scale and little detail provided to the royalist army, it is clear that such a source needs a reinterpretation, rather than be taken at face value.[100] We can tell that the choice of ground might have been prompted by lessons learnt at Marston Moor the previous summer, which was fought on open landscape with little cover, meaning that parliament was able to turn the flanks of the royalist positions.[101] Streeter and the Victorian antiquary Thomas Carlyle (who performed small scale excavation on the battlefield) believed that there was no evidence for the New Model

99   Ibid., p. 17.
100 Ibid., p. 17.
101 Ibid., p. 21.

Army forming up on the tactical high ground of Closter Hill, the slopes of which were covered by the Sulby Hedges and which was intersected by the main road, with streams dividing any climb. Instead, they believed that the New Model formed up at the bottom of the slope in the valley bottom, allowing dragoon forlorn hopes to advance along the hedges to the royalist positions, despite poor drainage, high agricultural land and a series of rabbit warrens breaking up any considerable advance from the parliamentarian right.[102] What might be clearer is that a combination of the two systems was employed and the parliamentarian line placed on an incline, the left moved forward to allow the maximum range of fire to be employed by John Okey's Dragoons, the right remaining on the hill top for ease of movement and bolstering of weak points within the line.[103] This forced a royalist withdrawal to the rear of the hill and Streeter depicted their left as squashed against the outer limits of Clipston village, not due to poor deployment but merely because Streeter has tried to place every unit within the limited space of the page. This has the effect of truncating the accurate scale available, while heightening the prestige of the New Model Army in depicting their right flank as overextending that of the royalists to make up for this cartographical flaw.[104]

However, this does not mean there was ample space on the battlefield, as the musket ball assemblage from the valley bottom shows that there is a clear 2,000-foot linear collection, rather than the calculated 2,850-foot frontage suggested by recorded orders of battle. This shows units combining together due to truncation from the bad landscape features on the right of the field, forcing the typical three to six-foot spacing between troops to be abandoned.[105] Other explanations for the abandonment of this drill book manoeuvre have included desertion and disease rates increasing after the siege of Leicester – the New Model Army's previous muster numbering 7,000 infantry and falling by 1,700 to 5,300 men.[106] Distinctive gaps with sparse representation of ordinance either side of this grouping may suggest the relative position of cavalry, although directly relatable identifiers are not discernible. However, small calibre musket balls, presumably identified as being fired from carbines, have been found along a 2,000-foot stretch left of the Sulby Hedges at the valley bottom, suggesting (as 20 feet was the recommended distance between divisions) that any likely cavalry evidence would be found 20 feet in front of this grouping.[107] For the right wing, the optimal frontage for the other half of calculated cavalry would be 4,000 feet, although a 700-foot gap between associated pistol ball scatters and a rabbit warren limits our current knowledge of the size of the parliamentarian cavalry numbers and distribution

102 Ibid., pp. 21, 224 and 229.
103 Ibid., pp. 21, 224 and 229.
104 Ibid., p. 232.
105 Ibid., p. 241.
106 Ibid., p. 241.
107 Ibid., p. 241.

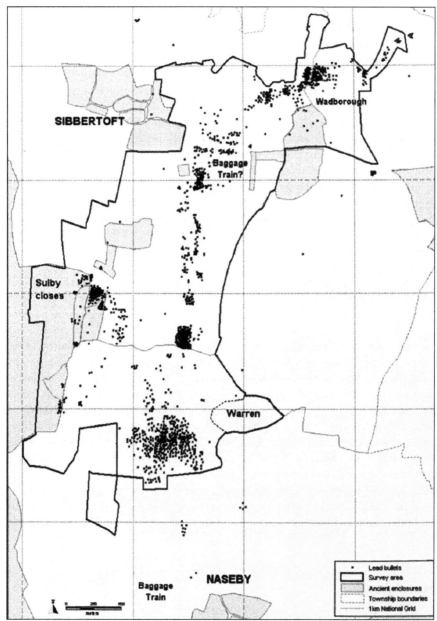

Figure 5.16 Metal detector survey of the Naseby battlefield, superimposed upon historic landscape, the elongated nature of the survey showing the fighting withdrawal and eventual collapse of discipline within the royalist army. (G. Foard, 'Integrating Documentary and Archaeological Evidence in the Investigation of Battles: A Case Study from Seventeenth-Century England', Unpublished PhD thesis, University of East Anglia, 2008, Fig. 7/284)

at Naseby.[108] Differing frontages throughout the parliamentarian lines clearly suggest that manuals may well have simply been regarded as guidelines to which military formations would adhere to in ideal circumstances, adapted when the surrounding terrain was inadequate.[109]

Further quandaries are raised as to the positioning of Okey's Dragoons during the battle, the majority of surviving accounts limiting their position to a simple skirmish line barriered by the Sulby Hedges. Streeter, however, despite his inadequacies, places Okey's dragoons crossing the barrier between Lankyford Hedge sheep enclosure and Sulby Hedge, even to the extent of further dragoon units being employed. This would have provided a good firing position across Broadmoor and the assumed line of advance of the royalist cavalry, although tactically too near to the parliamentarian line to be of any use, while also overlapping and limiting the use of parliamentarian cavalry. This suggests that Streeter has placed these troops too far forward, due to lack of space.[110] The issue is further confused by Okey himself, who maintained that his firing position was between Coate Green Pasture and Archwrong Close, on the border of Sibbertoft Parish.[111] However, the discovery of 80 musket balls directly between the two hedge system, with associated musket equipment and eight pewter bandolier tops, suggests that Streeter's positioning is the more accurate siting.[112] Furthermore, the mysterious second body is identified by an isolated accumulation of sixteen musket balls directly to the right of Okey's main position, suggesting that Fairfax was pushing harder on the royalist right than has previously been suggested.[113]

Initial skirmishes and clashes between the two sides can be identified by looking at sites near the field's edge connecting to original road lines. In this case, the road leading up the west of the Broadmoor ridgeline, along Gibbs Hill, has an isolated grouping of several musket balls, providing us with the image that the royalist deployment was not enacted in an easy and peaceable action but their tactical stance was continually harried in a running battle.[114] Looking towards the infantry centre, a scatter of 40 musket balls across Broadmoor Slope suggest further running engagements pushing towards the royalist centre as the New Model Army advanced from skirmishing forlorn hopes, although the low frequency of investigation means it is difficult to tell whether this was achieved in tandem or piecemeal.[115] The summit of Broadmoor Hill, however, completely lacks any archaeological material. This indicates that both lines completely engaged in hand-to-hand combat, pushing the royalist line

108 Ibid., p. 241.
109 Ibid., p. 242.
110 Ibid., p. 246.
111 Ibid., p. 246.
112 Ibid., p. 247.
113 Ibid., p. 247.
114 Ibid., p. 226.
115 Ibid., p. 251.

back to its second stop line, which is represented through a dense scatter along the hill top, possibly around 300 feet from each other.[116]

While investigation frequency is too low to identify individual unit spacing, by breaking down directly-related accumulations of musket balls, the ability to identify the space and extent occupied on a brigade-divisional level, and thus a generalised banding whereupon the broad position of a regiment was placed, allows the beginnings of direct predictive modelling with historiographical analysis using Streeter's distribution and Skippon's order of battle to provide absolute interpretation.[117] Thus, we must look to accounts to understand the varying positioning of particular troops at different times in the battle, as well as what troops still survived. For example, a gap just before the brow of the hill and the site of the royalist baggage train, roughly similar in dimension to those represented previously, might identify the position of Sir Marmaduke Langdale's troop of horse covering the royalist retreat. Likewise, a closely compact assemblage of musket balls on the rear slope of Broadmoor between Chapel Close and Pierce's Quick Close might show the position of the royalist baggage guards.[118]

A further way of identifying possible sites of regimental engagements and indeed last stands, such as those witnessed by Rupert's Bluecoat regiment, can be by locating, both traditionally and archaeologically, the site of mass graves. On the assumed position of the parliamentarian left flank, where Skippon's brigades are supposed to have been sited, Edward Fitzgerald discovered the site of a small massed grave in the 1850s. This discovery should be keyed into surrounding scatters of musket balls, associated frontage and numbers of troops.[119] A linear gap within this assemblage possibly relates to cavalry among these units, showing the final moments of organisation within the royalist army before routing northwards towards Sibbertoft.[120] A series of gradually diminishing linear correlations of musket balls running towards the summit of Broadmoor Hill start radiating towards period hedge lines and sunken lanes, which might indicate disordered troops radiating towards the areas of the greatest cover.[121] Certainly by the time we reach the northwest side of Clipston Parish and Wadborough Hill, an assemblage of over 130 musket balls with no clear alignment, delineation or order shows the final stand of the royalist army, the possible resting place of Rupert's own regiment and the total collapse of drill book etiquette and military science.[122]

Future studies would do well to take such examples to build a characterisation and model upon crowd dynamics and representation of the battlefield route within the archaeological record, a subject matter that is likely to produce more artefactual

116 Ibid., p. 263.
117 Ibid., p. 229.
118 Ibid., p. 278.
119 Ibid., p. 263.
120 Ibid., p. 275.
121 Ibid., p. 275.
122 Ibid., p. 279.

material and less historic material than most current battlefield studies. Naseby, while not presenting a coherently accurate representation of the archaeological yield and nature of finds due to varying survey techniques, clearly shows a battle late in the war that ultimately does away with the vagaries of uniform drill in favour of a hybrid, more effective characterisation according to the contemporary tactical limits, a subject deserving of its own research and modelling. While we can obviously make informed generalisations according to particular accumulations that mirror our supposed understanding of tactical formations according to distances and profile, our modelling system prepares us in no way for the unchoreographed level of movement associated with an army routing from the field. In this sense, with such a high level of artefacts and low level survey, there is little spatial analysis we can provide. However, at a lower level is this made any easier?

Conclusion

A study such as this cannot hope to cover or broach every piece of information that the military manual and its use could reveal. However, ordering and collating every single aspect of the soldier's life and existence, the military manual provides a valuable insight into life on the battlefield and if exploited correctly, can reveal a huge amount more about what these actions left behind. Through integrating programmes like Geographical Information Systems, available maps, metal detector finds, landscape regression and presumed distribution and extent of battle lines according to written accounts and historical interpretation, with developmental movement and extent of unit movement according to military practice of the time accounted for, the boundary rationale for historic battlefields might be improved. Rather than creating a static landscape filled with ruins and graves, it can become a place where the ebb and flow of history is clearly discernible and forces the clear portrayal of the landscape as we see it today. Such actions can further break down parts of the battlefield to include zones of influence relating to differing characterisation of actions. This allows different preservation rationale to be implemented to further preserve their remains but also extend the frequency of low level investigation to allow wider interpretation on these sites. This method of battlefield investigation has the scope to move interpretation of the typical battlefield from the blank field to a space where a number of ephemeral actions take place, in essence bringing these actions into contemporary consciousness.

Part III

Medicine and Welfare – Human and Equine

6

Ground-breaking pioneers or dangerous amateurs?
Did early modern surgery have any basis in medical science?

Dr Stephen M. Rutherford

Introduction

One of the key tenets for modern medical practice is the importance of 'Evidence-based Medicine', the foundation of medical practice on systematic clinical experience and empirical evidence of effective outcomes.[1] The concept of evidence-based medicine as a defined construct is relatively new, being developed in the 1990s, although using an evidence-base for medical practice is not in itself a recent phenomenon.[2] It is a common misconception, however, that evidence-based medical practice was absent from medical practice prior to the nineteenth century.

Early modern surgeons and physicians have a generally poor and unflattering image in the popular imagination. Anecdotes and tales of superstitious treatments, injudicious use of bloodletting and leeches, and barbaric operations performed without anaesthetic, all in unsanitary conditions, support this image of an ineffective and even dangerous practitioner. In particular, the common perception of medical practitioners in the early modern period precludes the use of effective, evidence-based methodologies; assuming a reliance instead on a reliance on folk medicine and superstitious and/or unproven practices. Indeed, Richard Gabriel in his history of military surgery largely dismisses the seventeenth century surgeon, especially the military surgeon, as being poorly trained, overly reliant on traditional theories and bizarre practices, and lacking in education or skill.[3] Indeed, the most common image used of medical

---

1   R. B. Haynes, P. J. Devereaux and G. H. Guyatt, 'Clinical expertise in the era of evidence-based medicine and patient choice', *EBM Notebook*, 7 (2002), pp. 36-8.
2   G. Guyatt *et al.*, 'Evidence-Based Medicine: A New Approach to Teaching the Practice of Medicine', *Journal of the American Medical Association*, 268 (1992), pp. 2420-5.
3   R. A. Gabriel, *Between Flesh and Steel: A history of military medicine from the middle ages to the war in Afghanistan* (Washington D.C., Potomac Books: 2013), pp. 65-85.

practitioners from this period, seen almost ubiquitously in museum displays and text-books alike, is the bird-beaked hood of the mid-seventeenth century plague doctor, an image which emphasises superstitious beliefs and practices. Yet a study of the writings of the practitioners themselves argues against this unfavourable image.

Surgeons, especially those involved in military conflict, have been at the forefront of medical innovation for many centuries.[4] It is a cliché that war drives innovation, but in the case of surgery this is certainly true. Roman and Greek military surgeons were accounted to be at the forefront of their fields, whilst the Crusades too led to the development of many effective techniques (principally through interactions with better-educated and more-effective Islamic physicians).[5] Even in more recent years, the Crimean War and American Civil War accelerated advances in anaesthetic use, amputation, and casualty care and processing.[6] The First and Second World Wars included significant advances in treatment of shock, reconstructive surgery, treatment of deep tissue wounds and blood transfusion, the use of sulphonamide drugs and antibiotics to combat infection, and treatment of post-traumatic stress disorder (shell shock).[7] Advances in surgical techniques, investigative procedures, blood diagnostic tests, casualty evacuation and battlefield first aid in Korea and Vietnam, and more recently in Iraq and Afghanistan, have all had impacts upon civilian medicine.[8] The seventeenth century seems to have been no exception.

4   P. B. Adamson, 'The military surgeon: his place in history', *Journal of the Royal Army Medical Corps*, 128 (1982), pp. 43-50; N. M. Rich, 'Military Surgeons and Surgeons in the Military', *Journal of the American College of Surgeons*, 220 (2015), pp. 127-35; B. A. Pruitt, 'Combat Casualty Care and Surgical Progress'. *Annals of Surgery*, 243 (2006), pp. 715-29.
5   Ibid., pp. 715-29; D. Dobanovački *et al.*, 'Surgery Before Common Era', *History of Medicine*, 20 (2012), pp. 28-35; P. D. Mitchell, *Medicine in the Crusades* (Cambridge, Cambridge University Press: 2004) pp. 31-40.
6   Gabriel, *Between Flesh and Steel*, pp. 133-7; M. M. Manring, A. Hawk, J. H. Calhoun and R. C. Andersen, 'Treatment of War Wounds, A historical review', *Clinical Orthopaedics and Related Research*, 467 (2009), pp. 2168-91; J. Laffin, *Combat Surgeons* (Stroud, Sutton: 1999), pp. 177-9; B. A. Pruitt, 'Combat Casualty Care and Surgical Progress', pp. 722-3.
7   R. M. Hardaway, '200 Years of military surgery', *Injury*, 30 (1999), pp. 387-97; T. Scotland and S. Heyes, *War Surgery 1914-18* (Solihull, Helion: 2012), pp. 101-13; B. Pichel, 'Broken faces: reconstructive surgery during and after the Great War', *Endeavour*, 34 (2010), pp. 25-9; L. G. Stansbury and J. R. Hess, 'Blood Transfusion in World War I: The Roles of Lawrence Bruce Robertson and Oswald Hope Robertson in the "Most Important Medical Advance of the War"', *Transfusion Medicine Reviews*, 23 (2009), pp. 232-6; D. B. Hoyt, 'Blood and War – lest we forget', *Journal of the American College of Surgeons*, 209 (2009), pp. 681-6; M. M. Manring, A. Hawk, J. H. Calhoun and R. C. Andersen, 'Treatment of War Wounds, A historical review', *Clinical Orthopaedics and Related Research*, 467 (2009), pp. 2168-91; P. H. Pinkerton, 'Canadian Surgeons and the Introduction of Blood Transfusion in War Surgery', *Transfusion Medicine Reviews*, 22 (2008), pp. 77-86; Laffin, 'Combat Surgeons', pp. 197-208.
8   B. A. Pruitt and T. E. Rasmussen, 'Vietnam (1972) to Afghanistan (2014): The state of military trauma care and research, past to present.', *Journal of Trauma and Acute Care Surgery*, 77 (2014), pp. S57-S65; Scotland and Heyes, *War Surgery*, pp. 51-82; Gabriel,

The impact of the British Civil Wars on the population of the British Isles was far greater than any subsequent conflict, with an estimated population loss of between 3 and 11.57% (compared to 3.04% and 0.64% in the First and Second World Wars respectively).[9] The writings of surgeons involved in the British Civil Wars reveal the extent to which surgery needed to adapt to a sudden and intense change in the requirements of medical practice. Weaponry in the seventeenth century was highly effective. A musket ball could pierce a steel breastplate or helmet, a sword cut could sever a limb, or at least cut straight to the bone.[10] Musket butts, heavy wooden stocks bound in iron, were favoured as a weapon of choice by Civil War musketeers when engaging in close-quarter combat and would result in concussion, craniofacial injuries, or other fractures.[11] Casualty numbers were high both in major conflicts and localised skirmishes. Yet there are examples of soldiers in the British Civil Wars who survived severe injuries, which does suggest that for some soldiers at least, medical care was effective. Such medical care would primarily be at the hands of the Surgeon, either one attached to the military unit or a civilian.[12] As the wars proceeded, these surgeons were able to practice their medical skills on a variety of patients with diverse and exceptional injuries, and thus many gained reputations as being highly effective. Moreover, the repetitious nature of many such injuries meant that a military surgeon would be able to observe the effects of their treatments on a large number of patients, therefore providing the environment for the development of an evidence-based approach to their practice.

This chapter will argue that far from being untrained and dangerous charlatans, military surgeons in the Civil Wars were potentially highly-skilled and well-trained individuals, despite their often lowly beginnings and lack of formal medical education. Indeed, this chapter will propose that many of the key approaches in contemporary surgery and medical care originate from the early modern period, in concert

---

Between Flesh and Steel, pp. 235-6; S. P. Cohen, C. Brown, C. Kurihara, A. Plunkett, C. Nguyen and S. A. Strassels, 'Diagnoses and factors associated with medical evacuation and return to duty for service members participating in Operation Iraqi Freedom or Operation Enduring Freedom: a prospective cohort study', *Lancet*, 375 (2010), pp. 301–9; D. Trunkey, 'Changes in Combat Casualty Care', *Journal of the American College of Surgeons*, 214 (2012), 879-91; A. Ramasamy, D. E. Hinsley, D. S. Edwards, M. P. M. Stewart, M. Midwinter, P. J. Parker, 'Skill sets and competencies for the modern military surgeon: Lessons from UK military operations in Southern Afghanistan.', *Injury*, 41 (2010), pp. 453–9.

9   I. Gentles, *The English Revolution and the Wars in the Three Kingdoms, 1638-1652* (London, Routledge: 2007), pp. 433-4; C. Carlton, cited in E. Gruber von Arni, *Justice for the Maimed Soldier* (Aldershot, Ashgate: 2001), p. 10.

10   A. Williams, D. Edge and T. Atkins, 'Bullet dents – "Proof Marks" or battle damage?', *Gladius*, 26 (2006), pp. 175-206, at p. 176 ; V. Florato, A. Boylston and C. Knüsel, eds, *Blood Red Roses: The archaeology of a mass grave from the Battle of Towton AD 1461* (Oxford, Oxbow Books: 2007), pp. 91-2.

11   R. Wiseman, *Severall Chirurgical Treatises* (London: 1676), p. 400.

12   Gruber von Arni, *Justice for the Maimed Soldier*, pp. 8 and 27.

with other scientific developments. Few, if any, paradigm-shifting breakthroughs in surgery or medical practice were made after the early modern period until the discovery of bacteria as a causative agent of disease and the development of anaesthetics in the mid-nineteenth century, safe and effective blood transfusions in the early twentieth century, and the development of antibiotics in the 1920s and 1930s. Far from being 'quacks', the surgeons of the early modern period, especially those who learned their trades in the conflicts of the Civil Wars, were pioneers of medical practice, with good understandings of physiology, anatomy, antiseptics, infection control and pharmacology, and much of their practice is still in evidence today with only modest refinements. In particular, this chapter aims to present evidence to show that practitioners in this period exhibited evidence-based practice. By making comparisons to later developments in history, this chapter aims to show that key methodologies of Civil War surgeons were forward-thinking and based on scientific principles and evidence-based methodology.

Medical Practitioners in the Seventeenth Century

There were three major branches of medical practice in the British Isles, and indeed most of Europe, during the early modern period: Physicians, apothecaries, and surgeons/barber-surgeons.[13] Added to this were local cunning men and women, as well as nursing practitioners (nursing also being considerably more advanced than is commonly assumed).[14] The definition between these three practitioners was significant.

Physicians were typically highly-educated individuals (primarily through a university education, often at a continental institution) whose primary focus was on *physic*, the maintenance of the internal workings of the body, bodily homeostasis and treatment of congenital conditions and diseases. The apothecary was the equivalent in many ways of the modern pharmacist, dispensing not only the chemicals prescribed by the physician but also offering inexpensive medical advice of their own to those who could not afford the fees of a physician.[15]

The surgeon's purview was invasive operations, the treatment of external ailments, wounds, fractures and the removal of bodily parts, as well as the letting of blood, application of enemas, some gynaecology and dentistry.[16] They were forbidden by

---

13   A. W. Sloan, *English Medicine in the Seventeenth Century* (Oreston, Carnegie: 1996), pp. 2-8.
14   Gruber von Arni, *Justice for the Maimed Soldier*, p.103-4 and 148-51.
15   Sloan, *English Medicine*, pp. 4-6 and 92-6; R. Jütte, 'A Seventeenth-Century German Barber-surgeon and his Patients', *Medical History*, 33 (1989), pp. 184-98, at p. 189.
16   L. McCray Beier, *Sufferers and Healers: The experience of illness in seventeenth-century England* (London, Routledge: 1987), pp. 12-13; A. L. Wyman, 'The surgeoness: the female practitioner of surgery 1400–1800', *Medical History*, 28 (1984), pp. 22-41, at p. 29. J. Cooke, *Mellificium Chirurgiae, or the Marrow of Chirurgery much enlarged, to which is added Anatomy* (London: 1676), p. 73.

law from treating the inner workings of the body.[17] As his role involved surgical activities undertaken without anaesthetic, the surgeon had a general reputation as being somewhat of a butcher and was feared accordingly. It is also worth noting that there were also examples of women as surgeons, some of whom were licenced by local guilds.[18] In some cases, through much of the medieval and early modern period, the surgeon was also a barber, hence the common term barber-surgeon. However, in England for much of the medieval period there were two distinct professions: the more-educated master surgeons and the less-formally-educated barber-surgeon, until the two were united by the Royal Charter of Henry VIII in 1540.[19] As the status of the profession increased in England and Scotland through the sixteenth century (the barber-surgeons achieved guild status in England in 1540 and in Edinburgh by 1505) and into the seventeenth century, the two aspects of the profession gradually split apart (a separation already observed in the College of Physicians and Surgeons of Glasgow, founded in 1519, which received Royal Charter in 1599, and which excluded barbers).[20] The schism between barbers and surgeons was finalised with the creation of the College of Surgeons in 1745 in England (granted the Royal Charter in 1800)[21] and The Royal College of Surgeons of the City of Edinburgh in 1778.[22] Within the London Company of Barber-Surgeons, during the mid-seventeenth century the two roles were quite distinct from each other, as shown by barbers and surgeons taking it in turns each year to be master of the Company of Barber-Surgeons.[23]

Unlike their physician peers, surgeons would not typically have been educated at University, but rather by apprenticeship to a senior practitioner, followed by an examination for obtaining a Guild licence, with the degree of challenge of that examination

---

17   Ibid., p. 12. Indeed the Company of Barber-Surgeons petitioned Parliament in 1624 for the right to be able to practice internal medicine, despite the monopoly the physicians had on that branch of medical practice: Anon, *To the most Honourable House of Commons, commonly called, the Lower House of Parliament. The humble petition of the masters or gouernors of the mysterie and comminaltie of barbers and chirurgions of London* (London: 1624).

18   Wyman, 'The surgeoness: the female practitioner of surgery 1400–1800', *Medical History*, 28 (1984), pp. 22-41.

19   J. Dobson, 'Barber into surgeon', *Annals of the Royal College of Surgeons of England*, 54 (1974), pp. 84-91, at pp. 84-5.

20   J. O. Robinson, 'The barber-surgeons of London', *Archives of Surgery*, 119 (1984), pp. 1171-5; I. MacLaren, 'A Brief History of the Royal College of Surgeons of Edinburgh', *Res Medica*, 268 (2005), pp. 55-56; J. Geyer-Kordesch and F. Macdonald, *The History of the Royal College of Physicians and Surgeons of Glasgow: Physicians and Surgeons in Glasgow, 1599-1858* (London, Hambledon Press: 1999), pp. ix-x.

21   Dobson, 'Barber into surgeon', p. 91.

22   MacLaren, 'Brief History', p. 56.

23   A. Griffin, 'Clowes, William, (1582–1648)', *Oxford Dictionary of National Biography* (Oxford, Oxford University Press: 2008), online edn, http://www.oxforddnb.com/view/article/5717.

varying depending on the nature of the licence.[24] The surgeon was also required to be licenced by the Church, usually *via* the office of the local bishop.[25] Regarding military surgeons, each regiment would likely have been allocated at least one surgeon (Gruber von Arni lists the names of the Surgeons noted for the regiments in Scotland in 1651-9, for example).[26] The records of various seventeenth century garrisons noted by Gruber von Arni in the Caribbean campaigns frequently note the presence of a surgeon general, master surgeon, surgeons and/or surgeons' mates; the latter being assistants and often apprentices or journeymen to the more senior practitioner(s).[27] Being of lesser status, the civilian surgeon would have been paid less than the physician.[28] However, within the army, the pay of surgeons and physicians appears to have been relatively similar, although they also appear to have charged for individual services outside of their standard remit, which would suggest that they supplemented their income with private work, even when salaried by the army.[29]

Communication within the profession is evident.[30] Discussion of published works and papers took place within the professional bodies of surgeons, as evidenced by William Clowes, son of the eminent naval surgeon, who introduced a ruling to the London Company of Barber-Surgeons in 1641 that lectures on surgery were to be read by approved surgeons only.[31] Works by William Clowes and John Woodall were aimed specifically at training younger surgeons, suggesting a collegiate environment within the profession.[32] The establishment of guilds of surgeons therefore suggests that there was a good level of communication between practitioners and potentially central repositories for printed works, as well as the sharing of experiences and ideas. The guilds also regulated the practice of their members; the Barber-Surgeons of York

---

24 McCray Beier, *Sufferers and Healers*, p. 12; Dobson, 'Barber into surgeon', p. 85; R. Magee, 'Medical practice and medical education 1500–2001: An overview', *Australia and New Zealand Journal of Surgery*, 74 (2004), pp. 272–6, at p. 275.

25 Dobson, 'Barber into surgeon', p. 85; McCray Beier, *Sufferers and Healers*, pp. 12-13.

26 Gruber von Arni, *Justice for the Maimed Soldier*, p. 228-31.

27 Ibid., pp. 8 and 34; E. Gruber Von Arni, *Justice to the Maimed Soldier, Vol. 2* (Nottingham, Caliver: 2015), pp. 22 and 62.

28 Ibid., p. 22-23; Jütte, 'A Seventeenth-Century German Barber-surgeon and his Patients', p. 189.

29 Gruber von Arni, *Justice for the Maimed Soldier*, pp. 8 and 54.

30 M. McVaugh, 'Richard Wiseman and the Medical Practitioners of Restoration London', *Journal of the History of Medicine*, 62 (2007), pp. 125-140, at pp. 129 and 131-2.

31 A. Griffin, 'Clowes, William, (1582–1648)', *Oxford Dictionary of National Biography* (Oxford, Oxford University Press: 2008), online edn, http://www.oxforddnb.com/view/article/5717.

32 As noted on the Prefaces of: A. Paré (transl. W. Hammond), *The Method of Curing Wounds made by Gun-shot. Also by Arrowes and Darts, with their Accidents* (London; 1617); H. C., *An Explanation of the Fashion and use of Three and fifty instruments of chirurgery* (London, 1631); H. Crooke (transl.), 'Μικροκοσμογραφια: A description of the Body of Man, together with the controversies thereto belonging' (London: 1631).

were regulated by the 'Searchers', formal officers of the Guild who would inspect the practice of practitioners in the city; a similar approach was noted on the Continent.[33]

Another aspect of significance for surgeons in the mid-seventeenth century was the intellectual environment of the time, especially in England. The seventeenth century, as well as being a period of considerable social and religious upheaval, was also a century in which science and medical understanding flourished. Courtier, poet and scientist Sir Francis Bacon (d. 1626) is largely credited with setting up the foundations of the scientific revolution in the British Isles, foundations which were then built upon with the foundation of the Royal Society in 1660. Leading natural philosophers of the time, such as Johnson, Harvey, Hooke and Boyle in England, as well as Fabry and Descartes in mainland Europe, began to make significant breakthroughs in chemistry, biology, medicine and physiology. In particular, physiology (although not yet termed as such) was gaining in momentum, leading some to begin to challenge the supremacy of Galen's theories on the workings of the body.[34] For example, William Harvey's treatise on the circulatory system (*Exercitatio Anatomica de Motu Cordis et Sanguinis in Animalibus*) was published in 1628, revolutionising the understanding of the human body, as did Francis Glisson's monograph on liver structure, *Anatomia hepatis*, published in 1654.

Anatomy too was fast becoming a mainstream science throughout the seventeenth century. Wholescale dissection of cadavers was formally authorised by Pope Clement VII in 1537, though it had been an occasional practice in key medical universities since the early fourteenth century, and so may already have been accepted practice in England before the split from Rome. Cadaveric dissection rose in popularity across Europe after Vesalius's pioneering work, *De humani corporis fabrica*, was published in the mid-sixteenth century. Both physicians and surgeons were keen to learn from the dissection of corpses and the College of Physicians but the Company of Barber Surgeons being the only two bodies permitted to undertake cadaveric dissection.[35] The surgeons' study of anatomy by dissection was codified in the charter of Henry VIII which established the London Company of Barber-Surgeons, who were granted four bodies of criminals per year to anatomise.[36] Though the conveyance of the criminal's

33   M. C. Barnett, 'The Barber-Surgeons of York', *Medical History*, 12 (1968), pp. 19-30, at pp. 21-2, 26 and 30; Jütte, 'A Seventeenth-Century German Barber-surgeon and his Patients', pp. 188 and 194-5.

34   T. Gale, *Certain works of Galens, called Methodus Medendi* (London: 1586).

35   S. B. Ghosh, 'Human cadaveric dissection: a historical account from ancient Greece to the modern era', *Anatomy and Cell Biology*, 48 (2015), pp. 153-69, at p. 158.

36   J. O. Robinson, 'The barber-surgeons of London', *Archives of Surgery*, 119 (1984), pp. 1171-5, at p. 1174; R. M. Ward, 'The Criminal Corpse, Anatomists and the Criminal Law: Parliamentary Attempts to Extend the Dissection of Offenders in Late Eighteenth-Century England', *Journal of British Studies*, 54 (2015), pp. 63–87, at p. 64; Ghosh, 'Human cadaveric dissection: a historical account from ancient Greece to the modern era', p. 159.

corpse to the anatomists was not always an easy one, and the crowd would on occasion remove the body before it could be transported away.[37]

By the mid-seventeenth century, dissective anatomy appears to have been accepted as commonplace for such practitioners. For example, the pages of 'The Printer to the Reader' immediately preceding the preface of the 1631 English extract by 'H. C.'[38] of Ambroise Paré's writings in *An Explanation of the Fashion and Use of Three and Fifty Instruments of Chirurgery* describe the body of a monstrously misshapen convict executed (ironically for the murder of the son of a Master Surgeon) in 1629 brought to the College of Physicians to be 'Cut vp for an Anatomy'.[39] In a pamphlet reporting the unsuccessful execution of Anne Greene in Oxford 1651, it is mentioned in a matter-of-fact manner that her body was taken, once hanged, to 'the College of Physicians, where all the learned Doctors and Chyrurgions [Surgeons] met to anatomise her'.[40] The event was only noted because, much to the surprise of the would-be anatomists, Anne's supposed corpse woke up when placed upon the anatomists' table! However, the casual manner in which the article refers to the fate of her body suggests that anatomical analysis by physicians and surgeons was common practice.

The level of anatomical knowledge evident in the various surgical treatises is significantly high, suggesting that the authors availed themselves of this learning opportunity, or had learned incidentally on-the-job. James Cooke's book, *The Marrow of Chirurgery*, contains an extensive, detailed and accurate section on human anatomy, whilst the translation of J. Berengarius's anatomical treatise Μικροκοσμογραφια [*Microcosmographia*]: *A description of the Body of Man* (published in English in 1664) was dedicated to the London Company of Barber-Surgeons, presumably to facilitate the training of their members.[41] Seminal works, such as those by Vesalius in his *De humani corporis fabrica*, whilst being far from cheap, had been available since the mid-sixteenth century (although there was no translation from the Latin of Vesalius's work at the time).[42] The level of anatomical knowledge, such as the blood vessels within the

---

37　Dobson, 'Barber into surgeon', pp. 88-9.
38　'H. C.' is Helkiah Crooke, Doctor of Physick, who translated several other surgical and anatomical texts of the period, such as Μικροκοσμογραφια: *A description of the Body of Man, together with the controversies thereto belonging* (London: 1631), a combination of the works of several authors but especially Gasper Bauinus and Andréas Laurentius, and 'σοματογραφια ανθροπινε [*somatograpia anthropine*]. Or A description of the body of man With the practise of chirurgery, and the use of three and fifty instruments. By artificiall figures representing the members, and fit termes expressing the same. Set forth either to pleasure or to profit those who are addicted to this study* (London: 1634).
39　H. C., *Explanation of the Fashion*, 'The Printer to the Reader'.
40　Anon., *A declaration from Oxford, of Anne Green a young woman that was lately, and unjustly hanged in the Castle-yard* (London: 1651), title page.
41　J. Cooke, *Mellificium Chirurgiae, or the Marrow of Chirurgery much enlarged, to which is added Anatomy* (London: 1676), pp. 305-48 and 377-442; Crooke, 'Μικροκοσμογραφια, pp. 95-156.
42　The first edition was published in 1543, the second edition in 1555.

body, the anatomy of ligaments, tendons and nerves, as well as the musculoskeletal system appear to be well-known to the authors of the surgical various texts.[43]

More significantly, understanding the roles of these structures, and how to treat damage to them, is also evident, such as the importance of avoiding trapping nerves or tendons during medical procedures[44] or of the significance of tendons and ligaments to the functioning of muscle and joints.[45] It is not unreasonable, therefore, to assume that many Surgeons, certainly in the mid- to latter-part of the seventeenth century, and especially in the major urban centres such as London and Edinburgh, would likely have been well-versed in anatomy, physiology and the workings of the human body in general.

Pioneering Surgeons of Note

This chapter will focus on the published works of several surgeons in the British Isles and mainland Europe as evidence for practice. In particular, there were a small number of highly influential individuals who published works of significance and longevity. Arguably the cornerstone of many surgical developments in this period was the works of Ambroise Paré (1510-1590), a French barber-surgeon active in the army during the mid-sixteenth century and surgeon to the kings of France from Henri II to Henri III.[46] Paré was highly respected, sufficiently so for Charles IX to reportedly have hidden him in a closet for safety during the St Bartholomew's Day massacre, for fear that his suspected Huguenot leanings would result in his murder.[47] Paré has been credited with several advances in surgery, pathology, orthopaedics and forensics, and

43   For example, a detailed description of the musculoskeletal system and circulatory system is included in Cooke, *Mellificium Chirurgiae*, pp. 424 and 411, respectively; Crooke, Μικροκοσμογραφια, pp. 96-160; H. Crooke (transl.), σοματογραφια ανθροπινε [*somatograpia anthropine*]. Or *A description of the body of man With the practise of chirurgery, and the use of three and fifty instruments. By artificiall figures representing the members, and fit termes expressing the same. Set forth either to pleasure or to profit those who are addicted to this study* (London: 1634), pp. 1-105; T. Johnson (transl.), *The workes of that famous chirurgion Ambrose Parey translated out of the Latine and compared with the French* (London: 1634), pp. 60-194.
44   'In the work of Extraction, take great care you lay not hold of some Nerve or Tendon, and so pluck them along with the Bullet': Wiseman, *Severall Chirurgical Treatises*, p. 412.
45   Wiseman, *Severall Chirurgical Treatises*, pp. 357-61; Cooke, *Mellificium Chirurgiae*, p. 434; Crooke, Μικροκοσμογραφια, pp. 907-25.
46   C. B. Drucker, 'Ambroise Paré and the Birth of the Gentle Art of Surgery', *Yale Journal of Biology and Medicine*, 81 (2008), pp. 199-202; P. K. Goya and A. N. Williams, '"To illustrate and increase Chyrurgerie": Ambroise Paré (1510-1590)', *Journal of Pediatric Surgery*, 45 (2010), pp. 2108-14.
47   According to Maximilien de Béthune, 1st Duke of Sully, Henri IV's Prime Minister; cited in P. Hernigou, 'Ambroise Paré's life (1510–1590): part I', *International Orthopaedics*, 37 (2013), pp. 543–7, at p. 546.

several of his works were translated into other languages.[48] His *Three and fifty instruments of chirurgery* was published in London in 1631 and therefore may have had a significant impact on the practice of surgeons in the mid-seventeenth century British Isles. Another documented surgeon from the Continent was Johannes Scultetus (or Schultheiss, 1595–1645), one of the first known trained surgeons in the German region (originally from Ulm, trained at Padua) and a surgeon during the Thirty Years War.[49] Scultetus was an expert in cancer surgery and developed the 'Scultetus binder' or 'many-tailed binder', a method of binding the body after surgery (for example after a mastectomy or abdominal hernia) to relieve tension on the wound, a method which remains in clinical use today.[50] Scultetus's work, the *Armamentarium chirurgicum*, was published posthumously and translated into numerous languages. It remained popular for decades, having a major impact on the education of barber-surgeons in many regions.[51] Scultetus himself was a strong advocate of better training for surgeons and barber-surgeons.[52] The *Armamentarium chirurgicum* contains over 100 individual examples of patients treated, making his book highly evidence-based.

There were also very notable practitioners in the British Isles during the late sixteenth and early seventeenth centuries. Thomas Gale (1507–1567) was a surgeon in the armies of Henry VIII (1544) and later Phillip II (1557), and was elected master of the London Company of Barber-Surgeons in 1561.[53] Gale was the author of *Certaine workes of chirurgie* (1563), the first printed surgical treatise to be written in English. Two surgeons of significant note in the latter part of the sixteenth and early seventeenth centuries were William Clowes (1543/4–1604) and John Woodall (1570–1643), each of whom had strong links to naval surgery, the former as part of Elizabeth I's navy (active during the Spanish Armada), the latter as Surgeon General of the East India Company.[54] Both developed ideas about treating scurvy and similar implications of long sea journeys and naval warfare. Clowes's *A Proved Practice for All Young*

48   P. Hernigou, 'Ambroise Paré III: Paré's contributions to surgical instruments and surgical instruments at the time of Ambroise Paré', *International Orthopaedics*, 37 (2013), pp. 975-80.

49   A. H. Scultetus, J. L. Villavicencio and N. M. Rich, 'The Life and Work of the German Physician Johannes Scultetus (1595–1645)', *Journal of the American College of Surgeons*, 196 (2003), pp. 130-9.

50   Ibid., pp. 136 and 137-8.

51   D. Schultheiss and U. Jonas, 'Johannes Scultetus (1595-1645). Urologic aspects in the 'Armamentarium chirurgicum'', *European Urology*, 34 (1998), pp. 520-5.

52   Scultetus, Villavicencio and Rich, 'Life and Work', pp. 132.

53   M. Satchell, 'Gale, Thomas (c.1507-1567)', *Oxford Dictionary of National Biography* (Oxford, Oxford University Press: 2008), online edn, http://www.oxforddnb.com/view/article/10297.

54   I. G. Murray, 'Clowes, William (1543/4–1604)', *Oxford Dictionary of National Biography* (Oxford, Oxford University Press: 2008), online edn, http://www.oxforddnb.com/view/article/5716; J. H. Appleby, 'Woodall, John (1570–1643)', *Oxford Dictionary of National Biography* (Oxford, Oxford University Press: 2008), online edn, http://www.oxforddnb.com/view/article/29902.

Surgeons was aimed at developing the skills of his peers, and he was a fierce propo-
nent for better standards in the (what he claimed at the time was a poorly-trained
and poorly-regulated) surgical profession. *The Surgions Mate*, published by Woodall in
1617, was targeted towards young naval surgeons and extremely influential.

There are there are two published surgeons from the Civil War period and beyond,
who are of prime significance to this paper. James Cooke (d. 1693-4) was surgeon to
Robert Greville, Lord Brooke, during the First Civil War (prior to Brooke's death
in 1643) and of other notables in Warwick during and after the Civil Wars.[55] Cooke
published several texts, *Mellficium chirurgiae, or the marrow of many good authors,
wherein is handled the Art of Chirurgery* in 1648, *Mellficium chirurgiae, or the Marrow
of Chirurgery* in 1655 and *Select observations on English bodies*. In 1657. The *Marrow
of Chirurgery* was reprinted six times until 1717, showing the longevity of his works.
Cooke's *Select observations on English Bodies* was based on the papers of the late Dr
John Hall, purchased from Hall's widow (William Shakespeare's daughter Susannah)
sometime between Hall's death in 1639 and her own in 1649.[56] This extensive collection of medical records is likely to have impacted on Cooke's own knowledge base and
informed his own medical practice.

The final major contributor whose practice informs this analysis is Richard
Wiseman, surgeon to the prince of Wales during the Civil Wars, including the battle
of Worcester in 1651, and sergeant surgeon to Charles as king after the Restoration.[57]
Wiseman's publications, *A Treatise of Wounds* in 1672 and his major work *Severall
Chirurgicall Treatise*s in 1676 (later renamed *Eight Chirurgical Tre*atises in 1696) were
of significant impact, the latter receiving five reprints up to 1734.[58] James Kirkup
describes Wiseman as bridging 'the gap between military and naval wound surgeons
of former generations and emergent civil surgeons'.[59] The key feature of Wiseman's
work, as with that of Cooke (though to a much greater extent than Cooke), is the

55   S. Wright, 'Cook, James (1571/2–1610)', *Oxford Dictionary of National Biography* (Oxford,
     Oxford University Press: 2004) online edn, http://www.oxforddnb.com/view/article/6139.
56   R. A. Cohen, 'Documents concerning James Cooke, surgeon, of Warwick', *Medical History*,
     1 (1957), pp. 168-73, at p. 168.
57   T. Longmore, *Richard Wisman: Surgeon and Sergeant Surgeon to Charles II* (London,
     Longmans, Green & Co: 1891); J. Kirkup, 'Wiseman, Richard (bap. 1620?, d. 1676)',
     Oxford Dictionary of National Biography (Oxford, Oxford University Press: 2008), online
     edn, http://www.oxforddnb.com/view/article/29792; L. Bakay, 'Richard Wiseman, a
     Royalist Surgeon of the English Civil War', *Surgical Neuroscience*, 27 (1987), pp. 415-18;
     M. McVaugh, 'Richard Wiseman and the Medical Practitioners of Restoration London',
     Journal of the History of Medicine, 62 (2007), pp. 125-40; A. D. Smith, 'Richard Wiseman:
     His Contributions to English Surgery', *Bulletin of New York Academy of Medicine*, 46
     (1970), pp. 167-82.
58   J. Kirkup, 'Wiseman, Richard (bap. 1620?, d. 1676)', *Oxford Dictionary of National
     Biography* (Oxford, Oxford University Press: 2008), online edn, http://www.oxforddnb.
     com/view/article/29792.
59   Ibid.

manner in which he uses case studies to evidence his practice, describing several hundred individual cases from his experience in the Civil Wars and in the Spanish navy. Not all of these case studies are clear successes, which makes Wiseman's approach particularly notable, as he is developing an evidence base for practice which does *not* work, as well as that which works effectively. It is approaches like Wiseman's and Cooke's that suggest that surgical practice in the mid-seventeenth century was not the poorly-evidenced and untrained charlatanry that its popular reputation would imply, but rather evidence-based medicine developed through a mixture of training, learning and trial-and-error.

It should be noted that the approach of this analysis is focused on a small number of practitioners only, and those who were fortunate, connected, or privileged enough to have positions of influence sufficient to enable their work to be published in print. It is likely that these individuals were unusual in their craft by being well-resourced and/or of sufficient skill to be noted by grandees sufficiently to be employed by them. Certainly there would have been a great many surgeons who did not share these fortunate circumstances and it is therefore difficult to generalise the findings presented here as applying to all practitioners of surgery, even those contemporary to the published surgeons. However, none of the authors of these treatises were men who hailed from particularly privileged backgrounds. Most do not appear to have had extensive (indeed any) formal medical education at university but rather learned their trade as apprentices and by experience. It is therefore not unreasonable to conclude that these individuals were not atypical of their peers, at least not to such an extent as to make this analysis invalid.

Key Early Modern Medical Concepts

At first glance, the terminology used by the early modern medical practitioner might seem arcane and their practices not based in any appropriate medical methodology. Whilst some of the superstitions of previous centuries were fading (though not completely lost), some traditional elements were still in evidence, such as the doctrine of signatures (which determined that herbal plants were likely to be shaped according to the part of the body they were designed to heal) and the Four Humours (blood, yellow bile, black bile and phlegm; the balance of which it was important to maintain for good health).[60] The reliance on the humours meant that cupping and bloodletting were still seen as effective medical practice (and remained so well into the nineteenth century). It also led to the terminology of blood flow as being referred to as 'heat' (restricted circulation, for example, leading to a lack of 'heat' to a body part). Similarly, there is some cognitive dissonance in understanding of medical and anatomical aspects. For example, despite an understanding of the nervous system, it was still understood that within the tooth resided a 'worm' (a misunderstood inter-

60   Sloan, *English Medicine*, pp. 25-6.

pretation of the nerve) which was fundamental to tooth pain.[61] Many of the surgical treatises and books of physic of the period contain treatments and recipes for ointments and medicines that cannot have any foundation in evidence-based practice. Yet many methods do appear to be effective and not too dissimilar to contemporary medical practice.

Health and Hygiene for the Common Soldier

The circumstances of a military campaign are unlike those of civilian life, but do have some parallels. Warfare in the mid-seventeenth century would have led to a high proportion of certain wounds: cuts and lacerations from swords, polearms and shrapnel; concussion damage from blows to armour, blunt weapons and impact from explosions; penetrative wounds from pikes and polearms, and gunshot injuries from muskets, pistols and artillery fire. Each of these wound types will be discussed below but first an important focus is on the common health and hygiene of soldiers on campaign. Deaths of military personnel from disease were common, typically plague and water-borne diseases (such as typhoid, dysentery or cholera) in summer, typhus in winter. Malnutrition would also have been a concern for a mobile military unit, as well as vitamin or mineral-related diseases such as scurvy or rickets. These conditions and diseases were significant killers, although many could potentially be avoided.

Several treatises exist that advise simple cautionary approaches that householders and soldiers may take to avoid common camp diseases such as the 'bloody flux' (dysentery) and typhoid,[62] diahorrea,[63] scurvy,[64] typhus,[65] sexually-transmitted diseases[66]

61   Greenspan, *Medicine: Perspectives in History and Art*, pp. 456-8.
62   B. A., '*A sick man's rare jewell*' (London, 1674), pp. 153-5; R. Elkes, *Approved Medicines of Little Cost, to preserve health and also to cure those that are sick*, pp. 21-3; G. Markham, *Countrey Contentments, or The English Huswife, containing The inward and outward Vertues which ought to be in a compleate Woman* (London: 1623), pp. 30-2; K. Digby, *Choice and Experimented Receipts in Physick and Chirurgery* (London: 1675), pp. 9-10 and 13; J. Cooke, *Supplementum Chirurgiae, or the supplement to the Marrow of Chyrurgerie*, (London: 1655), pp. 248 and 337; Cooke, *Mellificium Chirurgiae, or the Marrow of Chirurgery much enlarged*, (1676) p. 311; A. M., *A Rich Closet of Physical Secrets* (London: 1652), pp. 46-7.
63   Cooke, *Mellificium Chirurgiae, or the Marrow of Chirurgery much enlarged* (1676), p. 314; B. A., '*A sick man's rare jewell*' (London: 1674), pp. 156-9; A. M., *A Rich Closet of Physical Secrets* (London: 1652), pp. 44-5.
64   Elkes, *Approved Medicines of Little Cost*, pp. 19-21; B. A., '*A sick man's rare jewell*', pp. 46-50 and 68-81; Digby, *Choice and Experimented Receipts in Physick and Chirurgery*, pp. 23-4; Cooke, *Supplementum Chirurgiae, or the supplement to the Marrow of Chyrurgerie*, pp. 343-4, 350, 352 and 359; A. M., *A Rich Closet of Physical Secrets* (London: 1652), p. 69.
65   Elkes, *Approved Medicines of Little Cost*, pp. 25-6; Markham, *Countrey Contentments, or The English Huswife*, p. 9.
66   Generic term: Lue venerea; Primarily Syphalis, generally referred to as the 'Neopolitan [or Neapolitan] disease', 'French Pox' or 'Spanish Pox'; or Gonorrhoea, also referred to as 'The Clap' or 'Running the Reins'. B. A., '*A sick man's rare jewell*' (London: 1674), pp. 97-118;

and even plague.[67] Many of these remedies or preventative measures have a solid basis in modern medical practice. Richard Elkes's publication, *Approved medicines of little cost*, published in 1651, advised soldiers to carry a piece of iron in their snapsacks, so that it may be heated to red hot in a fire and dropped into water or beer to purify it.[68] Clearly, Elkes knew nothing of the bacteria that boiling water would kill but by empirical observation, it had been recorded that this approach was effective. Boiling water or beer with oak leaves or bark which contains strong tannins and tannic acid as a cure for dysentery.[69] The medicinal properties of tannins and other plant secondary metabolites have shown positive medical potential in recent years.[70] A solid broth of porridge oats is suggested to aid against diahorrea.[71] Elkes claimed two ingredients are useful to help treat the flux: salt and oatmeal. Salt might replace lost electrolytes from the body during diahorrea, oatmeal might help solidify the patient's stool. Elkes also recommended three 'earth remedies', essentially whole or powdered clay, for treating an upset stomach: 'Terra Sigillata (Terra Lemina), Bolarmonicke and Chalke'.[72] *Terra Sigillata* was a clay exported as a medicinal ingredient from the Greek island of Lemnos, *Bolarmonicke* from Spain and chalk was to be found readily all over the British Isles. The calcium, magnesium and silicon in these clays might have helped settle the stomach, much like milk of magnesia today. The recommended use of chalk (calcium carbonate) powdered in a drink to settle the stomach is directly equivalent to modern treatments of indigestion or heartburn.

Another ingredient seems far-fetched at first: dragon's blood. However, this ingredient was actually a resin from various exotic species of tree.[73] Powdered, dragon's blood could be used both as a pigment and a medicine. Thaspine, a key component of dragon's blood resin from the tree species *Croton lechleri*, has been proven to have

---

Cooke, *Mellificium Chirurgiae, or the Marrow of Chirurgery much enlarged* (1676), pp. 759-69 and 769-72; B. A., '*A sick man's rare jewell*', p. 116; Markham, *Countrey Contentments, or The English Huswife*, p. 50; Johnson, *workes of that famous chirurgion Ambrose Parey*, pp. 464-81; A. M., *A Rich Closet of Physical Secrets*, pp. 58-9.

67   Elkes, *Approved Medicines of Little Cost*, pp. 11-15; J. Woodall, *The cure of the plague by an antidote called Aurum Vitae*, (London: 1640); Anon., 'A treatise concerning the plague and the pox', in A. M., *A rich Closet of Physical Secrets* (London: 1652), pp. 1-113; Markham, *Countrey Contentments*, p. 9; Digby, *Choice and Experimented Receipts in Physick and Chirurgery*, pp. 40-3; Cooke, *Supplementum Chirurgiae, or the supplement to the Marrow of Chyrurgerie*, pp. 162-4, 192 and 283-412; Cooke, *Mellificium Chirurgiae, or the Marrow of Chirurgery much enlarged*, (1676) pp. 268 and 277; Johnson, *workes of that famous chirurgion Ambrose Parey*, pp. 535-75.

68   Elkes, *Approved Medicines of Little Cost*, p. 2.

69   Ibid., pp. 2-3.

70   K. T. Chung, T. Y. Wong, C.-I. Wei, Y. W. Huang and Y. Lin, 'Tannins and human health: a review', *Critical Reviews of Food Science and Nutrition*, 38 (1998), pp. 421-64.

71   Elkes, *Approved Medicines of Little Cost*, p. 2.

72   Ibid., p. 3.

73   The rather fanciful name refers to the bright scarlet-crimson hues of the resin, which could be used as a pigment as well as a medicine.

apoptotic properties (promotes cell death) in cancer tissue.[74] However, some of the recipes proposed do seem to be somewhat far-fetched. To protect against the plague, for example, Elkes recommended that one eats a small, walnut-sized amount each day of a paste made of powdered clay, walnuts, salt, figs, birthwort root, pimpernels, sorrel seed, purslane seeds and honey. None of these components have been suggested to have protective properties against *Yersinia pestis*, the bacterium that causes the disease, when ingested in any quantity, let alone one so small. So whilst some of these general remedies have some basis in effective medical practice, they are by no means universally so.

Antibacterial Agents

Even despite some of the more esoteric cures, many of the approaches suggested by these authors involve chemicals or processes that are mirrored today, where the bacterial cause of infection is known. This suggests that a large proportion of the remedies used were based on empirical evidence, rather than historical precedent and superstition. Principal among these are methods taken to either stem infection, or sterilise materials being used. Despite a lack of understanding of bacteria and the causative factors of infection and disease, it is commonplace to find the use of vinegar, red (and to a lesser extent white) wine, high-protein-level compounds (such as egg albumen) and other anti-bacterial compounds, such as poultices or honey.[75]

Vinegar has long been known as a cleaning and antiseptic agent, a 5% solution of acetic acid being an effective antibacterial agent. Vinegar was used in a diluted form either as oxycrate (vinegar/water mix) or as *posca* (an ancient vinegar/oxidised wine mix with water and herbs). The antibacterial properties of these acidic compounds is due to the reducing effect the acid has on bacterial enzymes and membranes.[76] No practitioners in the sixteenth or seventeenth centuries could have known this but clearly empirical evidence suggested that these agents were effective against infection, revealing a strong evidence base to their practice.

Alcohol is another effective antibacterial compound and alcoholic drinks were the preferred form of beverage for the very reason that it did not lead to disease. The use of wine, especially red wine, to soak bandages, 'tents' (rolled bandages used as separators in cut wounds) or swabs to clean wounds is so common in the writings that it suggests a near-ubiquitous usage. The use of red wine is far more common than white, possibly suggesting it was seen as more-effective. An explanation of this observation

74 W. Fayad, M. Fryknäs, S. Brnjic, M. H. Olofsson, R. Larsson, S. Linder, 'Identification of a novel topoisomerase inhibitor effective in cells overexpressing drug efflux transporters', *PLoS ONE*, 4 (2009), e7238.

75 Wiseman, *Severall Chirurgical Treatises*, p. 341.

76 B. S. Nagoba, S. P. Selkar, B. J Wadher and R. C. Gandhi, 'Acetic acid treatment of Pseudomonal wound infections--a review', *Journal of Infection & Public Health*, 6 (2013), pp. 410-15.

could possibly be due to the tannins in red wine, and also potentially due to the presence of resveratrol, an antibacterial and antifungal compound found in the skin of red grapes.[77]

Honey has been used as an antibacterial compound for millennia (there is evidence for its use in ancient Egypt) and has recently seen a resurgence in popularity due to the increase of antibiotic resistance.[78] The concentrated sugars in honey make bacterial survival impossible. Examples of the use of honey include boiling juice of Mullen in honey as a poultice to use on a wound after surgery for cancer, or in the treatment of 'great wounds'.[79] Similarly, high concentrations of protein (such as egg albumen) can have similar effects, and was frequently used as the basis for poultices.

Everyday compounds used in many of the treatments, therefore, did have effective properties and many are still in use today. It is likely that many of the other pharmacopeia and herbal remedies of the period had similarly effective properties, as the majority of modern pharmaceuticals are developed from plant-derived chemicals. Sufficient to say, that even though the practitioners of the time did not understand the mechanisms behind why these antimicrobial compounds worked, they were aware of their effectiveness and had an evidence base from which to base their continual use. The frequency in which they are referred to, and their ubiquity across different practitioners suggests that their use was effective and commonplace, including use of many chemicals that are still utilised today.

Cuts and Lacerations

A common weapon in the British Civil Wars was the sword. Swords were issued to all soldiers, though it was debateable the extent to which the cheap, mass-produced blades issued to common soldiery would have been used effectively. Even low quality blades could cut deeply into unprotected bodies, with good quality blades cutting bone-deep or potentially severing limbs. This was particularly the case for cavalry blades, with the added momentum of the speed of the rider behind them. Such deep

---

77   L. Frémont, 'Biological effects of Resveratrol', *Life Sciences*, 66 (2000), pp. 663-73; N. B. Bottaria *et al.*, 'Synergistic effects of resveratrol (free and inclusion complex) and sulfamethoxazole-trimetropim treatment on pathology, oxidant/antioxidant status and behavior of mice infected with *Toxoplasma gondii*, *Microbial Pathogenesis*, 95 (2016), pp. 166–74.

78   P. H. Kwakman, A. A. Te Velde, L. de Boer, C. M. Vandenbroucke-Grauls, S. A. Zaat, 'Two major medicinal honeys have different mechanisms of bactericidal activity', *PLoS ONE*, 6 (2011), e17709; M. D. Mandal and S. Mandal, 'Honey: its medicinal property and antibacterial activity', *Asian Pacific Journal of Tropical Biomedicine*, 1 (2011), pp. 154–60; N. J. Basson and S. R. Grobler, 'Antimicrobial activity of two South African honeys produced from indigenous Leucospermum cordifolium and Erica species on selected microorganisms', *BMC Complementary and Alternative Medicine*, 8 (2008) pp. 41-4.

79   Wiseman, *Severall Chirurgical Treatises*, pp. 104 and 347.

cuts would require significant medical procedures to close the wound and enable it to heal effectively.

Ligatures and Sutures

The texts have clear guidance for closing cut wounds. Two types of approaches are recommended: the use of ligatures and/or sutures. Ligature, a method of closing a wound by tying rather than stitching, was useful where an anatomical feature (such as a blood vessel or part of the body) required tying-off, or where stitching or suturing would not have been appropriate, possible or effective.[80] Ligatures could be either by a stout thread or a *rowler* (bandage). The basic ligature, the *Glutinative* or *Incarnative* ligature, used for 'simple, greene, and yet bloody wounds', used a bandage with either end wrapped around the body part, starting from the opposite side to the wound, crossing over the wound site, and then back again, secured again at the back to close the edges of the wound.[81] This is warned not to be too tight as to cause inflammation or pain, or so loose as to be ineffective. The second, the *Expulsive* ligature was designed to press out pus from an ulcer or infected wound, using a bandage that was wrapped initially loosely around the body, below the wound or ulcer but then ever tighter and tighter as it moved up over the limb or infected region, until it reached the infected area, thus providing pressure to expel the matter.[82] Finally, the *Retentive* ligature, used for wounds which could not be sutured or bound, or for areas such as the throat or belly, which was again a bandage, with pads beneath it, that pressed down upon the injured area.[83]

Where possible, a suture, or stitch, was used. Wiseman highlighted three types of suture: the *Incarnative*, the *Restringent* and the *Conserver*.[84] The *Incarnative* suture (termed the *Interpunctus* by Paré[85]), used for simple wounds, was a single or multiple whip-stitch, with the spacing of the sutures being the equivalent of a finger's width.[86]

> If the Wound be of two Fingers breadth, make one Stitch in the middle; if three fingers breadth, make two Stitches; if four fingers breadth, three Stitches; and so go on, making a Stitch less then the Wound is in number of fingers. Sometimes in declining Parts we make our Stitches at a little more distance.[87]

---

80   G. Keynes, ed., *The Apologie and Treatise of Ambroise Paré, 1585* (Chicago, University of Chicago Press: 1952), pp. 124-5; Wiseman, *Severall Chirurgical Treatises*, pp. 343-4.
81   Keynes, *Apologie and Treatise of Ambroise Paré*, p. 124.
82   Ibid., pp. 124-5.
83   Ibid., p. 125.
84   Wiseman, *Severall Chirurgical Treatises*, pp. 343-5.
85   H. C., 'Explanation of the Fashion', p12; Keynes, *Apologie and Treatise of Ambroise Paré*, pp. 128-9.
86   Cooke, *Mellificium Chirurgiae*, p. 433; H. C., 'Explanation of the Fashion', pp. 12-13.
87   Wiseman, *Severall Chirurgical Treatises*, p. 344.

This was a quick and strong stitch, made with a needle that had a 'three square point' (much like a modern leather needle) for efficient piercing of the skin, and to prevent ripping.[88] The guidance to space stitches a minimum of a finger's breadth apart is in keeping with the material technology of the time, where making fine steel needles, such as are used today, was not possible. Sutures of one centimetre or more apart were therefore the closest that would be possible when sewing through skin and tissue.

The second stitch, the *Restringent* stitch, useful for removing sutures and for internal wounds such as those of the bowel, was the same as a glover's stitch[89] (indeed Paré referred to it directly as the glover's stitch).[90] This stitch enabled a backbone of thread to follow the line of the wound, making the sutures easier to remove and the scar less noticeable.

The final stitch, the *Conserver*, was used for deep wounds which otherwise would have been too extensive for the sutures to hold without tearing. The stitch was '... made by one or more needles, having threed in them, thrust through the wound, the threed being wrapped to and againe at the head and the point of the needle...'.[91] The stitch could also be used on areas where the flesh was thin or weak, such as cuts to the face or treating a hare lip.[92] The *Conserver* used needles, pins or hardened quills, inserted laterally through the wound. These then had thread tied around them in a figure-of-eight pattern, pulling against the pins to draw the wound closed, rather than the lips of the wound, which would tear if used to close an extensive cut wound. The torsion caused here would support the wound until the flesh began to knit and then the wound itself could be closed by another stitch after this initial stage of healing. Such approaches to healing deep wounds were used in the treatment of deep lacerating wounds in the First World War, in Vietnam and were still in use in more recent military conflicts, such as the First Gulf War. The practice of these early modern surgeons, therefore, was sufficiently effective to have been continued for centuries thereafter.

Paré also defined two additional suture types, the *Gastroraphia*, used for deep belly wounds, and the dry suture, used primarily for cuts to the face.[93] The *Gastrographia* involved extensive packing of the wound as well as suture. The dry suture entailed two strips of linen or buckram glued to the skin on either side of the cut, with the sutures sewn through the cloth rather than through the skin, thus joining the two halves of

---

88   H. C., 'Explanation of the Fashion', pp. 12-14; Keynes, *Apologie and Treatise of Ambroise Paré*, pp. 127-129.
89   The equivalent of a modern 'blanket stitch'.
90   Keynes, *Apologie and Treatise of Ambroise Paré*, pp. 129; H. C., 'Explanation of the Fashion', p. 12.
91   Keynes, *Apologie and Treatise of Ambroise Paré*, p. 129.
92   Cooke, *Mellificium Chirurgiae*, p. 715; H. C., 'Explanation of the Fashion', p.13.
93   Keynes, *Apologie and Treatise of Ambroise Paré*, pp. 129; H. C., 'Explanation of the Fashion', pp. 13-14.

the wound without leaving a disfiguring scar. The surgeons were therefore able to adapt to the fact that their needles were not of fine quality by 21st century standards.

Another type of suture is also mentioned by Paré, who referred to it as the *Seton*.[94] In this treatment, a hole is pierced through the flesh using a red-hot needle or probe. This approach causes an eschar (a form of livid scar tissue) to line the hole, through which thread can be passed to hold the tissue together more-firmly. The *Seton* could then be threaded with a thick thread, linen or wool, in order to drain fluid from the affected area. The *Seton* has a direct modern equivalent in the form of the *shunt*, a fluid drainage tube used in the treatment of swelling, hydrocephalus and even in the treatment of cardiac disease.[95]

An interesting omission in many descriptions of practice is the use of cauterisation: the application of a red-hot cautery (cauterising iron) to sear and seal a wound or a vessel. Common in mediaeval surgery, the use of a cautery is only suggested to be used as a last resort.[96] Even in the repair of blood vessels, a glover's stitch is advised and cauterisation is only used when sutures or plugging the vessel is ineffective or insufficient.[97] Wiseman and Paré are similarly disdainful of the use of hot oil for cauterisation.[98] Indeed, Paré recounted how he accidentally identified that a mixture of egg yolk, rose oil and turpentine was a better means of treating a gunshot wound than boiling oil for cauterisation because he had run out of oil and had to improvise instead.[99] It appears that in the seventeenth century, cauterisation was used only when there was no alternative.

Delayed Primary Closure

One interesting procedure for the treatment of cut wounds appears, at first sight, rather confusing. At first, Wiseman advised, one should clean the wound and let it bleed:

> The weapon thus drawn out, cleanse it from Rags or ought else, and permit the wound to bleed, according to your judgement shall think fit, still having respect to the Constitution and Habit of the body, that what is in the small veins cut

94 Ibid., pp.14-15; Paré, *Method of Curing Wounds*, pp. 52-3.
95 A. K. Toma, M. C. Papadopoulos, S. Stapleton, N. D. Kitchen and L. D. Watkins, 'Systematic review of the outcome of shunt surgery in idiopathic normal-pressure hydrocephalus', *Acta Neurochirurgica*, 155 (2013), pp. 1977-80; S. M. Gifford *et al.*, 'Effect of temporary shunting on extremity vascular injury: An outcome analysis from the Global War on Terror vascular injury initiative', *Journal of Vascular Surgery*, 50 (2009), pp. 549-56.
96 Mitchell, *Medicine in the Crusades*, p. 116; Keynes, *Apologie and Treatise of Ambroise Paré*, p. 137; Cooke, *Mellificium Chirurgiae*, p. 433.
97 Wiseman, *Severall Chirurgical Treatises*, pp. 359 and 409.
98 Ibid., p. 359; Keynes, *Apologie and Treatise of Ambroise Paré*, p. 137.
99 Paré, *Method of Curing Wounds*, pp. 5-6.

asunder may flow out, as well as to hinder inflammation, as the generation of much matter.[100]

By allowing the wound to bleed, potential infectious agents could be removed from the wound site, although this would not be a certain method of removing all risk of infection.

Subsequently, the advice was not to close the wound but instead, to keep it open to the air. A 'tent' (a small rolled-up bandage) could be used to keep the sides of the wound apart until such a time as the surgeon deemed it fit to close the wound.[101] Wiseman advised that the wound be left open until it has the appearance of 'flesh long hang'd in the air'.[102] Paré also advised not to close the wound too soon.[103] Yet, interestingly, Cooke and other treatises did not advise this approach, so it may be that the practice was not universal and that certain military surgeons of the seventeenth century were perhaps pioneers in this practice.

The reason for keeping the wound open is to encourage 'proper digestion' of the wound. In other words, that it should produce pus and otherwise cleanse itself. By leaving the wound open, it encouraged the accumulation of lymph at the wound site and with it, the necessary white blood cells of the immune system to help fight infection. Closing the wound would merely trap the infection within the wound space and lead to sepsis. This approach (more recently termed 'delayed primary closure' or 'delayed primary suture') therefore accommodated for the lack of antibiotics in the fight against wound infection and was an approach that has remained in evidence ever since. In the Crimean War, George Husband Baird MacLeod recommended that wounds should be left open until 'all oozing has ceased from the cut surfaces'.[104] In the First World War, the approach for healing deep and infected wounds was to place the patient on a mattress that had been covered with a rubber sheet, then to drip sterile saline solution, or Dakin's Solution,[105] through the wound, drawn out by a muslin 'wick' on the lower side of the wound, much to the same effect.[106] Similar approaches were used in the Second World War. In his surgical manual, W. H. Ogilvie also advised that the wound be cleaned and packed with dressing/gauze soaked with 1/1000 flavine solution, then covered for 48-72 hours until it was 'pale and picked,

100 Wiseman, *Severall Chirurgical Treatises*, p. 341.
101 Paré, *Method of Curing Wounds*, p. 63.
102 Wiseman, *Severall Chirurgical Treatises*, p. 349
103 Keynes, *Apologie and Treatise of Ambroise Paré*, pp. 124-5; Wiseman, *Severall Chirurgical Treatises*, p. 325.
104 G. H. B. MacLeod, *Notes in the Surgery of the War in the Crimea; with remarks on the treatment of gunshot wounds* (London, Churchill: 1858), pp. 392 (see also pp. 322 and 352).
105 Dakin's solution, also known as 'Carrel–Dakin fluid', was a dilute solution of sodium hypochlorite (bleach; 0.4–0.5% v/v) and boric acid (4% v/v); Gabriel, *Between Flesh and Steel: A history of military medicine from the middle ages to the war in Afghanistan*, p. p217.
106 Scotland and Heyes, *War Surgery*, p. 68; D. P. Penhallow, *Military Surgery* (London, Oxford University Press: 1916), p. 73.

like salt beef'.[107] Ogilvie even goes so far as to name premature closure of the wound by suturing as the first of his '7 deadly sins of field surgery'.[108] Delayed primary closure has continued to be used even long after the development of antibiotics as a means to deal with wound infection, in Korea, Vietnam, in the Gulf and in civilian surgery, such as treating compartment syndrome and appendicitis.[109]

The use of delayed primary closure not only displays the competence of the seventeenth century practitioners but also highlights their understanding of the progress and impact of infection. It was to be another two centuries before bacteria were first identified as the causative agents of infection by Koch and others. Yet, the importance of cleansing the wound, or allowing it to cleanse itself, was clearly evident. The frequent advice for the use of 'rowlers' (bandages) that had been soaked in red wine or vinegar also shows that the authors understood the significance of antiseptic agents, though without any knowledge of the biochemical nature of their effects. The knowledge base of these practitioners, therefore, was far from basic when it came to wound treatment and aftercare. In the absence of a proper understanding of the causes of infection, or access to antimicrobial drugs, their approaches are quite remarkable and were probably highly effective. The need to cleanse the wound and to remove all foreign (and therefore potentially infectious) material from it was also highlighted in the other major wound form of the Civil Wars: gunshot wounds.

Gunshot Wounds

One of the characteristics of the Civil Wars, in contrast to most previous major conflicts within the British Isles, was the prevalence of small arms fire from muskets. Naval surgeons had needed to combat injuries sustained from firearms for well over a

107 W. H. Ogilvie, *Forward Surgery in Modern War* (London, Butterworth: 1944), p. 26.
108 Ibid. p. 32.
109 T. E. Rasmussen and R. M. Tai, *Rich's Vascular Surgery* (London, Elsevier Life Sciences: 2016), p. 9; V. E. Burkhalter, B. Butler, W. Metz, and G. Omer, 'Experiences with Delayed Primary Closure of War Wounds of the Hand in Viet Nam', *Journal of Bone and Joint Surgery*, 50A (1968), pp. 945-54; B. E. Leininger, T. E. Rasmussen, D. L. Smith, D. Jenkins and C. Coppola, 'Experience with Wound VAC and Delayed Primary Closure of Contaminated Soft Tissue Injuries in Iraq', *Journal of Trauma Injury, Infection, and Critical Care*, 61 (2006), pp. 1207-11; N. Chiverton and J. F. Redden, 'A new technique for delayed primary closure of fasciotomy wounds'. *Injury*, 31 (2000), pp. 21-4; J. Harrah, R. Gates, J. Carl and J. D. Harrah, 'A Simpler, Less Expensive Technique for Delayed Primary Closure of Fasciotomies', *American Journal of Surgery*, 180 (2000), pp. 55-7; F. J. Verdam *et al.*, 'Delayed Primary Closure of the Septic Open Abdomen with a Dynamic Closure System', *World Journal of Surgery*, 35 (2011), pp. 2348–55; B. Siribumrungwong, K. Srikuea and A. Thakkinstian, 'Comparison of superficial surgical site infection between delayed primary and primary wound closures in ruptured appendicitis', *Asian Journal of Surgery*, 37 (2014), pp. 120-4. M. C. Eliya-Masamba and G. W. Banda, 'Primary closure versus delayed closure for non bite traumatic wounds within 24 hours post injury', *Cochrane Database of Systematic Reviews*, 10 (2013), pp. 1-22.

century, and evidence for this is found in the collection of surgical implements found on the Mary Rose, which include probes and bullet extractors.[110] However, to most surgeons at the start of the Civil Wars, and to most civilian-trained surgeons, firearm wounds were unusual and they had little experience in their treatment. Paré offered insights into the diagnosis of a gunshot wound:

> In the beginning of the Curation, you ought first to know whether the wounds was made by Gun-shot or no; which is easie to be seene if the figure of the wound be round and livid in colour, and the naturall colour of the part is chaunged, that is to say, yellow, azure, liuid, or blacke. Also at the same instant that the patient receyved the blow, if he say that he felt an agravating pain, as if he had beene strooke with a great stone, or with a club, or as if a great burthen had falne upon the wounded part.[111]

Wiseman warned of the dangers of leaving inexperienced civilian surgeons to treat gunshot wounds, as they are easily mis-diagnosed. Wiseman observed that 'Where the bullet pierceth, it extinguishes the natural heat, and the lips of the wound are livid and blackish'.[112] This effect of a 'gunpowder tattoo' is indicative of a bullet wound.[113] Wiseman warned that a civilian surgeon, or one with no experience of gunshot wounds, would be likely to misdiagnose the blackened nature of the wound as gangrene and to try to treat the wound by 'inserting a pea and a poultice' into the wound, rather than investigating the wound appropriately.

The approaches displayed in the published writings were both effective and efficient. The main foci were on finding the bullet and material it had taken in with it, removing it without causing further damage, and how to treat the bullet hole afterwards. The musket ball used in the Civil Wars was spherical, made of lead, and typically fifteen to twenty millimetres in diameter (12-bore, the equivalent of 1/12lb or 38g in weight; although 10-bore (1/10 lb) was also not uncommon).[114] Fired by loose-grain black powder, the musket ball trajectory was typically of a low velocity (400-500 m/sec, compared to a modern rifle velocity of 1200-1700m/sec) with maximum range of up to 180 metres, the force of impact lessening with distance, so the *effective*

---

110 J. Gardiner, ed., *Before The Mast: The Archaeology of the Mary Rose* (Trowbridge, Cromwell Press: 2005), pp. 189 and 220-5.

111 Paré, *Method of Curing Wounds*, pp. 41-2.

112 Wiseman, *Severall Chirurgical Treatises*, p. 407.

113 M. Tokdemir, H. Kafadar, A. Turkoglu and T. Bork, 'Forensic value of gunpowder tattooing in identification of multiple entrance wounds from one bullet', *Legal Medicine*, 9 (2007), pp. 147-50.

114 V. Eyers, 'Ballistics of Matchlock Muskets', Unpublished MSc Thesis, Cranfield University, 2006. pp. 9, 12-13, 54; D. J. Blackmore, *Destructive and Formidable: British Infantry Firepower 1642 – 1765* (Croydon, Frontline, 2015), pp. 9-10.

range of the weapon was significantly less.[115] The low velocity, bullet shape, and the fact that lead in seventeenth century was softer than contemporary lead (which is now typically hardened with antimony), meant that the bullet was often lodged within the body after entry. A bullet will cause significant damage to the body as it travels through tissue, from the 'permanent cavity' (the tissue carved out by the passage of the bullet).[116] A modern conical bullet will typically yaw from side to side and in some cases flipping backwards as it travels within the body but with most high-velocity bullets, the trajectory of the projectile within the body is quite direct. A bullet will also induce a high degree of compression-related damage *via* the 'temporary cavity', due to the shockwave through the body caused by the displacement of tissue and momentum of the bullet.[117] A low-velocity bullet, such as a musket ball, is more prone to cause a wider secondary cavity and also to be affected by the varying densities of tissues within the body. When it strikes tissue of varying densities, a musket ball will likely veer off course, making it challenging to identify the pathway of the projectile; 'It being wonderful to consider how these Shots do twirl about' as Wiseman warned.[118]

An example of the variable trajectory of the musket ball can be seen in the wound received by Sergeant-Major-General Phillip Skippon of the parliamentarian army at the battle of Naseby, 1645. The bullet pierced his armour and entered his body on the right side of his breast, about six inches below the dorsal side of the armpit, and eventually excited in the small of the back, near the spine.[119] Similarly, a theoretical analysis of the symptoms of Admiral Lord Nelson, after he was shot at the Battle of Trafalgar, suggests that the bullet entered his body at the shoulder, lacerated the pulmonary artery, damaged the lungs and other internal organs, before lodging in the lower spine.[120] Whilst this case was 150 years after the Civil Wars, the shot was from a round lead ball from a smooth-bore musket and so would not have been dissimilar. The random path of the ball therefore posed considerable challenges for the surgeon.

---

115 Ibid. pp. 27-33, 41-42.
116 A. C. Szul, ed., *Emergency War Surgery: NATO Handbook, US revision 3* (Washington D. C., Unites States Government Printing Office: 2004); M. L. Fackler, 'Gunshot wound review', *Annals of Emergency Medicine*, 28 (1996), pp. 194-203; R. A. Santucci and Y.-J. Chang, 'Ballistics for Physicians: Myths about wound ballistics and gunshot injuries', *Journal of Urology*, 171 (2004), pp. 1408–14.
117 Ibid., pp. 1408-14.
118 Wiseman, *Severall Chirurgical Treatises*, p. 411.
119 Gruber von Arni, *Justice for the Maimed Soldier*, p. 179; I. Pells, 'Stout Skippon Hath a wound: the medical treatment of parliament's infantry commander following the battle of Naseby', conference paper given at 'Mortality, Care and Military Welfare during the British Civil Wars', National Civil War Centre, Newark, 7-8 August 2015.
120 D. Wang, W. S. El-Masry, M. Crumplin, S. Eisenstein, R. J. Pusey and T. Meagher, 'Admiral Lord Nelson's death: known and unknown – A historical review of the anatomy', *Spinal Cord*, 43 (2005), pp. 573–6.

Modern firearms typically have an exit wound which is usually larger, effusive and more-livid than the entry wound. However, this was not always the case with musket shot. Wiseman does describe an exit wound as being different to the entry wound,

> The figure of these wounds is always round. The Bullet forces the Flesh in with it, and the place by which it enters presently contracts closer; but its going out is more lax.[121]

However, frequently the musket ball would not pass through and so would need to be extracted from the body. Key to the process of extraction was locating the bullet, a procedure made challenging by the behaviour of the bullet within the human body. Contemporary accounts of bullet wounds support this observation. Either the surgeon's finger, or a long metal probe (with either a barrel or ball end) would be used to find the bullet, the latter relying on the difference in feel of metal striking bone or tissue, versus striking other metal.[122] The design of such probes (essentially a long metal rod of eight to twelve inches) had not changed since the early sixteenth century and remained largely unchanged until the turn of the twentieth century. The only alteration was that the improvement in material technology meant that the probe could be made lighter and more delicate in later years, as can be seen from extant examples, as well as illustrations in later military surgical manuals of the eighteenth and nineteenth centuries.[123] Interestingly, Wiseman suggested that when searching for the bullet, the surgeon,

> ... may guess by view of the wound the largeness of the bullet; and by comparing the one with the other make a choice of fit instrument for extraction...
>
>   Your main care in this work must be to find the bullet: But if you fail of it by searching into the wound with the probe then try if you can feel it by handling the parts about.[124]

This advice suggests that the initial approach should be to use an implement, rather than one's own fingers, which would be considerably more sensitive and tactile. Although Wiseman does not state his reasons, it is tempting to suggest that the main reason why one might use a probe, rather than a finger, would be because a probe might be less prone to carry infection into the wound. If the bullet could not be found

121 Ibid., pp. 573-6.
122 R. Wiseman, 'Severall Chirurgical Treatises'. (Norton and Maycock, London, 1676), p. 411.
123 Gross, *manual of Military Surgery*, p. 70; F. H. Hamilton, *A Practical Treatise on Military Surgery* (New York, Balliere Brothers: 1861), p. 139.
124 Wiseman, *Severall Chirurgical Treatises*, p. 411.

immediately, then often leaving it in place would lead to sufficient inflammation that its location became obvious.[125]

Once found, the bullet needed to be removed. The device used for bullet extraction could take two forms. A bullet extractor, or *Tirefond*, was a long metal tube containing a bore within it, with a screw-head at one end, which would be used to screw into the bullet, facilitating its removal.[126] Alternatively, tongs could be used, which were long and slender scissor-like implements, usually with either serrated or cupped ends, to clamp the ball. Various versions of these extractors existed, each with their own colourful and descriptive name, such as the 'Crowe's Bill' (with short, toothed fronds), 'Crane's Bill' (with longer, angles fronds), the 'Drake's Bill' (a long device with hollowed-out rounded ends operated by an internal baffle), the 'Parrot's Bill' (a long thin clamp, with a vice-like end operated by a screw) and the Swan's Beake' (which applies outwards pressure, like a modern rib spreader or Finochietto retractor).[127] Several of these implements remained fundamentally the same through the next several centuries but again, improved metallurgical technology leading to more delicate and precise instruments.[128] In removing the bullet, care was often advised not to clamp or pull either tendons or nerves, which hints at the high level of anatomical understanding which underpinned many of these procedures.[129]

Of fundamental importance in the treatments of gunshot wounds was the removal of any foreign matter that may have been taken in with the bullet. This may include dirt, hair and (most importantly) fragments of clothing. A soldier would have worn a shirt, a doublet and a coat, none of which would be particularly clean, and fragments of this cloth, if left inside the body, would hinder wound healing at best, cause septicaemia, fever and possibly death at worst.[130] Removal of 'Rags' seems to have been a fundamental priority in the advised procedures: 'Nay, while any of the Rags remain in the Wound, it will never cure, but the extraneous bodies drawn out, there is little difficulty in healing these Wounds if drest rationally', as Wiseman put it.[131] This was even more important than the removal of the bullet itself, which could sometimes be left within the body without causing too much further damage:

> Yet by the confession of those that allow Fire and Poison in it, the bullet may lie long there, and do little harm. Nay, I suppose there are not many but have heard of or seen bullets that, without grievance to the Patient, have continued lying long in the Fleshy parts of wounded men. Conceive this spoken of Leaden

---

125 Ibid., p. 411.
126 Paré, *Method of Curing Wounds*, pp. 50-1.
127 Ibid., pp. 45-50; H. C., *Explanation of the Fashion*, pp. 41-3.
128 Gross, *manual of Military Surgery*, p. 70; Hamilton, *Practical Treatise*, pp. 139-40.
129 Wiseman, *Severall Chirurgical Treatises*, p. 412.
130 Paré, *Method of Curing Wounds*, pp. 51-52.
131 Wiseman, *Severall Chirurgical Treatises*, pp. 410-11

bullets; for Iron or Brass cannot (by reason of their aptness to rust) remain without doing harm.[132]

This obsession with the removal of rags and foreign matter shows the extent to which the surgeons could link cause and effect to the causation of infection and sepsis. The high degree of prominence of it within the advice given in the texts similarly shows the degree of certainty with which this association was made. The understanding would have come primarily from observation, or from advice from older or more senior surgeons, which is a clear example of evidence-based medicine within these practitioners.

Fractures

Aside from cuts and penetrative wounds, another major wound type on a Civil War battleground would have been a fracture. Whilst the use of blunt weapons such as hammers or pollaxes was far less common than in previous centuries, musketeers would typically fight in close-quarters by using the iron-bound butts of their muskets, rather than swords. Therefore, cranial injuries, broken limbs and ribs would have been commonplace: 'Besides which there were various Fissures, Sedes, and some Fractures, with Depression, made by Sword, Musket-stock, &c.'.[133] Blunt force trauma could also be caused by edged weaponry striking armoured body parts, concussion from explosions, striking by shrapnel from mortar shells, by falls from horses or accidental damage.

Setting of a limb was a straightforward affair, despite not having access to plaster (such as is common for treating fractures today). Instead, setting the bone required splinting, using a leather cast, or wooden or metal splints, held in place with strapping or rowlers, and possibly a stiffened plaster equivalent made from egg white and resin.[134] Wiseman noted that it was important to ensure that the splint does not cause more damage to the limb by rubbing or cutting off circulation (or 'heat') to the limb, whilst Paré warned 'it may cause the member to become Atrophied or withered through the too long continuation of the said Rollers', which both display a practical understanding of the causes of sores and the implications of restricting circulation to extremities.[135]

A common cause of fractures was the secondary effect of gunshot wounds.[136] Low-velocity bullet wounds, such as those from black-powder weapons, when striking limbs could either cause severe bruising (easily mistaken for gangrene by

---

132 Ibid., p. 410.
133 Ibid., p. 400.
134 T. Gale, *Certain works of chirurgery, newly compiled*, (London: 1563), p. 58; Cooke, *Mellificium Chirurgiae*, p. 452; Keynes, *Apologie and Treatise of Ambroise Paré*, p. 168.
135 Wiseman, *Severall Chirurgical Treatises*, p. 443; Paré, *Method of Curing Wounds*, p. 66.
136 Paré (transl. Hammond), *The Method of Curing Wounds made by Gun-shot.* p.9

naïve surgeons) or subcutaneous fractures[137]or if it penetrated, be stopped by the bone and cause a cross-ways fracture in a diagonal cross shape from the strike point.[138] This diagonal fracture is a combination of the energy from the impact trying to find the fastest exit from the bone and also following the grain of the bone. The splintered fracture that results from such wounds are described, by contemporary authors, as being flake-like, or similar to fish scales, which could only be understood by extensive investigation and frequent experience of such injuries.[139] These fracture patterns were also found in later wars and even recognised up to the Second World War, although by the later twentieth century, the impact of the bullet was likely to cause more shattering of the bone than cross-hair fractures.[140] The treatment of shatter fractures from gunshots remained largely unchanged for many years, until resection of the bone became possible in the mid-nineteenth century, which enabled the shattered part of the bone to be removed and the bone to be reset as a shorter (but more stable and potentially-recoverable) limb.[141]

The major challenge with projectile-derived fractures is that the shattered nature of the bone is problematic to repair. The fact that there was an open wound, and potentially a projectile remaining in the wound site or the bone itself, was also a challenge for the surgeon. Wiseman advised that it is important to remove the bullet and repair the shattered limb before closure of the wound.[142]

Of importance to the treatment of a projectile-derived fracture, or a compound fracture where the bone has pierced the skin, is the need to dress or otherwise treat the wound whilst also maintaining traction on the limb. In Vietnam and more-recently, this was achieved by using an inflatable cast (a strip of inflatable sleeves which could wrap around and support the limb).[143] In earlier twentieth-century military surgery, this was enabled by the use of the Liston, Thomas and later the Tobruk splint, a personal traction device which held the limb at the top and bottom (e.g. the hip and the ankle) and then joined the two using steel or aluminium brackets, which could be slid apart from one another, then held in place with bolts to provide the traction.[144] The limb could then be supported by using a leather or similar sleeve for rigidity, whilst also providing access to the wound site when required. There is a

---

137 Paré (transl. Hammond), *The Method of Curing Wounds made by Gun-shot*. p.26, 79.
138 G. J. Ordog, J. Wasserberger and S. Balasubramanium, 'Wound Ballistics: Theory and Practice', *Annals of Emergency Medicine*, 13 (1984), pp. 1113-22; Penhallow, *Military Surgery*, p. 163.
139 Wiseman, *Severall Chirurgical Treatises*, p. 419.
140 Penhallow, *Military Surgery*, p. 163; Szul, *Emergency War Surgery*; Santucci and Chang, 'Ballistics for Physicians', pp. 1408-14.
141 Gross, *manual of Military Surgery*, pp. 87-8.
142 Wiseman, *Severall Chirurgical Treatises*, p. 421.
143 J. C. Clasper, 'Limb Injuries', in P. Mahoney *et al*, eds, *Ballistic Trauma* (London, Arnold: 1997), pp. 356-80.
144 Scotland and Heyes, *War Surgery*, pp. 154-5; Penhallow, *Military Surgery*, pp. 171-9; Ogilvie, *Forward Surgery*, p. 37.

direct equivalent suggested for similar wounds in the early modern period. The limb is supported inside either a leather or brass sleeve, or item of arm/leg armour, to which is attached long pins, with screws that enable them to be jacked apart to provide tractive force. This model is seen in writings from the 1530s through to 1640s.[145] Aside from the materials involved, the structure of these precursors of the Thomas and Tobruk Splint is identical to that used subsequently, which leads to the suggestion that either the later practitioners may have been building on innovations introduced by the seventeenth-century pioneers, or the seventeenth-century practitioners were utilising good medical practice which was also developed independently by later surgeons.

Amputation

If the limb, or part thereof, was too damaged or infected to be saved, then it needed to be removed in order not to damage the remainder of the body through sepsis. The removal of body parts through amputation was possibly the most feared and misunderstood of all operations undertaken by the surgeon. James Cooke highlighted this in the first sentence of his chapter on amputation: 'Dismembering is a dreadful Operation; yet necessary, that the dead part may not injure the living, nor procure death. *Sphacelus* [Gangrene] is the perfect *Mortification* of any part, invading not only the soft parts, but also the bones'.[146] He further went on to show a good understanding of the diagnosis of affected parts:

> The part is senseless, tough cut, if unseen by the party [patient]: the flesh is cold, flaggy, black, smells like a dead Carcass, the skin may be separated from the flesh, and flows therefrom viscid, green and blackish matter. There may be motion, the heads of the muscles being not affected, yet the work is not to be delayed. It may be taken off, either in the *sound* or *corrupt* part. The first is most use, and more secure.[147]

Quite apart from the common folk myth of the surgeon hacking off a limb with casual abandon, Cooke described meticulous preparations for the operation, which included bolstering the patient's ability to recover from the operation by providing high calorie diet (including egg yolks and sweet wine) and purgatives before operation.[148] Care was also taken to ensure a sterile operation site, with a requirement for a large bowl of ashes (a source of alkali such as lye, or sodium/potassium hydroxide), water and vinegar to clean the wounded area before and after, and bladders to cover the stump

---

145 W. Fabry (transl. J. Steer), *Gulielm Fabricus Hildamis, his experiments in Chyrurgerie* (London: 1643), pp. 57-64.
146 Cooke, *Mellificium Chirurgiae*, pp. 722-7.
147 Ibid., p. 722.
148 Ibid., pp. 722-3.

to keep it clean after the operation. Every precaution was also made to ensure that the operation was rapid and there were no unnecessary hiatuses in the procedure. Two bone saws were recommended (a spare therefore being immediately to hand in case of breakage), three needles (ideally ones which had not yet been used for any other purpose, and therefore sharp), several bandages of various kinds, and cloth buttons of various sizes that could be used to plug the ends of blood vessels.[149]

After applying a secure tourniquet (especially important if the limb contains large arteries), the flesh would be cut through to the bone with a dismembering or paring knife (a curved blade with the sharpened edge on the inside of the curve), which, Cooke suggested, some surgeons used red-hot.[150] The bone could then be cut using the saw, as close to the cut flesh site as possible. An eschar would be encouraged to develop by treating the cut site of the stump with a mixture of umber and lime, powdered and made into a paste using egg whites and ground hair (presumably the latter was to encourage aggregation of the poultice). The blood vessels would be plugged with cloth buttons made of tow (strong linen) dipped in *posca*. Alternatively, cauterising or suturing could be used (although the latter was less ideal due to the pressures exerted upon the sutured vessel, leading to rupture and haemorrhage within the stump). Bandaging the wound afterwards was done using rowlers dipped in oxycrate, the dressing kept unchanged for two to three days, then removed, cleansed of clotted blood and replaced with a second set of bandages, this time dipped in white wine. With each successive dressing, the aim was to try, ideally using dry stitches, to draw the edges of the stump together over the bone, after which, when the gap was sufficiently small, the tip of the stump could be stitched. Stitching of the stump was therefore not immediate.[151]

This procedure is remarkable in its attention to detail, hygiene, control of bleeding and the speed at which it should be performed. Management of infection, both of the flesh (which would cause septicaemia) or of the bone (which would cause osteomyelitis), are recognised as important considerations. The understanding of the latter affect, of infecting the bone, is quite remarkable as it reveals an extensive understanding of different entry routes for infections, of which bone-born infections are not obvious. Use of antibacterial compounds (alkali, vinegar or alcohol) also shows a deep understanding of the way in which infection could be controlled (as does the use of a red-hot dismembering knife), even though bacteria, as causative agents of infection, had not yet been identified. The emphasis on speed of the operation and then on quite intricate aftercare, also reveals a sophisticated approach which belies the butcher-like reputation that is characteristic of popular views of the profession. The emphasis on redundancy of equipment in the preparation is also significant and reflects on the

149 Ibid., p. 724.
150 Ibid. p. 723.
151 Ibid. pp. 724-5.

concerns of contemporary military surgeons in Vietnam and the Gulf Wars, who expressed concerns about the fragility of their surgical saws.

The amputatory procedure, whilst undoubtedly being a terrifying and dangerous procedure, especially in the absence of anaesthetics, was nevertheless as controlled as it could realistically be expected to be. Whilst the surgeons did not understand the basis of infection, they did clearly understand how best to control it and limit its impact. The amputation procedure in the seventeenth century was considerably more delicate than that in previous periods (where cauterisation of the stump was commonplace[152]) and indeed, the procedure remained largely unchanged after the development at the end of the seventeenth century of the 'flap amputation' method, using angled cuts through the flesh, rather than transverse ones, to produce flaps of skin that could easier be sewn together over the stump.[153] Many of the precautions established in seventeenth century practice were unchanged until the mid to late nineteenth century and the introduction of anaesthetics and rubbing alcohol or iodine for sterilisation, and the use of anaesthetics to calm the patient (which facilitated more rapid and effective procedures, as there was not also the need to hold the patient down during the operation).

Competence and effect

A key issue, and a problem when assessing the competence of early modern surgeons, is the lack of reliable medical records or specific data on patients. While some records of medical practitioners remain, such as the 1633-1663 casebook of London Surgeon Joseph Binns, the majority of references available regarding the efficacy practice are primarily eye witness accounts of survivors.[154] Such observations may themselves be naïve or unreliable, being either written by lay observers rather than medical professionals and often being embellished for political purposes (such as the detailed accounts of the wounding, treatment and recovery of Skippon in the popular press[155]). The other source of information is the writings of the surgeons themselves, which are subject to reporter bias and were often written many years after the events.

152　Mitchell, *Medicine in the Crusades*, pp. 116, 150, 192.
153　Two and three cut amputations, which used angled cuts rather than a single circular cut, were developed in 1715 and 1773 respectively. The approach of transverse cuts through the skin before removal of the muscle and bone, so that a soft-tissue flap covered the stump and there was therefore no skin tension over the amputated region ('flap amputation'), was developed by Lowdham in 1679, Verduyn in 1696, and later by Langenbeck in 1810 – see M. Sachs, J. Bojunga and A. Encke, 'Historical evolution of limb amputation' *World Journal of Surgery*, 23 (1999), pp. 1088-93.
154　McCray Beier, *Sufferers and Healers*, pp. 51-96.
155　I. Pells, 'Stout Skippon Hath a wound: the medical treatment of parliament's infantry commander following the battle of Naseby', conference paper given at 'Mortality, Care and Military Welfare during the British Civil Wars', National Civil War Centre, Newark, 7-8 August 2015.

Furthermore, it is impossible to determine which of those soldiers who died of their wounds did so because of poor or ineffective practice, of treatment arriving too late, or because the wounds themselves were beyond repair. Wiseman observed that thoracic wounds, and many abdominal wounds, are rarely able to be healed.[156] In this instance, it was a priority for the surgeon to make the patient as comfortable as possible, in order to make his remaining time alive more bearable.

However, one source of information can hint at the extent to which surgery was effective and that is to survey the extent of injuries which appeared to be survivable. Accounts of the recovery of notable figures, such as the well-documented injury and recovery of Skippon or the wounding of Sir Thomas Fairfax in the wrist at Adwalton Moor,[157] can identify injuries which were treated by medical professionals but which were not fatal. Similarly, the survivability of injuries can be inferred by assessing the range of injuries reported by maimed soldiers seeking pensions after the war. Data compiled by Hannah Worthen from Kent County Court records suggests a prevalence of injuries to either the limbs, the extremities (hands and feet) or the eyes.[158] Several petitioners are recorded as having sustained 'many dangerous wounds', suggesting that severe injury could be sustained without certain loss of life. A petition on behalf of John Tinkler of Durham, a gunner at Hartlepool, reveals that he survived blinding and the loss of both his arms.[159] Data summarised by Eric Gruber von Arni from the records of the admissions to the Chelsea Hospital in the early eighteenth century (1715-32) reveals survivors with injuries to the limbs (often several limbs simultaneously), damage to the head, back, abdomen, clavicle, groin and even removal of part of the peritoneum.[160] What is interesting about these last records is that of the fourteen cases, all of the patients sustained multiple injuries and all but four of them gained those injuries in different engagements, often over several years, showing that they had recovered sufficiently to continue serving in an active military capacity. The treatments these men had received clearly were effective, although it is perhaps telling that the majority of wounds presented by maimed soldiers seem to be damage to the limbs, which perhaps reinforces Wiseman's commentary that thoracic and abdominal wounds were difficult to treat and would most likely be fatal.

156 Wiseman, *Severall Chirurgical Treatises*, pp. 366-73.
157 A. Hopper, *'Black Tom': Sir Thomas Fairfax and the English Revolution* (Manchester, Manchester University Press: 2007), p. 228; I. J. Gentles, 'Fairfax, Thomas, third Lord Fairfax of Cameron (1612–1671)', *Oxford Dictionary of National Biography* (Oxford, Oxford University Press: 2008), online edn, http://www.oxforddnb.com/view/article/9092.
158 H. Worthen, 'The administration of war relief in Kent', conference paper given at 'Mortality, Care and Military Welfare during the British Civil Wars', National Civil War Centre, Newark, 7-8 August 2015.
159 Durham County Record Office, Q/S/OB 5 (Microfilm M7/2), Quarter Sessions Order Book, 1660-1668, fol. 72, ('The petition of John Tinckler of the city of Durham, 3 October 1660').
160 Gruber Von Arni, *Justice to the Maimed Soldier, Vol. 2*, pp. 198-9.

Early Modern Surgeons in Context

One characteristic which makes several of the published practitioners (especially Wiseman, and the German surgeon Johannes Scultetus[161]) particularly notable is their approach to describing their many treatments, providing clear evidence of the impact on specific patients. These descriptions are remarkable in that they often state that the approach taken did not produce the desired results. This approach is clearly one of 'evidence-based medicine'. This evidence-based approach is also characteristic of the scientific approaches adopted in the Enlightenment, first developed by Sir Francis Bacon and which are still in evidence in scientific endeavour today. As such, one can view these early surgical pioneers as pioneers of contemporary medical and scientific practice as well.

There are many instances of medical practice in these volumes that do not reflect procedures with a sound basis in science. The question, therefore, is why these practices were still adopted by reflective practitioners who were using an evidence base for their practice. It is notable that case studies are rarely given for any examples of practice that are *not* valid approaches, which leads one to tentatively suggest that in cases where an approach could not be proven by experience, then the traditional medicines or methods were applied by default. It is entirely possible that some of these treatments, recipes and poultices contained some element of pharmacologically-active ingredients but there are few obvious candidates for most. For example, Wiseman, as well as others, recommend the use of fat rendered from newly born puppies, which may have pharmaco-active properties, but this is highly unlikely.[162] In many cases, it is likely that what was at work was not an active ingredient in the medicine but rather the 'placebo effect' and the body actually self-healing. The placebo effect has been well documented, and evidence suggests that the more-interventionist the therapy, the stronger the placebo effect becomes.[163] It is entirely possible that for some less-serious complaints, the treatment itself was entirely incidental but were assumed to be effective on a *post hoc ergo proper hoc* basis, rather than by empirical proof.

Certainly the surgeons of the early modern period were still wedded to many of the ancient traditions of medicine, especially the concept of the four humours within the body, although there is a tentative sign that these more superstitious concepts were being explained through more rational observations, such as the access of blood to a wound providing heat and cleansing properties. Certainly they were not averse to challenging accepted dogma in the medical profession and, along with the scientific revolution of

---

161   Scultetus, Villavicencio and Rich, 'Life and Work', pp. 135.

162   Wiseman, *Severall Chirurgical Treatises*, p. 413.

163   M. Fässler, M. Gnädinger, T. Rosemann and N. Biller-Andorno, 'Placebo interventions in practice: a questionnaire survey on the attitudes of patients and physicians', *British Journal of General Practice*, 61 (2011), pp. 101–7, at p. 105; A. Hróbjartsson, M. Norup, 'The use of placebo interventions in medical practice – a national questionnaire survey of Danish clinicians', *Evaluation and the Health Professions*, 26 (2003), pp. 153–65, at p. 162.

which they were a part, they were establishing new methodologies of their own and identifying (and sharing) novel practices based on experience. In this, the military surgeon was ideally-situated to refine his practice, as he was provided with ample numbers of patients on whom to observe his effectiveness and the frequency of repetition of certain key injuries to be able to gather replicate observations of different patients.

It is, of course, dangerous to generalise and suggest that all practitioners in the seventeenth century were of equal capacity and training to those described here. Certainly Clowes and Gale seemed to consider their peers to be generally lacking in skill and Wiseman was quite dismissive of the skills of some civilian colleagues. It is also impossible to verify the claims of the surgeons against data or independent medical records. No patient records were kept, certainly not in a systematic manner, so it is impossible to follow individual treatments for all except the most celebrated of patients, such as Skippon.[164] Although Wiseman describes the treatment of his patients clearly, the accounts are, in many cases, twenty to thirty years after the event and so it is questionable whether all of the accounts are entirely accurate (though Wiseman is particularly vociferous that his memory can be trusted).[165] It is also possible that the reason the practitioners were published was because they were exceptionally-competent enough to have been noted by, and patronised by, grandees (Wiseman was surgeon to the prince of Wales, and later to him as Charles II, Paré was surgeon to the French royal family, Gale was close to two royal courts and Cooke was surgeon to Lord Brooke, earl of Warwick). It is therefore highly likely that the majority of surgeons were less capable and/or less well-trained. Certainly no printed work would detail examples of gross incompetence and so the published accounts and guides are not likely to be a true reflection of the profession as a whole.

However, the published writings do evidence practice which is not seen in earlier texts, and practice that is repeated and maintained for several centuries thereafter, albeit with occasional developments and refinements. As such, it is appropriate to see early modern surgeons of the mid-sixteenth to mid-seventeenth centuries as pioneers in their field, military surgeons especially so. For the following 200 years, their techniques were retained, largely unaltered, from their original methodologies. It was only the refinement of material technology that improved the surgical practices, with finer steel-working enabling needles, probes, knives, forceps and saws to be of better quality or more delicate and precise in nature. The fundamental usage of these instruments, however, was not changed significantly, which evidences the longevity of these practitioners' approaches. Far from being quacks, charlatans or dangerous amateurs, these individuals laid the foundations for surgery as a respected and effective medical profession.

---

164 Detailed patient notes were a key innovation of the Crimean War, enabling different army surgeons to follow the ongoing treatments of an individual, enacted previously by their peers.

165 McVaugh, 'Richard Wiseman', pp. 136.

7

'Dead Hogges, Dogges, Cats and well flayed Carryon Horses': Royalist hospital provision during the Civil Wars

Dr Eric Gruber von Arni

As the Marquis de Feuquières wrote in 1737, 'An army without good hospitals perishes easily, it being impossible that combat actions and sickness will not fill them often and all too abundantly'.[1] In this chapter, I shall examine the philosophy and measures adopted by the king and his council of war to provide hospitals and care for their army's sick and wounded.[2] Unfortunately, whereas the comprehensive records of their opponents survive in some quantity, most records of the royalist army were lost during the wholesale destruction when Oxford fell in 1646. Very few references to medical and nursing care in the royalist camp have survived and those that have refer mostly to Oxford between 1642 and 1643, the years of the so-called '*morbus campestris*', probably typhus.

With the king's council of war exercising a centralised command structure under the king's autocratic personal direction, a coordinated casualty care policy was a pipe dream. Such was their lack of awareness that the king's personal physician, William Harvey (who had been the first to accurately describe the circulation of blood), appears to have spent his time during the battle of Edgehill on 23 October 1642 having been delegated to look after the king's two young sons, Charles and James. After the battle, when the king's army moved towards Banbury, royalist casualties left behind found little sympathy amongst the local, predominantly parliamentarian, villagers. Most were transported to Oxford in wagons and deposited in various churches, almshouses, hostelries and private houses.

---

1   L. André, *Michel Le Tellier et l'Organisation de l'Armée Monarchique* (Paris, Felix Alcan: 1906), pp. 475-6.
2   The nature, membership and function of the king's council of war has been discussed at length in I. Roy, 'The Royalist Council of War, 1642-6', *Bulletin of the Institute for Historical Research*, 35 (1995), pp. 150-68.

After the king's abortive march on London in November, Oxford remained his chief headquarters until July 1646 and the centre of the royalist war effort in England. The court, officers and members of the government, as well as their servants, soldiers and families, all sought accommodation. This inevitably resulted in intense overcrowding and grossly insanitary conditions. By January 1644, in St. Aldate's parish alone, there was an average of more than five strangers resident in each of the 74 recorded house-holds.[3] The situation was well described by Lady Fanshawe in the following quotation:

> From as good a house as any gentleman of England had, we came to a baker's house in an obscure street, and from rooms well-furnished, to lie in a very bad bed in a garret, to one dish of meat, and that not the best ordered, no money, for we were as poor as Job, no clothes more than a man or two brought in their clothes bags: we had .... the sad spectacle of war, sometimes plague, sometimes sickness of other kinds by reason of so many people being packed together.[4]

The troops were unpopular and more than one churchwarden paid bribes to encourage them to move out of the town into the surrounding countryside.[5] When, in November 1642, the king retired from Turnham Green to Oxford, he left a strong garrison in Reading, a town that had endured a particularly high incidence of plague throughout the preceding four decades.[6] Following the town's surrender to the earl of Essex's army in April 1643, some 1,200 royalist soldiers withdrew towards Oxford, carrying the plague with them.

On 2 May 1643, the council of war announced that every wounded officer and soldier should be rewarded either with a pension, or be admitted to whatever hospitals and alms-houses remained within the king's area of control.[7] However, although the proclamation avoided specifying the amount of relief each wounded soldier would receive, it soon became obvious that the royal treasury could not possibly cope with the predicted financial burden and the proposals were effectively dropped when the royalist newsbook *Mercurius Aulicus* announced that they related 'only to the future and not likely to yield help and comfort ... for the present'.[8] Equally, many of the supposed hospitals and alms-houses in the surrounding towns and villages were under parliamentary control.

---

3   British Library [hereafter BL], Harleian MS 2125, fol. 66, p. 134v; S. Porter, 'The Oxford Fire of 1644', *Oxoniensis*, XLIX (1984), pp. 289-300.
4   L. Rice-Oxley, *Oxford Renowned* (Oxford, Methuen: 1925), p.126.
5   *Calendar of State Papers, Domestic Series* [hereafter CPSD], 1644, p. 10; Oxfordshire History Centre, Mss.d.d.Par (Churchwarden's Accounts for St. Aldate's and St. Michael's Parishes).
6   Oxfordshire History Centre, MSS. D.D. Par (Churchwarden's Accounts for St. Mary's parish).
7   *Mercurius Aulicus*, no. 18, 6 May 1643, pp. 226-7.
8   *Mercurius Aulicus*, no. 19, 13 May 1643, p. 235.

Figure 7.1 Culham Hill near Abingdon, viewed from the river Thames. (Author's photograph)

Also on 2 May, Facing the approach of Essex's army from Reading, the royalist army marched out of Oxford into an entrenched and fortified camp or 'leaguer' on Culham Hill, south-east of Abingdon.[9]

The Culham leaguer remained in being throughout May and into June, continually enlarged with earthworks, trackways and deep trenches. Some 700 defensive positions were excavated.[10] Troops were also moved into the leaguer from outlying garrisons until almost 20,000 soldiers were stationed on the hill, some accompanied by their families. Only 500 tents were provided, supplies were infrequent and, inevitably, poor sanitation, overcrowding, lack of food and suspect water brought disease. In addition, the hill's proximity to the river Thames was a mixed blessing as, in order to survive, soldiers, who normally drank water only as a last resort, were forced to drink from the river.[11] A graphic contemporary description of the river's contents was conveyed in the words of John Taylor, assistant water-bailiff at Oxford, which provided me with the title of this chapter:

9   National Archives [hereafter TNA], WO55/459, fol. 117 (Council to Sir John Heydon, 2 May 1643)
10   I. G. Philip, ed., *Journal of Sir Samuel Luke* (Oxford, Oxfordshire Record Society: 1950), I, p. 24.
11   Ibid., I, pp. 24 and 72.

I was commanded with the Water Baylie
To see the River clensed, both night and dayly
Dead Hogges, Dogges, Cats and well flayed Carryon Horses, Their noysom
Corpses soyld the water courses;
Both swines and stable dunge, Beasts guts and Garbage, Street durt, with
Gardners weeds and Rotten Herbage.
And from these Waters filthy puterfaction,
Out meat and drink were made, which bred Infection.[12]

The effects were soon evident. In St. Helen's parish, Abingdon, of the 184 burials during that summer of 1643, more than a third (66) were soldiers.[13] Several irate and influential commanders presented a nine-point petition to the king's council of war in an attempt to preserve the army's fighting strength. Amongst others matters, they requested a supply of shoes, stockings and better food, regimental wagons for use as ambulances and the establishment of a medical facility close to the leaguer accompanied by a physician and an apothecary.[14] The council of war responded by appointing Dr Francis Goddard as the physician and Thomas Clarges as apothecary.[15] In return, Goddard promptly pressed for the removal of the sick to a healthier location.[16]

Nuneham Balding (now Nuneham Courtney and Marsh Baldon) lay some five miles to the south of the city, not far from the Culham leaguer and an emergency hospital was established in the local manor.[17] On 2 June, the paymaster-general was instructed to release the back-pay owed to sick soldiers to Goddard for use in providing adequate food and treatment for them.[18] Additionally, the sheriffs of Oxfordshire and Berkshire were required to order local inhabitants to collect and deliver 60 flock beds, with sheets and other necessaries, to Nuneham for use by sick soldiers.[19]

The house at Nuneham soon proved inadequate and Goddard requested sufficient space to contain beds for all the sick because, he said, 'without great inconvenience, no

12 I.G. Philip, 'River Navigation at Oxford during the Civil War and Commonwealth', *Oxoniensis*, 2 (1937), pp. 152- 65, at p. 156.
13 St. Helen's, Abingdon Parish Register 1640-1678 (not deposited), St. Helen's Church, Abingdon; W. Bradbrook, 'The Church during the Commonwealth in the Abingdon Deanery', *Berkshire Archæological Journal*, 38 (1934), pp. 17-32.
14 BL, Harleian MS 6804, fol. 92 ('The Humble Desires of the Colonels to the King's Majesty', undated).
15 BL, Harleian MS 6852, fol. 74 (Orders of the council of war, 1643); BL, Harleian MS 6804, fol. 204 (Propositions for the medical care for the royalist forces, undated).
16 K. Park, 'Medicine and Society in Medieval Europe, 500-1500', in A. Wear, ed., *Medicine and Society* (Cambridge, Cambridge University Press: 1992), pp. 86-7.
17 M. M. D. Lobel, ed., *Victoria County History of Oxfordshire* (13 vols, Oxford, Oxford University Press: 1907- 96), 5, pp. 234-45.
18 BL, Harleian MS 6852, fol. 74 (Orders of the council of war, 1643).
19 BL, Harleian MS 6852, fols 72-3 (Orders of the council of war, 1643)

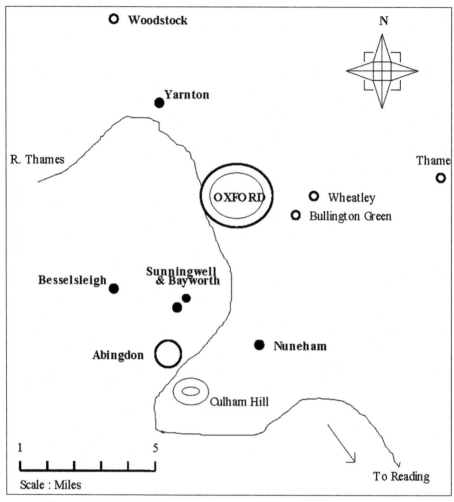

Figure 7.2 Locations of royalist military hospitals in the Oxford area, 1643-5.
(Author's drawing)

physick can be administered in straw and barns'.[20] He also suggested that the priests of
nearby parishes should appeal to their congregations for old linen and clothes so that
when soldiers were admitted to care they could receive clean garments whilst their
own were laundered.

20   BL, Harleian MS 6804, fol. 204 (Propositions for the medical care for the royalist forces,
undated).

The situation continued to deteriorate. The soldiers on Culham Hill were short of food and drink, discipline and morale were poor and desertions were frequent. Meanwhile, Essex and the parliamentary army had established a headquarters at Thame, eight miles east of Oxford. With an altered threat, the Culham leaguer was abandoned and the troops were moved to Bullington Green between Oxford and Wheatley.[21]

Exposure and disease had seriously depleted the king's troops, amongst whom over 3,000 men were described as 'so sick and weak that, if they were put to march, it is thought half of them were scarce able to march away'.[22] The facility at Nuneham was also vacated and transferred to the village of Sunningwell, a short distance north of Abingdon, where the local garrison had a hospital in the manor house of the Baskerville family.[23]

Eventually, a military hospital was established in the surviving portion of the former St. Mary's College, which stood in New Inn Hall Street, now known as Frewen Hall.[24] Again, unfortunately, documentation relating to the nature, quantity and quality of care provided there has not survived.

Subsequent orders from the council of war appear to have been drafted verbatim from recommendations expressed by Goddard regarding the severe outbreak of plague and typhus within Oxford. These included the opening of a third hospital at Yarnton Manor which was situated in a small, quiet village some four miles north-west of the city and was identified as a medical, or isolation, hospital to supplement the existing facilities at New Inn Hall Street and at Sunningwell.

The village was probably chosen because of its relative isolation and distance from the city as, whilst wounded patients requiring surgery continued to be treated in the city and at Sunningwell, henceforth infectious cases were sent to Yarnton. Unfortunately, the tragic effect of the presence of these patients in the village is graphically recorded in the parish registers, with 24 military and 26 civilian burials between May and August 1643.[25]

By 10 July 1643, the deaths in the Oxford garrison from sickness numbered 40 a week, besides those from other causes. Enormous difficulties were continually experienced with the on-going arrival in the city of casualties evacuated from battle-fields: 30 cartloads of injured soldiers from Prince Maurice's army following the battle of Lansdown, some 1,000 after the first battle of Newbury, whilst even more were to follow after the second battle of Newbury in October 1644. In July 1643, a review of hospital in-patients aimed at identifying those who could be discharged to care in the community had taken place and subsequently, a letter addressed to

21 A. Clark, ed., *The Life and Times of Anthony Wood* (5 vols, Oxford, Clarendon Press: 1891-1900), I, p. 100.
22 Philip, *Journal of Sir Samuel Luke*, II, pp. 90-102.
23 Clark, *Life and Times of Anthony Wood*, I, p. 270.
24 These buildings, now part of Brasenose College, were later renamed 'Frewen Hall'.
25 Oxfordshire History Centre, Mss.d.d.Par.Yarnton (Yarnton parish register, 1629-1721).

Figure 7.3 Frewen Hall. (Author's photograph)

Figure 7.4 Yarnton Manor. (Author's photograph)

the paymaster-general informed him that 469 soldiers had recovered and were fit to march.[26]

There was a continuing problem regarding the adequate supply of beds and bedding. Both the city's mayor and the county sheriff were pressed to provide as many sawyers as possible to prepare boards from newly-felled timber for the construction of more beds.[27] Even though Oxfordshire had been ordered to supply 300 beds, still more were required and, on 7 July 1643, an additional warrant was passed to the Sheriffs of Gloucestershire and Berkshire demanding beds and fresh straw from the inhabitants of villages bordering Oxfordshire.[28]

Although the patient capacity of the royalist hospitals is unknown, their staff establishment is shown in Table 7.1.

Table 7.1 Staff establishments and pay in Oxford's Military Hospitals, 1643

Appointment	Daily pay rate
Two female nurses	8d
Three overseers	6d
The commissary, John Bissell	5d
The physician's servant	2s 6d
The apothecary's servant	2s 0d

Source: BL, Harleian MS 6804, fol. 121.

The twelve women employed amongst the three hospitals were 'to act as nurses for the soldiers, to attend them and perform those offices which are necessary'.

The intense work in the three hospitals took its toll on everyone caring for the sick. Even so, William Barlow and Elizabeth Matthews, two employees at Yarnton found the time to marry in the manor chapel. The three senior hospital officers, Bowman, Clarges and Goddard, all reported exhaustion and overwork. For himself, Bowman complained that his burden was excessive and he was subsequently authorised to appoint two or three assistants with additional instructions that, in case of difficulties, he was to inform the council of war as soon as possible so that his patients did not suffer. Also overworked, Clarges found it necessary to write to the council secretary expressing, with wry humour, that he had 'by some subtle Philosophy, become a Doctor of Physick, two apothecaries, three overseers and twelve attendants' all rolled into one.

26   BL, Harleian MS 6852, fol. 163 (Council of war to Matthew Bradley, 29 July 1643).
27   BL, Harleian MS 6852, fol. 163 (Council of war to Matthew Bradley, 29 July 1643).
28   BL, Harleian MS 6852, fol. 115 (Council of war to the sheriffs of Gloucestershire and Berkshire, 7 July 1643).

With the war producing a continual flow of wounded men in addition to the victims of disease, Clarges and Goddard continued to press for implementation of Goddard's earlier requests for speedy surgical assistance. As Goddard complained, they were burying 'more toes and fingers than we do men'.[29] Hopefully, this indicated some measure of successful surgery. Eventually a surgeon and two mates were added to the hospital establishment.

By mid-June 1643, significantly increasing costs of providing care had caused the king to order the dean of Salisbury to form a committee to investigate and supervise the hospital accounts. An audit confirmed that the medical financial expenditure was not unreasonable and it was recommended that Goddard be provided with a constant cash float for paying hospital staff salaries.

On 17 July, John Bissell was appointed commissary for the sick, with instructions to pay the wages of soldiers in hospital less various deductions designed to offset the cost of care.[30] Soldiers in hospital would be entitled to three shillings a week. Of this, two were for the soldier and the remainder was retained towards the cost of medicines and the pay of doctors looking after him.

By November 1643, the royalist garrisons in Abingdon and Wallingford had been reduced to less than 800 men by disease whilst, on 14 December 1643, Oxford's over-crowding was exacerbated by further arrivals from Bristol and Winchester, the latter having survived the fall of Alton the day before.[31]

Garrisons lying at a greater distance from Oxford were forced to make their own local arrangements for casualty care. Insidiously, contagion spread westwards along major highways, assisted by the frequent movement of troops, particularly into the West Country. As an example, I have chosen to examine the outlying royalist garrison of Dartmouth in South Devon, some 140 miles from Oxford, where sick-ness appeared amongst the troops during the late autumn of 1643. Although most of Seymour's regiment were local men, some came from further afield. Throughout October, November and December, as the infection spread, hospital admissions were recorded in Seymour's accounts by treasurer John Tomasin.[32] On 20 October, Sir Edward Seymour, Dartmouth's newly appointed governor, found it necessary to convert a local estate, Mount Boone, into a garrison hospital. Seymour can have had few qualms about appropriating Mount Boone as the owner, Thomas Boone, was a

---

29   BL, Harleian MS 6804, fol. 203 (Thomas Clarges to Edward Walker, secretary to the royalist council of war, undated).

30   John Bissell was probably a Worcester man who was paid 5s a day for his services – see M. Toynbee, ed., *The Papers of Captain Henry Stevens* (Oxford, Oxfordshire Record Society: 1962), pp. 54-5.

31   S.R. Gardiner, *History of the Civil War* (4 vols, London, Windrush: 1987), I, p. 254.

32   R. Freeman, *Dartmouth, A New History of the Port and the People* (Dartmouth, Harbour Books: 1983), pp.66-72; P. Russell, *Dartmouth* (London, B. T. Batsford: 1950), pp. 108-18.

prominent local merchant, parliamentarian and a friend of Cromwell who was absent in London.[33]

In October, there were 20 in-patients. This figure rose to 30 in November and to 33 in December. Patients received medical attention from surgeon Richard Irish, whilst John Howe, a London divine, provided spiritual support and local women were recruited as nurses.[34]

Table 7.2 Admissions to Dartmouth Hospital, 20 October to 30 December 1643

Period covered	Number of people admitted
20-30 October 1643	23
1-30 November 1643	30
1-30 December 1643	33
Total	86

Source: Devon Record Office, Seymour MS 1392 M/L 1643, fols 8, 27 and 41.

Interestingly, Tomasin's accounts also provide an insight into the patients' diet, which, in this relatively isolated rural community, was demonstrably better than anything available in Oxford. It included beer, mutton, soup, bread, butter, sugar, prunes, fruit and pies.

Back in Oxford in November 1643, despite a continuing high number of patients, both sick and wounded, the council of war decided to dispense with the services of two surgeon's-mates and the apothecary's-mate. The Council claimed that they were under-employed and the dismissal of these men produced a saving of seven shillings a day. The Council also decided that the cost of caring for sick and wounded soldiers in outlying garrisons would henceforth be funded out of the county contributions or local taxes.[35] Lack of pay had reduced the morale of medical staff drastically, particularly amongst the long-serving regimental surgeons of the king's original army who had not been paid for months. Seven of them congregated in Oxford to petition the king for their arrears and, on 24 November 1643, Ashburnham, the treasurer at war, was ordered to provide them with £20 each on account.[36]

33   I. Palfrey, 'The Royalist War Effort Revisited: Edward Seymour and the Royalist Garrison at Dartmouth, 1643-4', *Transactions of the Devonshire Association*, 23 (1991), pp. 41-55.
34   Devon Record Office, Seymour MS 1392 M/L 1643, fols 8, 27 and 41 ('Dartmouth Garrison Accounts').
35   BL, Harleian MS 6852, fol. 225 (Council of war to the Constable and Churchwardens of Barrington and Rissington, 13 November 1643); BL, Harleian MS 6802, fol. 293 (Council of War to Surgeon Humphrey Paynton, 13 November 1644).
36   Described as belonging to the 'old regiments' of the army, the seven surgeons were Stephen Fawcett, Henry Johnson, Humphrey Paynton, John Robinson, James Rammage, Nicholas Thompson and John Thornhill: BL, Harleian MS 6852, fol. 210 (Council of war

All of these measures were undoubtedly a reflection of the king's desperately deteriorating financial situation. With bad beer, poor food and a shortage of fuel for fires, life in Oxford during the ensuing winter became particularly uncomfortable for the population and soldiers alike, though life was not without its humorous incidents. Soldiers are always eager to demonstrate initiative in finding new sources of liquid refreshment and three or four troops of horse managed to find alternative supplies by taking daily rides to Thame, a distance of some fourteen miles, for an hour or two's drinking in a more salubrious but seemingly well-supplied tavern.[37]

The winter brought a diminishing incidence of disease and the number of hospital in-patients fell accordingly. By March 1644, with the pace of work at Yarnton significantly reduced, the owner, Sir William Spencer, agitated for the return of his property. The council of war agreed and ordered Clarges and Bissell to transfer all the resident patients to Speaker William Lenthall's house at Besselsleigh, south-west of Oxford on the main road to Faringdon.[38] Naturally, Lenthall was not in any position to complain but Besselsleigh was to function as a hospital for a mere eleven weeks. On 30 May, Clarges was ordered to move his practice into the city and to continue caring for the sick under the directions of Dr Samuel Turner, the King's personal physician and physician-general.[39] Thenceforth, until the surrender of the city in the following year, the hospital in New Inn Hall Street provided the royal army's only static medical facility, with other, temporary houses being requisitioned as necessary.

Inevitably, the following summer of 1644 saw a resurgence of the plague and, in August, some sixteen cartloads of sick soldiers arrived in Oxford from Abingdon.[40] In an attempt to limit the spread of infection, the council changed its policy once more and directed that casualties could be dispersed amongst local communities with the proviso that only one, or at most two, houses in any town or village could be used for medical purposes. Unfortunately, the ensuing widespread dispersal of patients aided the spread of infection rather than containing it.

to John Ashburnham, Treasurer at War, 7 November 1643); BL, Harleian MS, fols 229-30 (Council of war to John Ashburnham, 27 November 1643).

37   Philip, *Journal of Sir Samuel Luke*, II, p. 57; J. Wright, *A Declaration of the Lords and Commons assembled in Parliament, concerning His Majesties late proclamation threatening Fire and Sword to all inhabitants in the County of Oxford and Berks* (London: 1644).

38   BL, Harleian MS 6852, fol. 41 (orders of the council of war, 1643); BL, Harleian MS 6804, fols 92 and 124 ('The Humble Desires of the Colonels to the King's Majesty', undated); Toynbee, *Papers of Captain Henry Stevens*, p. 35; CSPD, 1644-5, pp. 204-5; W. Page, ed., *Victoria County History of Oxfordshire* (13 vols, Oxford, Oxford University Press: 1907-96), 8, p. 209.

39   BL, Harleian MS 6802, fol. 198 ('Royal directions issued to Thomas Clarges, 30 May 1644').

40   Warwickshire County Record Office, 265/2 ('Transcription of MS Note by Sir William Dugdale in his Diary of 1644, A New Almanack and Prognosticator for the year of our Lord 1644'); BL, Harleian MS 6851, fol. 163 ('Papers of Edward Walker relating to the Civil War).

The king's court in Christ Church College was by no means immune to the unhealthy environment and significant losses were suffered by the royal household during the years 1642-6. Of these, the deaths included the king's comptroller, the keeper of the Great Seal, and two yeomen of the wardrobe. On 7 August 1643, even the Queen was reported as being very sick and one of her attendant ladies died in a room next to the Queen's bedchamber.[41]

Table 7.3 Royal Household burials in Oxford, 1642-6

Year	Number of burials
1642	1
1643	54
1644	26
1645	11
1646	3
Total	95

Source: Oxford Parish Records for All Saints, Christ Church, St. Aldate, St Ebbe, St Martin's, St Mary Magdalene, St Mary the Virgin, St Michael, St Peter le Bailey and St. Peter in the East parishes.

The morale of Oxford's population must have sunk to its lowest ebb when, on Sunday 6 October 1644, the most devastating fire of the Civil War years broke out there. Some 300 to 350 houses were lost, representing between a quarter and one third of the city.[42] Those made homeless by the fire could not be rehoused and faced the oncoming winter without a roof over their heads.[43] Many arriving casualties were diverted to Bristol or to Marlborough, where for some two weeks after the second battle of Newbury the king's council of war met and where Humphrey Paynter, paymaster-general, received instructions to purchase whatever medicines as were required by the army's physicians and surgeons – costs, naturally, being obtained by local taxation.[44]

The logistic, medical and environmental problems that faced Charles I's army throughout its occupation of Oxford were horrendous. The absence of an inherited infrastructure or ready-made hospitals, with poor administrative support, a shortage

41   Philip, *Journal of Sir Samuel Luke*, II, p. 130.
42   *CSPD*, 1644-5, pp.16 and 46.
43   S. Porter, 'The Oxford Fire of 1644', *Oxoniensis*, 49 (1984), pp.289-300; Toynbee, *Papers of Captain Henry Stevens*, p. 25.
44   BL, Harleian MS 6802, fol. 293 (Council of War to Humphrey Paynter, 13 November 1644); BL, Harleian MS 6804, fol. 92 ('The Humble Desires of the Colonels to the King's Majesty', undated); W. Money, *The First and Second Battles of Newbury and the Siege of Donnington Castle during the Civil War, 1643-1646* (London, Simpkin Marshall: 1884), *passim*.

of medical staff and gross overcrowding, not to mention the loss of backing from the College of Physicians (who favoured parliament), all ensured that the care and welfare of the king's sick and wounded troops compared badly with parliament's achievements. Widows and children appear to have been disregarded completely and simply referred to their home parishes for support, according to the vagrancy laws. These same parishes were themselves bowing under the weight of punitive taxation and the cost of 'free quartering' which left little or nothing for charitable causes.[45] Even allowing for their many disadvantages, whilst the doctors carried out their duties to the best of their abilities, the royal army's administrators allocated completely different priorities to the care of its sick and wounded compared with those adopted under parliament's commonweal – but that is another story.

45   The nationwide decline in charitable donations during the Civil War years has been eloquently described in W. K. Jordan, *The Charities of London* (London, George Allen & Unwin: 1960), p. 25 *et. seq.*; W. K. Jordan, *The Charities of Rural England* (London, George Allen & Unwin: 1961), p. 26 *et. seq.*

8

How did Waller lose Roundway?

Dr Christopher L. Scott

On 13 July 1643, Sir William Waller lost the Battle of Roundway Down. His army of some 5,000, comprising infantry, cavalry, dragoons and artillery was defeated by Henry, Lord Wilmot's cavalry force of no more than 1,800. Moreover Waller had the advantage of high ground and had warning in time to make his deployments, but still he lost. My presentation to the conference was an attempt to explain how this came about and in doing so offer some new thoughts on civil war cavalry. This is a summary of what I said, rather than an academic paper, as the full version will be published in a book on Roundway Down in the future.

Waller said of Roundway, 'This affair at Devizes was the most heavy that did ever befall me', so he was well aware of the magnitude of his failure.[1] So too were the enemy. The earl of Clarendon reported, 'This glorious day, for it was a day of triumph, redeemed the king's whole affairs, so that all clouds that shadowed them seemed to be dispelled, and a bright light of success [did] shine over the whole kingdom'.[2] Certain factions in Parliament openly blamed Waller for the reversal, especially the earl of Essex and his friends, so Waller had to cast around for someone else to share the blame.

1   W. Waller, 'Recollections', in H. Cowley, *The poetry of Anna Matilda* (London: 1788), pp. 103-39, at p. 131n; J. Adair, *Roundhead General: A Military Biography of Sir William Waller* (London, Macdonald: 1969), p. 95.
2   Edward Hyde, earl of Clarendon, *The History of the Rebellion and Civil Wars in England* (Oxford: 1731), II, Pt 1, p. 290.

Firstly, he chose God: '...it pleased the Lord to turn my victory into mourning, and my glory into shame...', which reflects on his fate-oriented Presbyterian leanings.[3] However, being an honest man he also accepted a degree of guilt:

> So sure was I of victory that I wrote to Parliament to bid them be at rest, for that I would shortly send them an account of the numbers taken and the numbers slain... My presumption upon mine own strength and former successes [was] most justly humbled at the Devizes by an utter defeat ...[4]

Thus his view of his share of blame was mainly for the sin of pride and overconfidence and nothing more. However, he was quick to shift real blame onto others, particularly his political enemies and those he saw as fickle friends.

> The proud have laid snares for me ... and set traps in my way...[5] At one time so full of my services they were going to make me General of all their forces, but a panic of my horse which deserted me, turned the tide of their good will, and Essex was taken again into favour.[6]

This was a defence of sorts but he had to find a convincing military answer for his military defeat, so he placed the strategic blame squarely on the shoulders of the earl of Essex, whom he insisted should have prevented Wilmot from leaving Oxford.

> My dismal defeat at Roundway Down was owing to those heart burnings and jealousies; for the General [Essex] suffered the enemies horse to pass quietly, and without molestation [from Oxford] ...this mischance of mine that had never happened had others done their duty.[7]

The tactical blame he reserved almost exclusively for his Horse saying 'a panic of my Horse, which deserted me...' He argued that they not only lost their nerve in action but it was so great and so total that it caused them not just to retire but to run away from the field.[8] So complete was this desertion that the royalists called the battle 'Runaway Down'.

---

3   Waller, 'Recollections', p.124.
4   Ibid., p. 123.
5   Ibid., p. 123.
6   Ibid., p. 138.
7   Ibid., p. 123.
8   Ibid., p. 138.

Beginning with Waller's Horse, how were 2,500 fairly experienced parliamentarian cavalry beaten by about 1,000 royalists?[9] The usual answer offered by most histories is that the royalists won Roundway because of:

1   The veteran status and expertise of the Oxford Horse.
2   The superiority of the royalist commanders.
3   The parliamentarians were stationary when the cavalry melee began thus giving the royalists impetus.
4   Cowardice of the Western Horse.

Each of these reasons has been well aired in public before.

However, I maintain that although all four of these reasons played a role in the victory, there were an additional two important factors. Firstly, parliamentarian cavalry tactics: the triumph of the Swedish system of Gustavus Adolphus over the Dutch system of William of Nassau.

The parliamentarian horse were deployed in a deep formation that was designed to facilitate the old-fashioned caracole. Lord Byron, in command of Wilmot's second brigade, tells us that the parliamentarians fought in this manner:

> By this time we were come very near to Waller's brigade. The command I gave my men was, that not a man should discharge his pistol till the enemy had spent all his shot, which was punctually observed. So that first they gave us a volley of their carbines, then of their pistols and then we fell in with them, and gave them ours in their teeth.[10]

Each troop of about fifty men formed in a close order block of eight troopers wide (files) in six ranks with officers at the front, rear and/or side. At one metre per horse frontage, a troop was thus eight metres wide, and at three metres per horse depth plus space between each rank, it was some twenty metres deep. Being typical of the parliamentarian army, both Colonel Robert Burgill's and Waller's regiments had about 350 strong in seven troops, with a total of 56 files in six ranks. Thus, at one metre per horse, a regiment was 56 metres wide and the horses were deployed one behind the other. This deployment was preferred over 'chequer-boarding' in order not to intermix troops in the fighting line. However, in order for each rank to peel off after firing to

---

9   Of the 1,800 royal Horse which presumably came onto the field, 300 were withdrawn for service in a forlorn hope and one third of the force under the earl of Crawford were kept in reserve and took no part in the action until the end when the outcome was in little doubt.

10   British Library, Additional MS 1103, d. 77/5 (Sir John Byron's relation to the secretary of the last western action between the Lord Wilmot and Sir William Waller); P. Young, 'The Royalist Army at the Battle of Roundway Down, 13th July, 1643', *The Journal of the Society of Army Research*, 31 (1953), appendix.

the rear so as to reload, a ten metre gap was left between each troop, enabling ranks to filter down both sides at the same time. Allowing for six troop intervals, the regiment's frontage was thus 116 metres wide.

According to Richard Atkyns, a troop captain who fought in Wilmot's brigade, the royalists formed in open order (two metres per horse) and three horses deep. So with each brigade having about 500 men, we arrive at a width of 167 files occupying some 334 metres of frontage.[11] Formed in line, they had only nominal troop and regimental intervals. Therefore, parliamentarian regiments drawn up to fire were about 120 meres per regiment wide. Even if the troop gaps were halved to five metres, each one was still overlapped on both sides and had a regularly pierced front.

At individual troop level when the two sides met, either in the full pell-mell crash advocated by some schools of cavalry historians or in the more moderate slow advance into contact argued for by others, each parliamentarian troop was soon overwhelmed by the royalists facing them, as seen in figures 8.1 and 8.2.

At regimental/brigade level, the individual troop fight was repeated all along the line. The result was that whatever regiment they faced, the royalists were able to both meet the line head on and then flow down the gaps to engage the flanks of its constituent troops, whilst some men without an enemy to engage were able to hook around the formation and fall upon its rear.

In those troop intervals, those on the left flank of the defending troop were caught on their bridle arms, whilst those in the centre files could not use their swords at all. Although the melees were hard fought and rather protracted, the end result was never in doubt.

The second important factor in determining the outcome of Roundway Down was the condition of the horses. Byron states that:

> Yet they would not quit their ground, but stood pushing for it a pretty space, till it pleased God, I think to put new spirit into our tired horse as well as into our men. So that, though it were up the hill and that a steep one, we overbore them, and with that violence, that we forced them to fall foul upon other reserves of Horse that stood behind to second them.[12]

The key phrase here is 'put new spirit into our tired horse'.

Waller's cavalry had spent a long time on campaign in 1643 and had been out in one theatre or another since the spring:

---

11 The royalists were grouped in three brigades with rather *ad hoc* regiments formed from various individual troops, many of which fought alongside each other for some time

12 British Library, Additional MS 1103, d. 77/5 (Sir John Byron's relation to the secretary of the last western action between the Lord Wilmot and Sir William Waller); Young, 'Royalist Army at the Battle of Roundway Down', appendix.

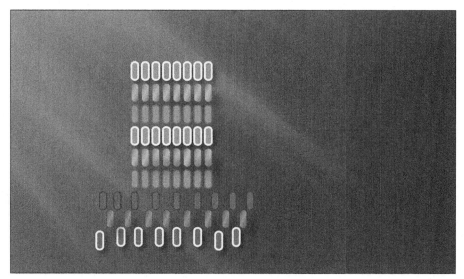

Figure 8.1 When the royalists attacked only part of the force was met head on in the initial clash.

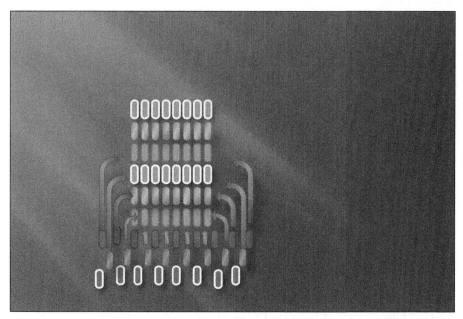

Figure 8.2 The rest of the force then came into play. The second rank filtered through to equalise the frontage and others poured down the interval to attack the flanks. The third rank replaced casualties.

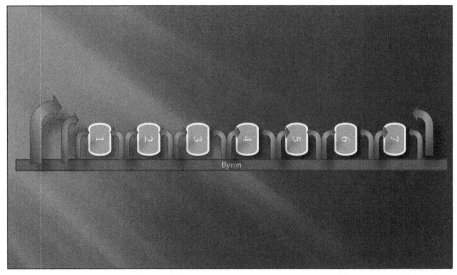

Figure 8.3 The overall effect was that of swamping and overawing the parliamentarian regiment.

Western Horse:

March, April:	Skirmishing across Cornwall.
May:	Battle of Stratton chased out of Cornwall.
June:	Skirmishes across Devon and Somerset.
	Actions at Glastonbury and Wells, followed by a march to Bristol.

Waller's Horse:

March:	March from Southeast to the West.
	Taking of Malmesbury and Battle of Highnam.
June:	Campaign to Worcester, then to Bristol and Bath.
	Action at Chewton Mendip.
	Beating up of Quarters around Frome.

And for the ten days of July before the battle of Roundway, the whole force was involved in:

Monday 3 July:	Action on the Bathford Road.
Tuesday 4 July:	Standoff above Swainswick.
Wednesday 5 July:	Battle of Lansdown.
Thursday 6 July:	Retirement into Bath.
Friday 7 July:	Advance to Chippenham.
Saturday 8 July:	Action at Bromham.
Sunday 9 July:	Action at Rowde.

Monday 10 July:	March onto Roundway Down.
	Day Action on Coatfields.
	Night Action at Beckhampton.
Tuesday 11 July:	Repulse of sorties.
Wednesday 12 July:	Supporting assaults.
Thursday 13 July:	Battle of Roundway.

They had been very busy indeed. Wilmot's Horse on the other hand had had a far easier time of it. Based in and around the royalist capital of Oxford, they too had seen some action:

Wilmot's Horse:

| February: | Rupert's venture into Hampshire resulted in a skirmish near Alton with some losses. Fell back into quarters around Oxford. |
| March to July: | Not worked hard over the late spring and most probably kept in stables; exercised in patrols when needed and were watered and fed. |

And for the July days leading up to the battle:

Tuesday 11 July:	Left Oxford and surrounding villages.
Wednesday 12 July:	Rendezvous and rest in Marlborough.
Thursday 13 July:	Battle of Roundway.

The looking after of horses is a complex business. Seventeenth century horse husbandry was not all that different from that of the modern day but it cannot be emphasised too much that for cavalry horses, condition is everything – especially if one's life depends on it – and there are several important dos and don'ts:

1   Cannot be ridden hard all day.
2   Need a lot of good clean water.
3   Should be prevented from grazing, as grass is a poor substitute and can cause gastric problems.
4   Must have regular feed, especially oats, barley, corn and hay plus some root vegetables.
5   Ideally, they should have clean bedding and their lines cleared of dung almost daily.
6   Need regular grooming:
   a.   Coat must be short to reduce sweating.
   b.   Coat must be brushed to clear parasites and the skin examined for cuts and sores and treated quickly to prevent infection.
   c.   Hooves cleared of debris and oiled to prevent hoof rot.
   d.   Nostrils, ears and anus cleaned.
   e.   Harness and tack had to be kept supple to prevent rub sores.

It is both arduous and time-consuming work keeping a horse in top condition.

Waller's horse just never had the time or the right situation to keep their horses in fighting fit condition. They had been worked hard for months and deprived of proper care. Wilmot's horses were in far better condition. Byron might well say '…it pleased God, I think to put new spirit into our tired horse…' but actually it was the grooms and ostlers of Oxfordshire!

In conclusion, yes, Waller lost Roundway because the Oxford Horse were more experienced and probably much better horsemen. Wilmot and Byron understood their trade better than Sir Arthur Haselrig and Sir Edward Hungerford. The royalists had the impetus in melee and the Western Horse broke and ran, some even before they came into action. However, it was also because the Dutch firepower system was inferior to the cold steel of the Swedish system, the deployment for the former playing into the hands of the latter. Moreover, the royalist horses were in far better physical condition. I submit that these last two were possibly the more telling factors!

Index

Wolverhampton Military Studies

www.helion.co.uk/wolverhamptonmilitarystudies

Submissions

The publishers would be pleased to receive submissions for this series. Please contact us via email (info@helion.co.uk), or in writing to Helion & Company Limited, 26 Willow Road, Solihull, West Midlands, B91 1UE.

Titles

Lightning Source UK Ltd.
Milton Keynes UK
UKOW06n1316180117
292351UK00005B/23/P

9 781911 096443